THE CENTRAL LIBERAL TRUTH

The Central Liberal Truth

How Politics Can Change a Culture
and Save It from Itself

LAWRENCE E. HARRISON

OXFORD

UNIVERSITY PRESS

2006

OXFORD
UNIVERSITY PRESS

Oxford University Press, Inc., publishes works that
further Oxford University's objective of excellence
in research, scholarship, and education.

Oxford New York
Auckland Cape Town Dar es Salaam Hong Kong Karachi
Kuala Lumpur Madrid Melbourne Mexico City Nairobi
New Delhi Shanghai Taipei Toronto

With offices in
Argentina Austria Brazil Chile Czech Republic France Greece
Guatemala Hungary Italy Japan Poland Portugal Singapore
South Korea Switzerland Thailand Turkey Ukraine Vietnam

Copyright © 2006 by Lawrence E. Harrison

Published by Oxford University Press, Inc.
198 Madison Avenue, New York, NY 10016
www.oup.com

Oxford is a registered trademark of Oxford University Press

Library of Congress Cataloging-in-Publication Data
Harrison, Lawrence E.
The central liberal truth : how politics can change a culture
and save it from itself / Lawrence E. Harrison.
p. cm.
Includes bibliographical references and index.
ISBN-13: 978-0-19-530041-3
ISBN-10: 0-19-530041-6
1. Culture. 2. Culture—Political aspects.
3. Social values. I. Title.
HM621.H37 2006
306'.01—dc22
2005026379

3 5 7 9 8 6 4 2
Printed in the United States of America
on acid-free paper

For Patsy—Again, and always

CONTENTS

Acknowledgments   ix

Preface   xi

Introduction   1

1 The Riddle of Hispaniola   21

2 Disaggregating "Culture"   35

3 Models and Instruments
  of Cultural Transmission/Change   57

4 Religions and Progress   87

5 Culture in Action I   120

6 Culture in Action II   142

7 Patterns of Cultural Change   163

8 Success and Failure   184

9 Conclusion: Guidelines
  for Progressive Cultural Change   206

Notes   227

Appendix: Biographical Sketches   245

Index   255

ACKNOWLEDGMENTS

I OWE A GREAT DEBT OF GRATITUDE to the Fletcher School at Tufts University, and particularly to its dean, Stephen Bosworth, for providing the Culture Matters Research Project with an ideal home for research, conferences, and writing.

The versatility, energy, and effectiveness of my assistant at Fletcher, Lupita Ervin, merit special mention. She managed the administrative and financial aspects of the project and attended to the myriad details of two major conferences, always efficiently and always with a smile. I also wish to acknowledge Fran Parisi's assistance in financial management.

The project was made possible through the generous financial support of the Smith Richardson Foundation, the John Templeton Foundation, the Donner Foundation, the Sidney Swensrud Foundation, Dr. John Templeton, and Max Thelen.

The following people read the manuscript and provided valuable comments: Giacomo Bernardi, James Fox, Mariano Grondona, Robert Hefner, Jerome Kagan, Stephen Lewis, and Alex Shakow.

The book has been the beneficiary of the skillful and sure editorial hands of George Scialabba in Cambridge, Massachusetts, and Sara Safransky at the Oxford University Press. I also want to thank Joellyn Ausanka for her helpful role in coordinating production of the book.

I want to take special note of the crucial role played by Tim Bartlett, my editor for *Culture Matters* at Basic Books and at the Oxford University Press for *The Central Liberal Truth*. He has served as critic, supporter, intellectual foil, and friend, and I am enormously grateful to him.

Some sixty people were involved in the Culture Matters Research Project, from which this book and two companion collections of essays flow. But *The Central Liberal Truth* reflects my own views, with which other participants in the project may or may not agree.

I want to take note of the role played in my life by my parents, David Albert Harrison and Jennie Levin Harrison, and by my brother, Robert Arthur Harrison, all of whom have been deceased for many years; by my grandparents, and by all who came before.

But my greatest debt is to my wife, Patricia Crane Harrison, to whom this book is dedicated. She was a constant source of encouragement, ideas, helpful criticism, and relevant clippings from the *New York Times*. Her grace and charm—and timely reminder notes to me—contributed immeasurably to the success of the two major Culture Matters Research Project conferences. But my debt to her goes far beyond the Research Project and this book. She has given me the happiest years of my life. Her final gift to me was a lesson in how to face death with dignity, grace, and courage. She passed away on November 9, 2005.

PREFACE

From 1962 to 1982, I was an official of the United States Agency for International Development (USAID). During those two decades, I directed USAID missions in five Latin American countries: the Dominican Republic during and after the 1965 revolution;[1] Costa Rica (1969–71), where I had also served in 1964–65; the Regional Mission for Central America, in Guatemala (1975–77); Haiti (1977–79); and Nicaragua, where I arrived one week after the Sandinistas took power in 1979 and remained until mid-1981. I also worked in the Latin American Bureau of USAID in Washington from 1962 to 1963 and from 1971 to 1975.

I started my career in USAID in 1962 at the time of President Kennedy's Latin American initiative, the Alliance for Progress, with the presumption, widely shared by my colleagues, that Latin America was "in trouble" because the United States had neglected it. Ironically, the dominant explanation in Latin America and amongst academic communities around the world for Latin America's underdevelopment in the 1970s and 1980s was Dependency Theory: Latin America was poor, unjust, and authoritarian not because it had been *neglected* by the United States but because it had been *exploited* by the United States.

After I had worked in Latin American countries for a few years, it became apparent to me that the "neglect" view was both naïve and arrogant, a conclusion reached at about the same time by Teodoro

Moscoso, first U.S. coordinator of the Alliance for Progress and an architect of Puerto Rico's Operation Bootstrap. A sign on the wall of his office in the State Department in the early 1960s read "Please be brief. We are twenty years late." Later he would write: "The Latin American case is so complex, so difficult to solve, and so fraught with human and global danger and distress that the use of the word 'anguish' is not an exaggeration. The longer I live, the more I believe that, just as no human being can save another who does not have the will to save himself, no country can save others no matter how good its intentions or how hard it tries."[2]

What also became increasingly apparent to me was a pattern of problems that were common, in greater or lesser degree, to all the countries in which I worked, among them disrespect for the law, unbridled exercise of authority, lack of cooperation with one another, passivity when encountering problems, lack of civic consciousness, lack of trust, and pursuit of narrow personal interest. To be sure, these shortcomings are found in all human societies, including the United States. But the *degree of intensity* of the problems in Latin America seemed to me to be much greater. And the problems were clearly linked to Latin America's difficulties consolidating democracy and social justice, and producing prosperity for its people. The array of fundamental problems that we associate with underdevelopment was, I believed, deeply rooted in the minds of Latin Americans.

I found these same problems in particularly high profile in Haiti, which is not really a Latin American country but an African-American country. During my two years there (1977–79), a friend gave me a copy of the Venezuelan writer Carlos Rangel's book *Del Buen Salvaje al Buen Revolucionario* (*From the Noble Savage to the Noble Revolutionary*).[3] In it, Rangel argues that Latin America's "failures," to use his word, are chiefly the consequence of its Iberian cultural heritage. Rangel incurred the wrath of the Latin American intellectual and political establishments at the time, but many prominent Latin Americans, Octavio Paz, Mario Vargas Llosa, Mariano Grondona, and Carlos Alberto Montaner among them, subsequently came to similar conclusions.

Rangel's book helped to crystallize my own thoughts on the causes of Latin America's problems. My subsequent two years in Nicaragua with the Sandinista government confirmed the relevance of my conclusions to a revolutionary environment. So I decided to retire from the foreign service to pursue these thoughts in a scholarly setting. I wrote to Samuel Huntington, then director of the Center for International Affairs at Harvard University, whom I had known for several years, and told him of my interest in writing a book on the role of culture in Latin America's evolution. That letter led to three two-year stints at the Center for International Affairs during which I wrote three books: *Underdevelopment Is a State of Mind* (1985), *Who Prospers?* (1992), and *The Pan-American Dream* (1997). Starting with *Who Prospers?*, my focus broadened to the role of culture, for good or for bad, in other parts of the world.

In April 1999, I organized a symposium at Harvard at which a group of scholars, journalists, politicians, and development practitioners met under the auspices of the Harvard Academy for International and Area Studies, chaired by Samuel Huntington, to discuss the relationship between cultural values and human progress—the thesis that values, beliefs, and attitudes are a key but neglected factor in understanding the evolution of societies and that the neglect of cultural factors may go a long way toward explaining the agonizingly slow progress toward democratic governance, social justice, and prosperity in so many countries in Africa, Latin America, the Islamic world, and elsewhere. Many of the participants in the symposium believed that understanding how culture influences the behavior of individuals and societies, and what forces shape cultural change, could accelerate the pace of progress.

During the final session of the symposium, we considered what might be done to inculcate or strengthen the values and attitudes that nurture progress. No one at the symposium believed that culture is genetically determined; rather, all believed that culture is acquired—transmitted from generation to generation through the family, the church, the school, and other socializing instruments.[4] But it was clear that we were not prepared to address cultural change and what promotes or impedes it. We did not have a satisfactory understanding of the components of "culture" that would allow us to look at *how* culture influences the behaviors that promote progress. The participants in the symposium agreed that culture changes, but many were uncomfortable discussing measures to encourage or facilitate cultural change.

The papers prepared for the symposium were published in 2000 in the book *Culture Matters*, coedited by Samuel Huntington and me, which had a far broader impact than its co-editors expected. Its success made it possible to revisit those unanswered questions raised at the last session of the Harvard symposium. By the spring of 2002, two years after the publication of *Culture Matters*, we had raised enough money to make a research program possible. Since then, more than 60 professionals from around the world, mostly scholars but also journalists, development practitioners, politicians, and business people, have participated in the Culture Matters Research Project (CMRP), administered by the Fletcher School at Tufts University.[5]

The Central Liberal Truth, which distills the CMRP, thus culminates more than two decades of research and writing about the role of cultural values, beliefs, and attitudes in the evolution of human societies, and another two decades of work in the field. The goal of the project is the creation of guidelines for strengthening the values and attitudes that nurture human progress.

I want to stress as forcefully as I can that the guidelines contained in the final chapter of this book will only prove useful when political, intellectual, and other leaders *within* a society conclude that some traditional values and attitudes are obstacles to bringing about the kind of society that aspires to democratic governance, social justice, and prosperity. Any efforts to impose the guidelines from outside, whether by governments or development assistance institutions, are likely to fail.

THE CENTRAL LIBERAL TRUTH

The central conservative truth is that it is culture, not politics, that determines the success of a society. The central liberal truth is that politics can change a culture and save it from itself.

—Daniel Patrick Moynihan

Introduction

I am convinced that the luckiest of geographic circumstances and the best of laws cannot maintain a constitution in despite of mores, whereas the latter can turn even the most unfavorable circumstances and the worst laws to advantage. The importance of mores is a universal truth to which study and experience continually bring us back. I find it occupies the central position in my thoughts: all my ideas come back to it in the end.
— Alexis de Tocqueville, *Democracy in America*[1]

THE INFLUENCE OF CULTURAL VALUES, beliefs, and attitudes on the way that societies evolve has been shunned by scholars, politicians, and development experts, notwithstanding the views of Tocqueville, Max Weber, and more recently Francis Fukuyama, Samuel Huntington, David Landes, Robert Putnam, and Lucian Pye, among others. It is much more comfortable for the experts to cite geographic constraints, insufficient resources, bad policies, and weak institutions. That way they avoid the invidious comparisons, political sensitivities, and bruised feelings often engendered by cultural explanations of success and failure. But by avoiding culture, the experts also ignore not only an important part of the explanation of why some societies or ethno-religious groups do better than others with respect to democratic governance, social justice, and prosperity. They also ignore the possibility that progress can be accelerated by (1) analyzing cultural obstacles to it, and (2) addressing cultural change as a remedy.

The influence of culture on the way that societies evolve is central not only to the goal of reducing poverty and injustice around the world. It is also a key factor in foreign policy, with particular relevance to the Bush administration's keystone policy of promoting democracy: "[the] values of freedom are right and true for every person, in every society."[2] If culture matters in making democracy work, as Tocqueville insists, and as the disappointing experience of the United States in promoting democracy (e.g., in Latin America) suggests, then the keystone is likely to crumble under the pressure of cultures averse to democracy, as in the Arab countries, not one of which has yet produced stable democracy.

Some fundamental questions about what drives human progress cannot be answered without considering the role of culture and/or cultural change. For example:

- Why have democratic institutions failed to take root in any Arab country?
- Why have the Confucian societies of East Asia experienced transforming rates of economic growth?
- Why are East Asian immigrants so successful wherever they migrate?
- Why are Jews so successful wherever they migrate?
- What explains the "miracle" of Spain's transformation from a traditional autocracy to a modern Western European democracy?
- Why do the Nordic countries lead the rest of the world in most indicators of progress?
- Why have Haiti and the Dominican Republic, two countries that share the Caribbean island of Hispaniola, followed such divergent paths?

Other Factors Matter, Too

CULTURE CAN BE CRUCIAL, but it is only one factor, if an important one, in play in human progress. Geography, including climate and resource endowment, also matters, not only in its direct impact on economic development but also through its influence on culture. Jared Diamond makes a compelling case for the powerful influence of environment in his best-selling *Guns, Germs, and Steel,* but he leaves space for culture: "Among other factors [explaining why some societies have advanced more rapidly than others] cultural factors . . . loom large. . . . Human cultural traits vary greatly around the world. Some of that cultural variation is no doubt a product of environmental variation. . . . But an important question concerns the possible significance of local cultural factors unrelated to the environment. A minor cultural feature may arise for trivial, temporary local reasons, become fixed, and then predispose a society toward more important cultural choices. . . . "[3]

That colder climates forced humans to plan ahead to get through the winter, while humans in tropical zones had no such problem, must surely be relevant in explaining why most poor countries are found in the tropical zones; and it may also be relevant in explaining why the warmer portions of some countries—for example, the south of Italy, the south of Spain, the south of the United States—are poorer than the colder portions.

Ideology and governmental policies can also profoundly influence the pace and direction that development takes: toward or away from democracy and social justice, toward or away from sustained rapid economic growth. In contrast with Italy, Spain, and the United States, the northern part of Korea is poor, the southern part rich. This reversal is largely because, in the North, an ideology and the policies that flow from it are hostile to economic development and political pluralism, while the ideology and policies of the South have proven conducive to economic development, which in turn has nurtured democracy. This is a case where ideology and economic policy seem to matter much more than culture. Yet even in such cases, culture is in play. North Korea's authoritarian government is in part a product of the same authoritarian current in Confucianism that produced the autocracies of Mao Zedong and his predecessors and successors in China—and the progressive authoritarianism of Lee Kuan Yew in Singapore. And, as we shall see, ideological shifts have played a key role in cultural change in several countries.

The role of political leaders with a vision of a better society can also play a crucial role. The Meiji leadership in late-nineteenth-century Japan, Mustafa Kemal in Turkey following World War I, and Franklin

Roosevelt in the United States of the 1930s and '40s all brought about transforming change—in a political and economic sense, to be sure, but in a cultural sense as well. A more recent example is the crucial role played by Mikhail Gorbachev in the demise of the Soviet empire and the movement, rapid in some of its components and slow in others, toward democratic capitalism.

I note in passing that each of these leaderships came to power at a time of national crisis, validating an observation by Samuel Huntington, "Societies . . . may change their culture in response to major trauma."[4] The corresponding crises: Japan's awareness of its technological backwardness and vulnerability in the wake of the arrival of Commodore Perry's flotilla in Tokyo Bay in 1853; the collapse of the Ottoman Empire in World War I; the Great Depression and World War II; the failure of Communism to produce prosperity, and increasing evidence that the West was winning the Cold War.

Generally, however, what I wrote in *Underdevelopment Is a State of Mind* twenty years ago remains valid: "the cultural environment importantly influences the process through which leaders gain their positions, the priorities they apply in shaping policies, and the people, institutions, and practices they use to execute those policies"—not to mention culture's influence on the leaders themselves.[5]

Success can also breed cultural change that slows the pace of economic growth. Such has been the case in Japan in the 1990s and the first years of the twenty-first century, and it may also be true of some European countries, too, as symbolized by France's move to a 35-hour work week. The *New York Times* recently noted that Norway's "bedrock work ethic" is caving in as a result of the country's affluence.[6] These cases evoke the kind of post-industrial culture that Ronald Inglehart has analyzed: "Having attained high levels of economic security, the populations of the first nations to industrialize have gradually come to emphasize . . . values [other than prosperity]; these groups give higher priority to the quality of life than to economic growth."[7] I am reminded of Thomas Mann's early novel of a north German commercial dynasty, *Buddenbrooks*, in which the dynastic fortune is dissipated through lack of interest in business in third and fourth generation offspring; also a Chinese adage that covers three generations: From rags, to riches, to ruin.

The foregoing is not a full cataloguing of the noncultural factors that influence how societies evolve. But it does address significant factors, some of which, for example, ideology in North Korea (and in East Germany) have trumped culture. Culture is one of several relevant factors. But in many cases, it may be the crucial one.

"Imperialism," "Colonialism," and "Dependency"

I spoke at a World Bank poverty-reduction conference after publication of *Culture Matters*, which was for several years a bestseller at the World Bank bookstore. After my presentation, a South African woman strongly criticized my comments, characterizing them as "blaming the victim." I have heard this comment often during the past two decades. What it means is that the problems of Third World countries—the "developing" or "underdeveloped" countries of Africa, Asia, and Latin America—are the consequence of irresponsible, abusive, exploitative colonial powers in the cases of Africa and Asia, or the comparably destructive behavior of "Yankee imperialism" in Latin America. The latter view was at the heart of Dependency Theory, which dominated interpretations of Latin American underdevelopment in universities around the world in the 1970s and 1980s and is still alive and well in some Latin American universities today. Some colonial regimes, for example Belgium in the Congo, are clearly deserving of the opprobrium evoked by the word "colonialism." But in other cases, the net of positive and negative aspects of colonialism may be positive. I share the judgment of Nobelist economist Sir Arthur Lewis, a black from the Caribbean island of St. Lucia: "The best empires have added greatly to human happiness; they have established peace over wide areas, have built roads, have improved public health, have stimulated trade, have brought improved systems of law, have introduced new technical knowledge, and so on. Whereas the worst empires have brought pillage, and slaughter and slavery in their train."[8]

With respect to Latin America, the symbol par excellence of Yankee imperialism and the "ruthless"[9] behavior of American companies was the United Fruit Company. Yet, as we shall see in chapter 6, United

Fruit was advantageous to the countries in which it operated not only in economic terms but also by promoting progressive cultural change.

The "victim" self-image, whether warranted or not, is self-defeating, particularly if the "victimizer" is no longer present, as in the case of formerly colonial countries that have enjoyed independence for almost half a century—many African countries—or more than a half-century with respect to India and Pakistan. The only hope for the victim is for compensation or reparations from the victimizer. Lucian Pye has described Dependency Theory as "demeaning and despairing."[10] And Bernard Lewis's words are also relevant: "When people realize that things are going wrong, there are two questions they can ask: One is, 'What did we do wrong?' and the other is 'Who did this to us?' The latter leads to conspiracy theories and paranoia. The first question leads to another line of thinking: 'How do we put it right?'"[11] David Landes adds, "In the second half of the twentieth century, Latin America chose conspiracy theories and paranoia. In the second half of the nineteenth century, Japan asked itself, 'How do we put it right?'"[12]

Defining "Culture"

WHAT DO WE MEAN BY "CULTURE"? "It has been defined in myriad ways," as a recent World Bank study observes.[13] We commonly hear references to "popular culture," which includes food, entertainment, and clothing styles, among other dimensions. And "culture" often brings to mind literature, art, and music—"high" culture. But for our purposes, culture is the body of values, beliefs, and attitudes that members of a society share; values, beliefs, and attitudes shaped chiefly by environment, religion, and the vagaries of history that are passed on from generation to generation chiefly through child rearing practices, religious practice, the education system, the media, and peer relationships. Those values, beliefs, and attitudes are disaggregated in a 25-factor typology of progress-prone and progress-resistant societies presented in chapter 2.

Culture is powerfully influenced by religion, and the cultures discussed in this book are defined, at a broad level of generalization, by the predominant religion or ethical code: Protestant, Catholic, Orthodox Christian, Jewish, Islamic, Confucian, Hindu, and Buddhist. These are roughly comparable to the "civilizations" that Samuel Huntington analyzes in *The Clash of Civilizations and the Remaking of World Order*, although he groups together the European Protestant and Catholic countries and the British offspring countries (the United States, Canada, Australia, and New Zealand) as "the West."[14] However, our analysis will go beyond these general categories to specific countries within "civilizations," and even to some provinces, cities, towns, and ethnic groups.

Over the generations, culture develops a powerful momentum, but it is susceptible to change. Attitudes and beliefs are more susceptible than values: examples are the transformation of attitudes on race in the United States in recent decades, and the not uncommon shifting of political beliefs, or ideologies, from one political party to another. Values, on the other hand, are the bedrock of culture, and they usually change more slowly than attitudes and beliefs. An example is the central Confucian value of filial piety—the responsibility of the child to honor, respect, and obey the father. But rapid modernization in Japan, South Korea, Hong Kong, Singapore, and now China itself has shaken even that bedrock value.

How does culture influence the way that societies progress? Cultures can be thought of as overlays on a universal human nature, overlays that go a long way toward explaining the behavioral differences that are reflected in the divergent political, social, and economic evolution of societies, for example of Western Europe and the Arab countries.[15] Relevant is an observation from the widely read *Arab Human Development Report 2002*, commissioned by the United Nations Development Program and Arab Fund for Economic and Social Development:

> Culture and values are the soul of development. They provide its impetus, facilitate the means needed to further it, and substantially define people's vision of its purposes and ends. Culture and values are instrumental in the sense that they help to shape people's hopes, fears, ambitions, attitudes and actions, but they are also formative because they mould people's ideals and inspire their dreams for a fulfilling life for themselves and future generations. There is some debate in Arab countries about whether culture and values promote or retard development. Ultimately, however, values are not the servants of development; they are its wellspring . . .

Governments—Arab or otherwise—cannot decree their people's values; indeed, governments and their actions are partly formed by national cultures and values. Governments can, however, influence culture through leadership and example, and by shaping education and pedagogy, incentive structures in society, and use of the media. Moreover, by influencing values, they can affect the path of development.[16]

Throughout this book, I will be generalizing about cultures and religions. That is inevitable in a project that seeks a deeper understanding of what constitutes "culture," how it influences behavior, and what might be done to modify it. But one must be mindful that cultures are not homogeneous; that all cultures have, in Robert Hefner's words, "their own internal pluralism, variety, or rival 'streams.'"[17] Moreover, individual variation exists in all cultures: progress-prone people will surely be found in progress-resistant cultures, and vice versa. Nevertheless, there is compelling evidence, for example from Geert Hofstede's comparative analyses of cultural differences in IBM offices around the world,[18] and the World Values Survey, which assesses values and value change in some 65 countries, that meaningful patterns exist in the values, beliefs, and attitudes of nations, and even "civilizations," that make generalizations both valid and useful.

Defining "Progress"

ANY ATTEMPT TO DEFINE "PROGRESS" is likely to collide with the views of people who subscribe to cultural relativism, the theory that each society or culture must define its own ideas "about what is true, good, beautiful, and efficient"[19] and that cultures are neither better nor worse, simply different. Cultural relativism was at the root of the American Anthropological Association's opposition to the 1948 United Nations Universal Declaration of Human Rights on the grounds that it was an ethnocentric imposition of the West on the rest of the world.[20] Yet the declaration today provides us with a definition of progress that is substantially accepted well beyond the boundaries of "the West":

- The right to life, liberty, and security of person
- Equality before the law

- Freedom of thought, conscience, and religion
- The right to take part in . . . government . . . directly or through chosen representatives
- [The right to assure that] the will of the people [is] the basis of the authority of government
- The right to an [adequate] standard of living
- [The right to] adequate medical care and necessary social services
- The right to education

No one can argue that the UN Declaration is fully "universal." Surely, there are individuals and groups who would disagree with one or more of the components of progress. However, a majority of the world's people surely would agree with the following assertions, which are a restatement of the declaration:

> Life is better than death.
> Health is better than sickness.
> Liberty is better than slavery.
> Prosperity is better than poverty.
> Education is better than ignorance.
> Justice is better than injustice.

Contrary Views

IN THE PRECEDING DISCUSSION OF "PROGRESS," I mentioned the opposition of some anthropologists to the culture matters thesis on the grounds that "progress" and "development" are impositions of the West on the rest of the world, as in the case of the UN Universal Declaration of Human Rights.

University of Chicago anthropologist Richard Shweder expresses such views in his *Culture Matters* essay "Moral Maps, 'First World' Conceits, and the New Evangelists." Shweder identifies himself as a "cultural pluralist" who believes:

[in] "universalism without uniformity," which is what makes me a pluralist. . . . I believe that there are universally binding values but that there are just too many of them (e.g., justice, beneficence, autonomy,

sacrifice, liberty, loyalty, sanctity, duty). . . . I believe that all the good things in life can't be simultaneously maximized. I believe that when it comes to implementing true values there are always trade-offs, which is why there are different traditions of values (i.e., cultures) and why no one cultural tradition has ever been able to honor everything that is good.[21]

Shweder continues:

Throughout history, whoever is wealthiest and the most technologically advanced thinks that their way of life is the best, the most natural, the God-given, the surest means to salvation, or at least the fast lane to well-being in this world. . . . Dazzled by our contemporary inventions and toys (e.g., CNN, IBM, Big Mac, blue jeans, the birth control pill, the credit card) and at home in our way of life, we are prone to similar illusions and the same type of conceits.[22]

Shweder is critical of "Radical relativists—those who believe that anything goes."[23] But it is clear that his brand of cultural pluralism is close to radical relativism, or what the Canadian sociologist Rhoda Howard refers to as "cultural absolutism—a philosophical position that declares a society's culture to be of supreme ethical value. It advocates ethnocentric adherence to one's own cultural norms as an ethically correct attitude for everyone except loosely-defined 'Westerners.'"[24] Shweder is an outspoken supporter of female genital cutting as an authentic cultural practice: at a lecture he gave on Martha's Vineyard a few years ago, he described how young girls approach the cutting procedure with a very positive attitude in part "because their mothers and grandmothers had had the same experience."[25]

In a footnote to his *Culture Matters* chapter, Shweder has this to say:

Among the many fascinating remarks heard at the [1999 Harvard] conference were several "indigenous" testimonials from cosmopolitan intellectuals out of Africa and Latin America. These representatives from the "Third World" played the part of disgruntled "insiders," bearing witness to the impoverishment of their own native cultures, telling us how bad things can be in the home country . . . For most globe-hopping managers of the world system, including cosmopolitan intellectuals from out of the "Third World," travel plans mean more than ancestry . . .

After all, whose voice is more "indigenous"? The voice of a "Western-educated" M.B.A. or Ph.D. from Dakar or Delhi, who looks down on his or her own cultural traditions and looks up to the United States for intellectual and moral guidance and material aid? Or the voice of a "Western" scholar who does years of fieldwork in rural villages in Africa or Asia and understands and sees value in the traditions of "others"?[26]

The Camerounian economist Daniel Etounga Manguelle, author of a chapter in *Culture Matters* entitled "Does Africa Need a Cultural Adjustment Program?"[27] responded:

> As a "disgruntled insider" and "cosmopolitan intellectual" from Africa, I . . . comment on Richard Shweder's note . . . with some diffidence. After all, I am responding to a Western scholar who identifies himself as more "indigenous" than I am because he "has done years of fieldwork in rural villages in [the Third World]."
>
> I have to confess that I failed to receive the "intellectual and moral guidance and material aid" I expected at the Harvard symposium, so I am going to tell the truth: We Africans really enjoy living in shantytowns where there isn't enough food, health care, or education for our children. Furthermore, our corrupt chieftancy political systems are really marvelous and have permitted countries like Mobutu's Zaire to earn us international prestige and respect.
>
> Moreover, it would certainly be boring if free, democratic elections were organized all over Africa. Were that to happen, we would no longer be real Africans, and by losing our identity—and our authoritarianism, our bloody civil wars, our illiteracy, our forty-five year life expectancy—we would be letting down not only ourselves but also those Western anthropologists who study us so sympathetically and understand that we can't be expected to behave like human beings who seek dignity. . . . We are Africans, and our identity matters!
>
> So let us fight for it with the full support of those Western scholars who have the wisdom and courage to acknowledge that Africans belong to a different world.[28]

THE THESIS THAT CULTURE MATTERS makes a lot of economists uncomfortable. As the former World Bank economist William Easterly, author of *The Elusive Quest for Growth*, wrote, in reviewing my book *Who*

Prospers? "maybe there is a lot to be said for the old-fashioned economist's view that people are the same everywhere and will respond to the right economic opportunities and incentives."[29] Easterly's view ignores the fact that, in multicultural countries where the economic opportunities and incentives are available to all, some ethnic or religious minorities do much better than majority populations, as in the case of the Chinese minorities in Indonesia, Malaysia, the Philippines, and Thailand—and any other place to which the Chinese have migrated, including the United States. Why has the "Washington Consensus" prescription of democratic capitalism worked well in India and poorly in Latin America (with the exception of Chile[30]), where socialism, and even authoritarian socialism in the case of Venezuela, appears to be alive and well? Cultural factors may not be the whole explanation, but surely they are relevant.

In his recent book *The End of Poverty*, economist Jeffrey Sachs attacks the culture matters thesis in these words:

> Many people take for granted that poverty and wealth are simply a reflection of societal values. One recent study [Daniel Etounga-Manguelle's essay in *Culture Matters*] attributed African poverty to a dislike of work, suppression of individualism, and irrationality; another study [Lionel Sosa's *The Americano Dream*, cited in Samuel Huntington's *Who Are We?*[31]] identified the main obstacles to Mexican-American upward mobility as "resignation of the poor [to poverty]," "low priority of education," and "mistrust of those outside the family." The idea that whole societies are condemned to poverty because of their values has a long history, but one that is seldom useful.[32]

Yet earlier in *The End of Poverty*, Sachs has this to say:

> Even when governments are trying to advance their countries, the cultural environment may be an obstacle to development. Cultural or religious norms in the society may block the role of women, for example, leaving half of the population without economic or political rights. . . . Similar cultural barriers may apply to religious or ethnic minorities. Social norms may prevent certain groups from gaining access to public services (such as schooling, health facilities, or job training minorities. . . . A . . . possible reason for continued poverty in the midst of growth is cultural.[33]

Sachs's self-contradiction, noted in the *New York Times* review of his book, reflects his longstanding ambivalence on the significance of culture.[34] Prior to his participation in the 1999 *Culture Matters* Harvard symposium, he expressed the view that culture was one of several factors influencing economic outcomes. But at the symposium, he presented a paper ("Notes on a New Sociology of Economic Development"— chapter 3 in *Culture Matters*) that downplayed the role of culture. In a subsequent debate with me at the Council on Foreign Relations in New York in 2001, he reluctantly agreed that culture probably did matter in Russia's economic collapse,* and when he addressed my class at the Fletcher School the following year, he acknowledged that culture was a factor in Haiti's dismal history (see chapter 1).

The reluctance of many economists to confront culture reflects in part the difficulty of quantifying cultural factors and identifying clear patterns of cause and effect. Moynihan's aphorism underscores the complexity one faces in dealing with culture: in the central *conservative* truth, culture is a cause of national success (or failure); in the central *liberal* truth it is an effect of politics and policy. In *Making Democracy Work*, Robert Putnam traced the roots of the Italian north's progress and the south's backwardness to the emergence of communes in the north and the authoritarian Norman presence in the south almost a thousand years ago.[35]

But in the shorter run, culture is *acted upon* by numerous factors, among them leaders, policies, traumas, economic forces, social movements (like that led by Martin Luther King), the media, and books. The key role of books is exemplified by the Uruguayan writer José Enrique Rodó's *Ariel*.[36] First published in 1900, *Ariel* presents two characters from Shakespeare's *The Tempest* to allegorize Latin America and the United States: the comely, spiritual, artistic, moral Ariel is contrasted with the ugly, vulgar, pragmatic, money-grubbing Caliban. *Ariel* is still popular in Latin America today, 105 years—and millions of copies— after it was first published. It has powerfully reinforced the anti-capitalist values and anti-American attitudes of generations of Latin American intellectuals.

---

*Federal Reserve chairman Alan Greenspan said a few years ago that he used to assume that capitalism was "human nature." But in the wake of the collapse of the Russian economy, he concluded that "it was not human nature at all, but culture."

I hope that the evidence and analysis contained in this book and the two companion volumes of CMRP essays (*Developing Cultures: Essays on Cultural Change* and *Developing Cultures: Case Studies*, both published by Routledge) will persuade skeptical economists about the utility of cultural analysis. Four of the essay authors are economists: James Fox (development assistance and cultural change in *Essays on Cultural Change*); David Hojman (Chile), Stephen Lewis (Botswana), and Yoshihara Kunio (Japan) in *Case Studies*. So are CMRP advisory board members Morris Altman, Robert Hodam, and Timur Kuran.

In his book *Asia Per Capita*, Yoshihara identifies the following ways that culture influences economic development:[37]

- Culture determines individual preference structure.

- Culture is also an important determinant of people's attitudes toward public order and the ethics of government officials.

- Culture affects institutions by shaping the ideological basis for legislation or policy.

- A strategy for sustainable economic growth requires an appropriate cultural policy.[38]

The Marshall Plan Panacea

THE CONVENTIONAL ECONOMIC development strategies of the past half-century, chiefly devised by development assistance institutions like the World Bank and scholars, emphasized market incentives, trade and investment, competitiveness, employment-intensive manufacturing, agricultural productivity, appropriate technology, institution building, health, education, and infrastructure, among others. These have generally had beneficial results but have rarely produced transforming rates of economic growth. Critics like Jeffrey Sachs blame the rich countries for not contributing enough money for development assistance, above all the United States, which has devoted a declining percentage of its GNP to foreign aid since the Marshall Plan era. Sachs reminds us that the accepted target for rich country development assistance is 0.7 percent of GDP and that in 2004, U.S. development assistance totaled about $15 billion, or 0.14 percent of GNP.* (At 0.7 percent, the figure would have been $75 billion.)[39] Sachs believes that if the flow of aid to poor countries were doubled, extreme poverty could be cut in half.

In the wake of crises around the world in recent decades, for example Central America in the 1980s, Afghanistan in 2001, Iraq in 2003, experts have called for "a new Marshall Plan" to accelerate the pace of development, on the assumption that larger volumes of foreign aid would bring about economic transformations that until now have eluded most poor countries.[40] Through the Marshall Plan, a three-year program that began in 1948, the United States provided grants totaling $13 billion in food, machinery, and other products for reconstruction of 17 European countries. To coordinate the program, the Organization of European Economic Cooperation, precursor of the European Union, was established.

In fact, a similar approach, with heavy flows of external resources and the active participation of recipient countries in decisions on policies and resource allocation, has been tried in a different setting—Latin America—though with scant results. The Alliance for Progress, inaugurated by President Kennedy and Latin American leaders in 1961, was designed with the Marshall Plan in mind, although with fewer resources—$20 billion ($10 billion in development assistance, $10 billion in private investment) over 10 years. (To be sure, much of the Marshall Plan resources went not for development but for reconstruction of a devastated Europe.) By the early 1970s, Latin America was supposed to have been well on the road to democracy, prosperity, and social justice. Conditions in Latin America today, more than forty years later, demonstrate that the Alliance for Progress did not succeed.

Why did the Marshall Plan succeed in Europe, and why was Japan transformed into a democracy after World War II, while comparable efforts in Latin America failed? And why should we be skeptical of Marshall Plan rhetoric in connection with our involvement in Afghanistan and Iraq? Devastated though they were after World War II, Western Europe and Japan still possessed the indispensable resources for

---

*Immigrant remittances to Latin American countries, largely from the United States, totaled roughly $45 billion in 2004—exceeding all foreign direct investment and foreign aid combined according to a recent Inter-American Development Bank study cited in a *Los Angeles Times* editorial of May 21, 2005.

human progress: large numbers of educated, trained, resourceful people who had once before succeeded in producing high levels of prosperity based on a combination of entrepreneurship, technological advances, sophisticated public and private institutions, advanced educational systems, and infrastructure and productive capacity that had survived the war. The prewar condition of Western Europe and Japan, and the speed of postwar recovery (and, in Germany and Japan, the transition to democracy) were the result of value systems that are prone to progress. I agree with Jeffrey Sachs and others that increased levels of development assistance are desirable. But substantially higher levels of assistance, for example in Central America following the Sandinista Revolution in Nicaragua in 1979, cannot assure transforming rates of economic growth in the absence of sustained good policies and institutions that work, both of which may depend on cultural change.

"Racism," Human Nature, and Culture

AMONG THE MOST SERIOUS CRITIQUES of attempts to link culture with development is that they are racist. A comment of Jeffrey Sachs's is relevant: "[A] main problem with cultural interpretations is that they are usually made on the basis of prejudice."[41] It's important to note that nothing in this book is based on any kind of genetic or racial theory of culture. As far as we know, culture has nothing to do with genes or race. It is acquired by each generation and transmitted through child rearing, family, churches, schools, the media, and peer relationships, among other things. Culture changes, genes probably do not, at least not in the time frame and context with which we are concerned.[42]

Haiti and Barbados are cases in point. Both are largely populated by the descendents of slaves imported from the same area of West Africa. During colonial times, both were sugar colonies, one French, one British, dependent on slave labor. The Haitian slaves fought for and won their independence from France early in 1804 (see chapter 1), while Barbados remained a British colony until 1966. Starting early in the eighteenth century, and reflecting the liberalization of British society more generally, the Barbadian slaves became increasingly acculturated to British values and institutions and gradually gained political influence that culminated in the twentieth century with political dominance over the island.

The contrasts today between Haiti and Barbados are startling. Barbados receives a perfect score for political rights and civil liberties from Freedom House, a respected democracy assessment organization, while Haiti is judged "not free." On the 2003 UN Human Development Index, Barbados is number 27—ahead of Singapore and South Korea—while Haiti is number 150 of 175 countries. Culture matters. Race doesn't. Moreover, labeling cultural arguments as "racist" blocks access to a potentially important instrument of progress—cultural change.

The Culture Matters Research Project

THE CENTRAL LIBERAL TRUTH is an effort to take the cultural paradigm from theory to practice in the form of concrete guidelines for action. To produce these guidelines, we identified three tasks, each requiring answers to a fundamental question:

Task 1. What are the values and attitudes that influence the political, economic, and social evolution of societies?

Task 2. What are the instruments and institutions that transmit cultural values, beliefs, and attitudes, and how amenable are they to application or modification for the purpose of promoting progressive values?

Task 3. What can we learn about the role of culture and cultural change from case studies, including studies of societies that have experienced political, economic, and social transformations?

To address these issues, the CMRP recruited 65 experts from 22 countries around the world. Most were university professors—30 universities were represented—but the group also included representatives of research institutions or foundations, journalists, government officials, and various other professions. (Brief biographical sketches of the participants are found in the Appendix.) Fifty-one of the participants prepared papers for two conferences at the Fletcher School, one that was held in March of 2003, the second in March of 2004. The conferences were also attended by the 14 members of an advisory board.

With respect to the values and attitudes that matter (Task 1), the CMRP has produced a model, or typology, of cultural values that derives principally from the work of the Argentine journalist and writer Mariano Grondona. This typology, which is discussed in chapter 2, comprises 25 factors that are viewed very differently in cultures conducive to progress and those that resist progress. By disaggregating "culture," the typology offers specific value, belief, and attitude targets for change.

The instruments and institutions of cultural transmission and change (Task 2) include child-rearing practices, several aspects of education, religion, the media, political leadership, and development projects. Harvard psychologist Jerome Kagan coordinated the papers dealing with child development, including his own and another on child rearing and other papers on character education, civic education, and education reform. The papers on religion address Buddhism, Catholicism, Confucianism (not a religion but an ethical code), Hinduism, Islam, Judaism, Orthodox Christianity, and Protestantism. The media papers cover news and opinion journalism and entertainment television. The paper on the role of political leadership was written by a politician, former governor of Colorado Richard Lamm. The two papers on development assistance include a broad overview of the impact on values, beliefs, and attitudes of traditional development activities, and a description and assessment of a specific project designed to increase political participation. These essays were published in January 2006 by Routledge as *Developing Cultures: Essays on Cultural Change*, co-edited by Jerome Kagan and me.

The guidelines for the case studies encouraged the writers to explore both sides of the Moynihan aphorism: how culture influences the success and failure of societies, and how politics, defined broadly to include individual and group initiatives as well as political action, can change a culture. The 27 papers cover Africa (Botswana, South Africa, and a Yoruba community in Nigeria); East Asia (China, Japan, Singapore, Taiwan); Eastern Europe and Orthodox countries (Russia, the city of Novgorod in Russia, Georgia, and former members of the Soviet Bloc); India; Islamic countries (Egypt, Indonesia, Pakistan/ Bangladesh, and Turkey); Latin America (Argentina, Brazil, Chile, Mexico, and Venezuela); and the West (African-Americans in the United States, Ireland, Italy, the Province of Quebec, Spain, and Sweden). These essays are being published by Routledge late in 2005 as *Developing Cultures: Case Studies*, co-edited by Peter Berger and me.

Structure of the Book

CHAPTER 1 EXPLORES THE POWER OF CULTURE through the history of Hispaniola, an island shared by Haiti and the Dominican Republic—two countries of contrasting cultures. Chapter 2 examines the 25-factor model/ typology of progress-prone and progress-resistant cultures to facilitate understanding of what we mean when we refer to "cultural values, beliefs, and attitudes" and how culture shapes the behaviors that influence how a society evolves politically, economically, and socially.

Chapter 3 begins with two models of cultural change that explain *how* culture operates with other factors to influence behavior. It then gives an overview of the instruments and institutions of cultural transmission and/or change: child rearing, education, the media, and leadership. The fifth institution, religion, is so salient in its impact on culture and so varied that I devote a separate chapter to it.

Chapter 4 addresses the key role played by religion and includes an analysis of the performance of 117 countries grouped by predominant religion with respect to ten indicators of progress, along with an overview of the eleven CMRP papers that address religions.

Chapters 5 and 6 review the 27 Task 3 case studies broken down by region or, in the sense that Samuel Huntington has used the word, civilizations: societies that share "values, beliefs, institutions, and social structures."[43] Chapter 5 includes Africa, Confucian (East Asian) countries, India, and Islamic countries. Chapter 6 includes Latin America, Orthodox/Eastern European countries, and the West.

Chapter 7 identifies and explores the patterns of change that emerge from the Task 3 case studies: the key role of leadership; the importance of openness to new ideas; the utility of finding or inventing continuities with the past; the crucial role of education; the impact of economic policy; the constructive role of foreign investment; the cultural utility of home ownership; the key role of a professional civil service.

Chapter 8 examines initiatives or programs designed to promote cultural change: Peru's Institute of Human Development, which promoted the "The Ten Commandments of Development" in Peru and other Latin American countries; anti-corruption campaigns supported by the National Strategy Information Center, a nongovernmental organization in Washington, D.C.; a project to promote political participation in Bolivia; a campaign to promote punctuality in Ecuador; USAID's efforts to promote democracy in Latin America; the transformation of Bogotá Colombia; philanthropy; American and other schools abroad; and an assessment of the cultural impact of traditional development programs.

Chapter 9 concludes the book with guidelines for progressive cultural change in several key areas: child rearing and education; religious reform; government policies; development assistance institutions; universities; media; and the private sector.

1

The Riddle of Hispaniola

I OFFER THE FOLLOWING COMPARISON of Haiti, a former French slave colony, and the Dominican Republic, a former Spanish slave colony, to demonstrate that culture matters. The two countries share the island of Hispaniola, largely neutralizing geography, climate, and environment as possible explanations for their divergent histories.

During the first half of the nineteenth century, Haiti was far more powerful and affluent than the Dominican Republic, yet today Haiti is by far the poorest country in the Western Hemisphere, while the Dominican Republic is a far more progressive society, albeit demonstrating the political, economic, and social debilities common to most Ibero-American countries—the countries that were once colonies of Spain and Portugal.

The Island of Hispaniola

THE CARIBBEAN ISLAND OF HISPANIOLA is one of the four islands of the Greater Antilles, flanked by Cuba and Jamaica to the west, and Puerto Rico to the east.

Its northern shore falls on the twentieth parallel of north latitude—well into the tropical zone, which extends east across the Atlantic

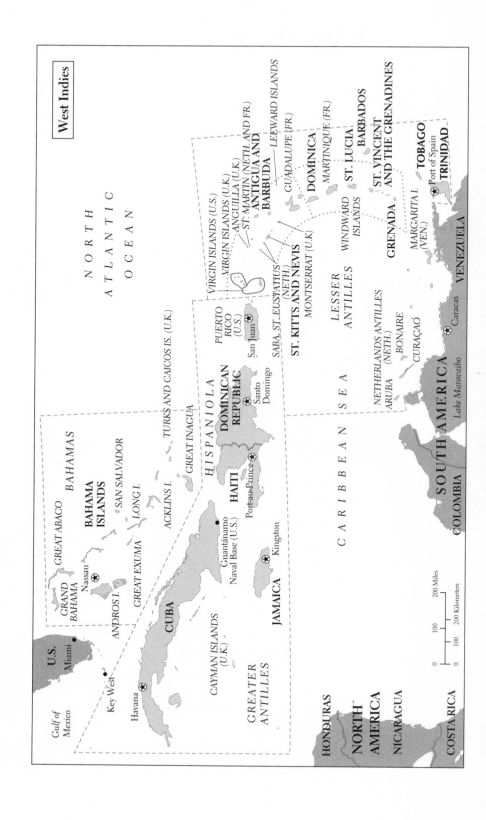

West Indies

through the sub-Saharan Sahel countries of Africa; southern Saudi Arabia; central India; northern Myanmar (Burma), Thailand, and Laos; the Chinese island of Hainan, not far from Hong Kong; across the Pacific through the island of Hawaii, continuing into Mexico passing near Mexico City and through the Yucatan Peninsula back into the Caribbean, where it touches Cuba at Santiago and Guantánamo Bay before completing its full circle.

Hispaniola is the twenty-third largest island in the world, 29,418 square miles, roughly the size of Austria or South Carolina. The Dominican Republic, on the east side, occupies slightly less than two-thirds of the island's total area; Haiti, on the west, slightly more than one-third.

Rich agricultural lands are found on both sides of the island, although the Dominican Republic is somewhat better off in this respect. The Cibao Valley in the north-central region of the Dominican Republic is the most extensive fertile area on the island. But Haiti is also endowed with flat, rich lands: the Northern Plain, surrounding the city of Cap Haitien along the Atlantic Coast; the valley of the Artibonite River, which empties into the Gulf of La Gonave, the body of water that separates the northern and southern peninsulas, or jaws, that dominate Haiti's geography; and the Cul-de-Sac, a rich valley just to the north of the capital city of Port-au-Prince. Gold and nickel are mined in the Dominican Republic. Haiti's only significant mineral endowment was bauxite deposits, depleted decades ago.

When Christopher Columbus arrived at Hispaniola in December 1492, it was populated by the Taino Indians, members of the Arawak family, whose lands extended back down the Lesser Antilles to northeastern South America. The Taino civilization was less advanced than those of the Aztec, Maya, and Inca, on the Central and South American mainland.

Columbus's second expedition, late in 1493, established Spanish control over the island, and the Indians were effectively enslaved to work in gold and silver mines. Their numbers began to drop precipitously as a consequence of overwork, physical cruelty, and above all their susceptibility to diseases arriving with the Spaniards, for which the latter had developed substantial immunity but against which the Tainos were defenseless. By one estimate, there may have been about six hundred thousand Tainos in 1492; in 1508, the number had dropped to sixty thousand, and by 1518, there were only three thousand survivors.[1]

The demise of the Tainos left a labor shortage, and the Spaniards began importing African slaves in large numbers. Sugar production began to surge and mining declined, leaving most African slaves to work the land. By 1540, however, Spain's interest had shifted to Mexico and Peru, where precious metals were abundant. Hispaniola slipped into the backwaters of the Spanish Empire.

Spain's inattentiveness left Hispaniola vulnerable. It was first attacked by the British in 1586 when Francis Drake occupied the capital city of Santo Domingo and pocketed a substantial ransom from the Spaniards, and then again in 1625, when French, Dutch, and British privateers established a base on the island of Tortuga (*La Tortue* in French) off the northwestern shore of Hispaniola. When the Spaniards failed to oust them, the French established their control over the island and then extended their presence to the western third of Hispaniola. French domination of what came to be called St. Domingue was confirmed by the Treaty of Ryswick with Spain in 1697.

In the eighteenth century, St. Domingue grew rich on agriculture driven by slave labor. In 1776, Adam Smith observed: "The French colony of St. Domingue . . . is now the most important of the sugar colonies of the West Indies, and its produce is said to be greater than that of all the English sugar colonies put together."[2] Fourteen years later, a slave uprising triggered a revolution, led by the fabled Toussaint L'Ouverture, that concluded with the bloody defeat and ouster of the French in 1803. The Republic of Haiti declared its independence in 1804 under General Jean-Jacques Dessalines, successor to Toussaint.

At the time of Haiti's independence, its population was more than half a million, of whom more than 85 percent were slaves. Santo Domingo, the eastern two-thirds of Hispaniola, with a population of fewer than one hundred thousand,[3] had ceased to be a Spanish colony, having been ceded to France by Spain in 1795. The Haitian slave rebellion had overwhelmed the Spaniards and then the French, and the only remaining French garrison on the island controlled the city of Santo Domingo. With the help of the British, the Spaniards regained control of the eastern two-thirds of Hispaniola from the Haitians in 1809, but in 1821, the colony proclaimed its independence from Spain, which scarcely resisted. A few months later, the Haitians under President Jean Pierre Boyer invaded the Dominican side and met little opposition. The entire island was unified under Haitian dominion for two decades.

The overthrow of Boyer in 1843 triggered a rebellion by the Dominicans that led, the following year, to their establishing an independent Dominican Republic.

Hispaniola in the Twenty-first Century

ONE HUNDRED AND SIXTY YEARS LATER, at the beginning of the twenty-first century, the Dominican Republic is a fairly representative Latin American country of about nine million people. Throughout much of the nineteenth and twentieth century, its history was characterized by dictatorships, civil strife, slow and inequitably distributed economic development, and high levels of corruption. The United States intervened twice, militarily, in the twentieth century: first, at the time of World War I, concerned that the country's chaotic politics and economic mismanagement rendered it vulnerable to a German presence in the Caribbean approaches to the Panama Canal; and again in 1965, when a revolution erupted that Washington feared could lead to another Cuba.[4]

Since 1965, the Dominican Republic has moved somewhat erratically, as have so many Latin American countries, toward democratic governance. Over the last four decades, politics were dominated by three-time President Joaquín Balaguer, who died in 2002 at the age of 95. In Freedom House's 2003 rankings of countries, the Dominican Republic scores 2 for both political rights and civil liberties on a scale of 1 to 7, in which 1 is fully free.

Haiti's history since it retreated to its original and current borders in 1844 has been unrelievedly dismal. A parade of self-seeking, incompetent, corrupt, and often brutal chiefs of state has continued into the twenty-first century. In a realization of the Malthusian prediction—that population tends to increase at a faster rate than its means of subsistence and that unless it is checked by moral restraint or disaster widespread poverty and degradation inevitably result—population growth has outstripped Haiti's natural resources, while land erosion, resulting chiefly from the clearing of trees, has left a scarred landscape. The border between Haiti and the Dominican Republic is vividly apparent from the air: brown and denuded to the west, green and treed to the east. Haiti's population today totals about seven million people.

Many hundreds of thousands of Dominicans and Haitians have left their native countries and live, legally or illegally, in the United States. Many Dominicans pass through neighboring Puerto Rico, where they either remain or continue on to the mainland. Large numbers of Haitians live in Canada, France, and the Dominican Republic.[5] As in the Dominican Republic, the United States intervened twice, militarily, in Haiti in the twentieth century: first, at the time of World War I, with the same concern for the security of the Panama Canal; and again in 1994–95, to return the elected president Jean-Bertrand Aristide to power after he had been ousted by the Haitian military in September 1991, having served just eight months of his term.[6] In 2004, Aristide, now generally viewed as non-democratic and corrupt, was forced out by a violent uprising of opponents, including former allies, and the U.S. military returned to escort him out of Haiti and to help pacify the country. However, the violence and chaos continue as of this writing.

Two Haitian chiefs of state, François Duvalier, dictatorial president from 1957 to 1971, and Jean-Bertrand Aristide, arrived in power with the reputation of liberal reformers, only to revert to the traditional abuse of power. Freedom House ranked Haiti as "not free" in 2003 with scores of 6 for both political rights and civil liberties.

Far richer and more powerful than the Dominican Republic and its predecessor Spanish colony in the eighteenth century and the first half of the nineteenth, Haiti is today the poorest country by far in the Western Hemisphere. The striking reversal of the two countries is apparent from the following data, mostly taken from The United Nations *Human Development Report 2003:*[7]

Table 1.1

Indicator	Dominican Republic	Haiti
Human Development Index (combines health, education and prosperity factors; 1 is best, 173 is worst)	94	150
Life expectancy at birth	67 years	49 years
Adult literacy	84%	51%
School enrolment as % of school-age people	72%	52%
Corruption—from Transparency International's Corruption Perceptions Index 2004:		
145 countries with #1 (Finland) cleanest	87	145
GDP per capita calculated by purchasing power parity	$7,020	$1,860

Explaining the Reversal

WHAT EXPLAINS THE STRIKING REVERSAL? Let's first explore the most common explanations for differences in the way that societies have evolved—environment and geography.

As I mentioned in the introduction, historian Jared Diamond has made a compelling case that environmental factors chiefly explain different paths of development. Prominent among these factors are climate, including temperature variations and rainfall/snowfall patterns; natural resource endowment, including the extent of arable land, the availability of domesticable animals, mineral deposits, and waterways that facilitate trade; and number of mountain ranges that impede communication.

Jeffrey Sachs reaches a similar conclusion: "Two basic [geographic] patterns stand out. First, the temperate regions of the world are vastly more developed than the tropics. . . . Second, geographically remote regions—either those far from the coasts and navigable rivers or mountainous states with high internal and international transport costs—are considerably less developed than societies on coastal plains or navigable rivers. Landlocked states in general face the worst problems."[8]

In pondering why some countries are rich while others are poor, and why some evolve democratically while others don't, geography is an indispensable first consideration. But exceptions to the geographic presumption are numerous. The island of Hispaniola is a case in point. There are some differences in the natural environment between the eastern side of the island (the Dominican Republic) and the western side (Haiti), but they are relatively small compared to the similarities, and insufficient to explain the dramatic reversal of their fortunes.

If we follow the tropical latitudes occupied by Hispaniola around the world, we note some further contrasts, partly explained, to be sure, by environmental variations. Several of the countries are poor and often authoritarian in their politics, such as the Sahel countries of sub-Saharan Africa, Myanmar, and Laos. Saudi Arabia is rich in oil but authoritarian. India is poor—albeit now with a growing economy—but democratic. Thailand has prospered and moved toward democracy. China's economy has been growing at a phenomenal pace for a quarter of a century, but its politics remain authoritarian. Mexico has prospered, and prolonged one-party rule has recently given way, haltingly perhaps, to the politics of pluralism, though it remains far behind its neighbors to the north, the United States and Canada. Cuba, half a century ago relatively prosperous but inequitable and autocratic, is today poor, equitable, and autocratic.

Two islands in the same latitudes as Hispaniola stand out: Hong Kong and Hawaii. Hong Kong, when still a British colony in the last half of the twentieth century, experienced an economic miracle. Today, it is part of China, and as prosperous as France. Its people's preference for democracy is a continuing headache for Beijing. The island of Hawaii, part of the state of Hawaii, enjoys the prosperity and freedom of the United States.

In other latitudes, the limits of geographic determinism are also apparent. One finds very different conditions in the neighboring Central American countries of Costa Rica, relatively prosperous and democratically stable, and Nicaragua, poor and with a long history of civil war and dictatorship. No dramatic differences exist in their physical environment; indeed, Nicaragua has an advantage in natural resource endowment.

The contrasts between Argentina and Canada, and Argentina and Australia, are also relevant. All three are large, resource rich, substantially or wholly in the temperate zone (interestingly, more than one-third of Australia is in the tropics), and relatively underpopulated. All three were the object of heavy British investment in the nineteenth century. Today, Argentina's per capita GNP is less than one-half that of Canada and Australia. Canada and Australia are among the world's most stable democracies, while Argentina's political history is largely authoritarian and filled with strife and instability.

Canada and Russia occupy essentially the same latitudes. There are significant geographic and demographic differences between the two, but there are also many similarities, including rich mineral deposits, petroleum among them. The economic and political contrasts are dramatic. Per capita GNP in Canada is roughly six times greater. It is tempting to blame the economic gap—not to mention the political one—on seven decades of Communism. But according to economic historian Angus Maddison, Russia was even further behind Canada in 1913 than in 1989.[9] And, of course, Russia had known nothing throughout its history but highly centralized, authoritarian politics.

Let's look to another part of the world that confounds geographic explanations of economic development: East Asia. How can we explain the fact that the countries experiencing the fastest economic growth in the second half of the twentieth century were all "Confucian"—including Hong Kong and Singapore, both in the tropics?*

The Power of Culture

How else can the striking reversal of Haiti and the Dominican Republic be explained? I debated Jeffrey Sachs twice in 2001, the first time at a Harvard discussion series, the second time at the Council on Foreign Relations in New York. I raised the Haiti–Dominican Republic contrast in the first debate as evidence of the power of culture and distributed the following table to make the case that Haiti is much closer culturally to Africa than it is to the neighboring Dominican Republic. I selected Benin because it is in the Dahomey region of Africa, from which came most of the slaves imported into both sides of Hispaniola in the sixteenth, seventeenth, and eighteenth centuries.

Table 1.2
Benin, Haiti, and the Dominican Republic
(Source: World Bank, World Development Report 1999/2000)

Indicator	Benin	Haiti	Dominican Republic
Per capita GNP	$380	$410	$1,770
Child malnutrition	29%	28%	6%
Child mortality per 1000	149	125	47
Life expectancy (years)	53.5	53.5	71
Illiteracy	60%	55%	18%
Urban dweller access to sanitation	60%	43%	89%

I argued that among the common cultural features that relate Haiti to Dahomey is the animist religion known as Voodoo (usually referred to by scholars as "Vodun"), and like many similar animist religions in

---

*"Confucian" will be used throughout this book to describe those countries—China, Korea, Japan, Singapore, Taiwan—that have been profoundly influenced by Chinese culture, which has, in turn, been profoundly influenced by Confucianism, which is not a religion but an ethical code. Of course other influences on Chinese culture are also in play, Buddhism, Taosim, and ancestor worship among them.

Africa, Voodoo has features that resist progress. Voodoo is not a religion that concerns itself with ethical issues: ". . . the notions of sin and a moral law . . . are alien to Vodun."[10] Its followers' destinies are believed to be controlled by hundreds of spirits, the *loa*, very human and capricious, who must be propitiated through ceremonies if one is to realize one's desires. Voodoo is a species of the sorcery that Camerounian economist Daniel Etounga-Manguelle identifies in *Culture Matters* as one of the principal obstacles to progress in Africa.[11] "A society in which magic and witchcraft flourish today is a sick society ruled by tension, fear, and moral disorder. Sorcery is a costly mechanism for managing conflict and preserving the status quo, which is, importantly, what African society is about."[12] Voodoo discourages initiative, rationality, achievement, education, and a number of other factors that are discussed in the following chapter.

Voodoo is practiced mostly by poor Haitians, who make up the vast majority of the country's population. But upper-class Haitians also feel its influence. A Haitian colleague at the USAID mission who has an advanced degree from a U.S. university once said to me, "If *any* Haitian, myself included, ever tells you that they totally reject Voodoo, they are lying." My Haitian son-in-law, who holds a graduate degree from Harvard, agrees. He tells me that his early exposure to Voodoo often colors his reactions to events.

The impact of Voodoo on Haiti is conveyed vividly by Wallace Hodges, an American Baptist missionary who lived in Haiti for 20 years, in a 1981 article in the *Baltimore Sun*:

> [Dr. Hodges] has developed a theory as to why Haiti . . . is one of the poorest [countries] in the world. It is a theory based on culture, not race; on belief, not ability. It puts the blame for Haiti's plight squarely with the Voodoo spirits that still hold dominant influence over the lives of [the Haitians]. . . . Haiti . . . "has a special vision of the world" created by its African roots and tempered by its experience of slavery. "Haitians see the nature of events much differently than we do." The basic difference is that the Judeo-Christian tradition makes man responsible for his destiny. "By internalizing guilt, we hold ourselves responsible for what happens, and what to do about it." In contrast, the Haitian externalizes his guilt. He attributes everything, the good as well as the bad, to the spirits. *Since this limits his responsibility . . . it also limits his potential* (my emphasis).

At its simplest, it means that if a Haitian steals a jug of milk from Dr. Hodge's hospital, he has no shame because he believes he was given the opportunity by the spirits. On a more complex level, it means that there is a limit to . . . how organized the society can become, how advanced its agriculture can be.

"A [Haitian] child is made to understand immediately that everything that happens is due to [the spirits]. He is raised to externalize evil and to understand he is in continuous danger. . . . People believe that the real reason Haitians want to [emigrate] is that they are afraid of the government. That is superficial. They are afraid of each other. You will find a high degree of paranoia in Haiti. . . ."[13]

But Voodoo is not the only progress-resistant force at work in Haiti. Hodges's reference to slavery is relevant to the contrast between the two neighboring countries. The treatment of the slaves in French St. Domingue was particularly brutal. And the uprising through which they won their freedom left them immediately in charge of their destiny. Their value system was largely shaped by African culture, of which Voodoo was a prominent component, and by slavery. Nobel Prize–winning economist Sir Arthur Lewis, himself a descendent of African slaves, wrote that those who had experienced slavery, both master and slave, "have inherited the idea that work is only fit for slaves."[14]

In backwater colonial Santo Domingo, "master and slave relied upon each other for company and support, and the chains were in this way gradually lightened."[15] Confirmation of the contrasting treatment of slaves can be appreciated from the racial makeup of the two countries today: Haiti has a small white and mulatto upper class, while the large majority underclass is black. The Dominican Republic has a small white upper class while the masses are predominantly mulatto.

But the slavery experience has left scars on the cultures of both countries. The Venezuelan writer Carlos Rangel observes: "It is not surprising to find that a number of factors inhibit the development of societies formerly based on slavery: the passive resistance to work that is the earmark of the slave; the absurd prestige of idleness that afflicts his master; and, finally, a rhythm of life so little concerned with punctuality. . . ."[16]

Jeffrey Sachs has argued that two major non-cultural factors adversely affected Haiti: (1) the precipitous drop of world sugar prices following the introduction of sugar beets in Europe during the second half of the nineteenth century, and (2) the U.S. marine occupation of Haiti from 1915 to 1934.[17] But the marines also occupied the Dominican Republic, from 1916 to 1924, setting the stage for the Trujillo dictatorship.[18] And as a consequence of the break-up of Haiti's plantations into small plots by Presidents Alexandre Pétion and Jean Pierre Boyer between 1806 and 1843, Haiti ceased to export sugar for several decades, while the Dominican Republic became an increasingly important sugar exporter in the second half of the nineteenth century.

What other factors might explain Haiti's lack of progress? Bad leadership is one obvious candidate. The only Haitian leaders with a claim to greatness were Toussaint L'Ouverture, leader of the slave rebellion, and Alexandre Pétion (1806–18), a social innovator far ahead of his time who provided health care for all, benefits for pregnant and nursing women, and security for the elderly. But with the exception of Pétion, Haiti has never had a president fully committed to modernizing the country. Haitian leaders have reflected their culture rather than trying to change it. Once again we are reminded of the parallels between Haiti and Africa, where anti-democratic, oppressive, self-serving leadership has been common.

Explanations that emphasize policies and institutions arrive at a similar dead end. The policies will inevitably reflect the agenda of a self-seeking, authoritarian leader—and the culture that both nurtured him and may have produced many other similar leaders. Those of us who have worked at institution-building in countries like Haiti are well aware of the frustrations that attend such efforts when mired in a culture that resists modernization. Such societies confirm the truth of Daniel Etounga-Manguelle's observation: "Culture is the mother. Institutions are the children."[19] Though as we shall see, it *can* be the other way around.

During the past two centuries, the two countries that share the island of Hispaniola have flip-flopped. How can one understand this reversal other than as a reflection of a set of values and attitudes derivative of African culture, including an animist religion, and of the slavery experience, that resist democratization, prosperity, and justice? If one asks how slavery can be relevant if it ended two hundred years ago, one need only recall Robert Putnam's conclusion in *Making Democracy Work* that the culture of the Italian south is still influenced by the Norman presence *nine hundred* years ago.

How else can Haiti's tortured history be explained? Some observers cite the heavy indemnity the French extracted from Haiti in 1825 for reestablishment of relations (originally 150 million francs over 5 years, later reduced to 60 million francs over 30 years) as a major cause of Haiti's poverty.[20] It is also true that, for several decades after its independence, Haiti was ostracized by other Western Hemisphere nations, the United States among them, out of fear that Haiti's successful slave rebellion would spread to their own slaves. With respect to the United States, that policy changed at the time of the Civil War—official recognition was extended in 1862. Others have argued that Haiti's problems are largely the result of a mulatto upper class that identifies itself with the former French masters and treats black Haitians as inferior beings.[21] (When I lived in Haiti, a mulatto neighbor once said to me of the black Haitians, "You know, they really are subhuman.") But while the color divide remains a divisive force in Haiti, for a good part of Haiti's history, black chiefs of state, "Papa Doc" Duvalier among them, ran the country in an authoritarian manner similar to that of mulatto chiefs of state.

While these and other factors may be relevant, none of them, even collectively, is adequate to the task of explaining the unending dysfunction of Haitian society. What *can* explain Haiti's predicament is a set of cultural values, beliefs, and attitudes, rooted in African culture and the slavery experience, that resist progress.

What are these values, beliefs, and attitudes? In the next chapter, we break down "culture" into 25 components that are viewed very differently in societies that are prone to democracy, justice, and prosperity, and societies that resist them.

JARED DIAMOND'S SEQUEL to *Guns, Germs, and Steel* was published early in 2005—*Collapse: How Societies Choose to Fail or Succeed.*[22] In it he explores several cases to explain how the interplay of environment and policy influences historic outcomes. Diamond, too, devotes a chapter to Haiti and the Dominican Republic. At the beginning of that chapter he writes:

> Why were the outcomes so different in the two countries, and why is it Haiti rather than the Dominican Republic that went into steep decline? Some environmental differences do exist between the two halves of the island and made some contribution to the outcomes, but that is

the smaller part of the explanation. Most of the explanation has to do with differences between the two peoples in their histories, attitudes, self-defined identity, and institutions, as well as between their recent leaders of government. For anyone inclined to caricature environmental history as "environmental determinism," the contrasting histories of the Dominican Republic and Haiti provide a useful antidote. Yes, environmental problems do constrain human societies, but the societies' responses also make a difference. So, too, for better or worse, do the actions and inactions of leaders.[23]

Diamond goes on to analyze the different responses in the two sides of Hispaniola, principally with respect to environmental factors and choices. The narrowness of this focus deters him from analyzing the broader array of differences, for example in education, health, infrastructure, and more generally the patterns of institutional debility. Had he pursued a broader approach, he would, I believe, have perceived that the patterns of "choices" and patterns of "leadership" are so striking—and not only in recent history—as to suggest a common denominator, which is culture.

2

Disaggregating "Culture"

... two aspects of culture have struck me as particularly relevant in the flat world. One is how outward your culture is: to what degree is it open to foreign influences and ideas? ... The other, more intangible, is how inward your culture is ... to what degree is there a sense of national solidarity and a focus on development, to what degree is there trust within the society for strangers to collaborate ... and to what degree are the elites in the country concerned with the masses ... ?

—Thomas Friedman, *The World Is Flat*

OVER SEVERAL YEARS OF THOUGHT AND OBSERVATION, the Argentine scholar and journalist Mariano Grondona evolved a theory of development that is captured in a group of cultural factors that affect progress. These factors constitute a typology in which cultures that are favorable to economic development are contrasted with cultures that resist it. As Grondona puts it, "It is possible to construct two ideal value systems: one including only values that favor economic development and the other including only values that resist it. . . . Neither of these value systems exists in reality, and no nation falls completely within either of those two value systems. However, some countries approach the extreme favorable to economic development, whereas others approach the opposite extreme."[1]

Table 2.1
Typology of Progress-Prone and Progress-Resistant Cultures

Factor	Progress-Prone Culture	Progress-Resistant Culture
WORLDVIEW		
1. Religion	Nurtures rationality, achievement; promotes material pursuits; focus on this world; pragmatism	Nurtures irrationality; inhibits material pursuits; focus on the other world; utopianism
2. Destiny	I can influence my destiny for the better	Fatalism, resignation, sorcery
3. Time orientation	Future focus promotes planning, punctuality, deferred gratification	Present or past focus discourages planning, punctuality, saving
4. Wealth	Product of human creativity is wealth expandable (positive sum)	What exists (zero-sum) is wealth; not expandable
5. Knowledge	Practical, verifiable; facts matter	Abstract, theoretical, cosmological, not verifiable
VALUES, VIRTUES		
6. Ethical code	Rigorous within realistic norms; feeds trust	Elastic, wide gap twixt utopian norms and behavior = mistrust
7. The lesser virtues	A job well done, tidiness, courtesy, punctuality matter	Lesser virtues unimportant
8. Education	Indispensable; promotes autonomy, heterodoxy, dissent, creativity	Less priority; promotes dependency, orthodoxy
ECONOMIC BEHAVIOR		
9. Work/achievement	Live to work: work leads to wealth	Work to live: work doesn't lead to wealth; work is for the poor
10. Frugality and prosperity	The mother of investment	A threat to equality because those who save will get rich, provoking envy
11. Entrepreneurship	Investment and creativity	Rent seeking: income derives from government connections
12. Risk propensity	Moderate	Low
13. Competition	Leads to excellence	Is a sign of aggression, and a threat to equality—and privilege

Table 2.1 (*continued*)
Typology of Progress-Prone and Progress-Resistant Cultures

Factor	Progress-Prone Culture	Progress-Resistant Culture
14. Innovation	Open; rapid adaptation to innovation	Suspicious; slow adaptation to innovation
15. Advancement	Based on merit, connections	Based on family and/or patron connections

SOCIAL BEHAVIOR

16. Rule of law/ corruption	Reasonably law abiding; corruption is prosecuted	Money, connections matter; corruption is tolerated
17. Radius of identification and trust	Stronger identification with the broader society	Stronger identification with the narrow community
18. Family	The idea of "family" extends to the broader society	The family is a fortress against the broader society
19. Association (social capital)	Trust, identification breed coopera-tion, affiliation, participation	Mistrust breeds extreme individualism, anomie
20. The individual/ the group	Emphasizes the individual but not excessively	Emphasizes the collectivity
21. Authority	Dispersed: checks and balances, consensus	Centralized: unfettered, often arbitrary
22. Role of elites	Responsibility to society	Power and rent seeking; exploitative
23. Church-state relations	Secularized; wall between church and state	Religion plays major role in civic sphere
24. Gender relationships	If gender equality not a reality, at least not inconsistent with value system	Women subordinated to men in most dimensions of life
25. Fertility	The number of children should depend on the family's capacity to raise and educate them	Children are gifts of God; they are an economic asset

Four participants in the Culture Matters Research Project have expanded Grondona's typology to include political and social as well as economic development: Irakli Chkonia, Ronald Inglehart, Matteo Marini, and I. Their expansion also incorporated the subheadings World View, Values and Virtues, Economic Behavior, and Social Behavior. It's important to keep in mind Grondona's characterization of the typology as "idealized"—a simplification of a complex system. There is no such thing as a monolithic culture; all cultures have crosscurrents to their mainstreams. That is as true of the Argentine/Latin American culture that served as Grondona's model for the progress-resistant column in the typology as it is for American culture, which served as the progress-prone column. Robert Hefner's words, cited in the introduction, bear repeating: ". . . this theme [of variety within cultures] allows us to recognize that even in relatively progress unfriendly cultures, there are alternative streams at work, some of which may contain bits and pieces of progressive values."[2] As we will see, cultural change may be facilitated by reference to a progressive cultural tradition, even if out of a country's mainstream.

The political scientist Ronald Inglehart has tested Grondona's 25 elements of culture with data from the World Values Survey, a periodic assessment of values and attitudes over two decades that now covers 81 countries and 85 percent of the world's population. I will reference his findings in reviewing the typology. In general, "these empirical findings tend to support the Progress Typology—sometimes very strongly."[3] Of the 25 factors, 11 receive "strong confirmation" from the World Values Survey data; 3 receive "moderately strong confirmation"; there is "no significant support" for 2; and no data are available for 9. As Inglehart stresses, "the World Values Survey was not designed to test the Progress Typology. But it was designed to provide a comprehensive exploration of all important realms of human values, and consequently it does tap most . . . of the domains included in the Progress Typology."[4] Inglehart's colleague Miguel Basáñez has since developed a questionnaire tailored to the CMRP typology that was tested in Guatemala in 2005.

Bassam Tibi, who wrote papers on Islam and Egypt that appear in the companion *Developing Cultures* volumes, presented the typology at a conference in Abu Dhabi. As I address the typology components, I will draw on some of his comments as well as those of Inglehart and author Michael Novak. I will also refer to Haiti, a prototype of the progress-resistant model.

Worldview

1. Religion

Religion can be a powerful force for progress to the extent that it nurtures rationality and objectivity, encourages accumulation of wealth, and promotes ethical behavior consistent with the goals of the UN Universal Declaration of Human Rights. The foregoing statement captures the essence of the Protestant ethic to which Max Weber attributed the rise of capitalism. It reverberates in many subsequent factors: for example, destiny, ethical code, education, work, frugality, entrepreneurship, and innovation.

Religion—in the case of the Confucian countries, an ethical code—is a principal source of values, which may persist long after religious observance has declined (witness the highly successful Lutheran Nordic countries, where the religion is no longer widely practiced). Those values can be either nurturing of or resistant to democracy, social justice, and economic development. In *Democracy in America*, Alexis de Tocqueville notes: "[The British settlers] brought with them into the New World a form of Christianity which I cannot better describe than by styling it a democratic and republican religion. This contributed powerfully to the establishment of a republic and a democracy in public affairs; and from the beginning, politics and religion contracted an alliance which has never been dissolved."[5]

If a religion nurtures irrationality, like Voodoo, inhibits or is ambivalent about material pursuits, like Catholicism, and focuses on the other world, its adherents are likely to be indisposed to economic development. But they are also likely to be susceptible to a passivity, a resignation in which authoritarianism and injustice thrive. With the great early centuries of Islam in mind, Bassam Tibi says, "In reading the Qur'an and studying its precepts . . . I . . . find in Islam a deep commitment to rationalism and achievement as well as to the pursuit of worldly affairs . . . but I miss this spirit among contemporary Muslims."[6] As Haiti is prototypical of a progress-resistant society, Voodoo is prototypical of those religions that nurture irrationality.

As Ronald Inglehart put it, "Strong emphasis on religion is negatively correlated with progress. Societies in which religion is linked with rationality, material pursuits, and a focus on this world tend to attach much less importance to religion."[7] (The United States, where a substantial majority of citizens are believers, in contrast to Western Europe, is an exceptional case.) Inglehart's words echo the poignant plaint of John Wesley more than two centuries ago: "I fear, wherever riches have increased, the essence of religion has decreased in the same proportion. Therefore I do not see how it is possible . . . for any revival of true religion to continue long. For religion must necessarily produce both industry and frugality, and these cannot but produce riches. But as riches increase, so will pride, anger, and love of the world in all its branches."[8]

2. Destiny

Tibi again finds language in the Qur'an that he interprets as supporting the progressive view of destiny: "Whatever good befalls you . . . it is from Allah; and whatever ill from yourself."[9] However, one could argue that those words are ambivalent: if good can only come from Allah, then the idea that humans are largely responsible for their destiny is undermined, even if the Qur'an assigns the avoidance of ill to humans. In any event, Tibi concludes, "the fatalist worldview can be observed at work in reality, even though belied by . . . Islamic revelation."[10]

3. Time orientation

Progressive cultures, such as Protestant and Confucian societies, focus more on the future than progress-resistant societies. Orientation toward the future implies the possibility of change and progress, and that possibility, as Weber stressed, must be realizable in this life. Calvinism forces the eyes of the faithful toward the future. So do the basic tenets of Judaism: "Judaism clings to the idea of progress. The Golden Age of Humanity is not in the past, but in the future."[11] Progress-resistant cultures often focus on the present or a glorious past, as in the case of Mexico's evocation of the glories of pre-Colombian civilizations. Such a time emphasis discourages planning and saving. Usually in such cultures, punctuality and the efficient use of time are not highly valued.

4. Wealth

In Protestant/Calvinist societies, where one's state of grace is confirmed by prosperity, culture overrides human nature, and, as Weber stressed, accumulation of wealth is encouraged. The zero-sum worldview discourages initiative since anyone's gain is someone else's loss. In many traditional societies, a "crabs in a barrel" psychology is operative: people who "get ahead" are pulled back with a variety of sanctions, including redistribution of their wealth to the community. Human nature is affronted when another does better than oneself; this dark recess of human nature is probably also the source of *schadenfreude*, the satisfaction one derives from another's problems.

The zero-sum worldview is common to peasant societies around the world, according to anthropologist George Foster, who perceives a "Universal Peasant Culture" dominated by the "Image of Limited Good," which he defines as follows: "By 'Image of Limited Good,' I mean that broad areas of peasant behavior are patterned in such fashion as to suggest that peasants view their social, economic, and natural universes—their total environment—as one in which all of the desired things in life such as land, wealth, health, friendship and love, manliness and honor, respect and status, power and influence, security and safety, *exist in finite quantity* and *are always in short supply*. . . . Not only do these and all other "good things" exist in finite and limited quantities, but in addition *there is no way directly within peasant power to increase the available quantities*."[12]

5. Knowledge

If a society doesn't respect facts, it is at an enormous disadvantage not only in terms of productivity, competitiveness, and economic development but also in building democratic and just institutions. Modernization depends on appreciation of and adaptation to the scientific approach. This is particularly true of facts or interpretations that challenge self-esteem and identity.

Values/Virtues

6. Ethical code

The rigor of the ethical code profoundly influences several other factors including rule of law/corruption, radius of identification and trust, and association. While these latter three factors fall under "social behavior," the ethical code is also highly relevant to economic behavior as well. A rigorous ethical code engenders behaviors that nurture trust, and trust is central to economic efficiency, as Weber stresses when he speaks of Benjamin Franklin's ethical exhortations.[13] That the Nordic countries do so well on economic indices (for example, Finland, Sweden, Denmark, Norway, and Iceland all appear among the top ten countries on the World Economic Forum's 2004 Growth Competitiveness Index) is almost surely related to the fact that they score comparably well in the World Values Survey data on trust. Conversely, Haiti's poverty almost surely reflects the absence of an ethical code in Voodoo, which breeds high levels of mistrust.

Democracy appeared first and most enduringly in countries where the value of fair play, central to the Anglo-Protestant tradition, had taken root—Britain and its offspring being good examples. This was a key element of the congeniality between American culture and democracy that Tocqueville perceived. With respect to the much later consolidation of democracy in Catholic countries, I note Weber's observation: "The God of Calvinism demanded of his believers not single good works, but a life of good works combined into a unified system. There was no place for the very human Catholic cycle of sin, repentance, atonement, release, followed by renewed sin."[14]

7. The lesser virtues

A job well done, tidiness, courtesy, and punctuality are lubricants of both the economic and politico-social systems. The lesser virtues can translate into hard economic data: punctuality is practiced in all of the top 15 countries on the World Economic Forum's competitiveness rankings, 12 of which are Protestant and 3 Confucian (Taiwan, Singapore, and Japan).

"Punctuality is not a Latin American comparative advantage," says *The Economist* in an article about a national punctuality campaign inaugurated by Ecuadoran president Lucio Gutiérrez, who appeared at the launching ceremony, "but at the last minute."[15] *Participación Ciudadana* (Citizen Participation), the civic organization that initiated the campaign, estimates that tardiness costs Ecuador upwards of $700 million per year—more than 4 percent of GDP.

The punctuality campaign in Ecuador was the subject of a subsequent article in *The New Yorker* in which the author, James Surowiecki, writes: "Attitudes toward time tend to pervade nearly every aspect of a culture. In hyperpunctual countries like Japan, pedestrians walk fast, business transactions take place quickly and bank clocks are always accurate. . . . In other words, Ecuadorans . . . are trying to revolutionize the way they live and work. . . ."[16]

In this context, Tibi mentions a definition of IBM by an Egyptian wag: *Inshallah* (God willing); *Bukra* (tomorrow); *Ma'lish* (it doesn't matter).

8. Education

The value attached to the education of both men and women is powerfully linked to modernization. The value attached to education is influenced by religion or ethical code: Protestantism and Judaism promoted education to facilitate reading of the bible by congregants, in contrast to Catholicism (the high levels of literacy in Scotland in the seventeenth century and low levels in Ireland are a case in point).[17] In Confucianism, learning occupies the highest rung on the prestige ladder, witness the mandarin scholars who were so powerful in imperial China. Another example of the Confucian emphasis on education is Japan—in 1905 more than 90 percent of Japanese elementary school age boys *and girls* were in school, among the highest percentages in the world at the time.[18]

Economic Behavior

9. Work/Achievement

Work as a vehicle for achieving the good life is another value shared by Protestantism and Judaism. In mainstream Catholic doctrine, derivative of classical Greek/Roman philosophy, the good life is found in spiritual matters, contemplation, and artistic achievement. Work, particularly manual work, is beneath the dignity of the elite and is relegated to the lower classes. Low prestige attaches to economic activity, as many writers, Weber, Edward Banfield, and Mariano Grondona among them, have observed.[19] Particularly when combined with the Catholic doctrinal preference for the poor ("It is easier for a camel to go through the eye of a needle than for a rich man to enter into the kingdom of God," Matthew 19:24), it is easy to understand why Catholic ambivalence about capitalism persists to this day.

The Catholic ordering of values was substantially shared by the Confucian countries until the second half of the nineteenth century in the case of Japan and the second half of the twentieth century in the cases of South Korea and China, and the latter's derivative societies: Taiwan, Hong Kong, and Singapore. For reasons of national security and prestige, economic activity, which was traditionally the lowest rung on the Confucian prestige ladder, below scholars, soldiers, and farmers, has been promoted to high prestige—witness Chinese Communist leader Deng Xiaoping's exhortation: "To get rich is glorious." The effect has been to liberate those values that Confucianism shares with the Protestant ethic: education, merit, frugality, achievement, the lesser virtues. As we shall see in chapter 6, a similar value transformation with respect to economic activity has occurred in the Catholic—now sometimes referred to as "post-Catholic"—societies of Ireland, Italy, Quebec, and Spain.

World Values Survey data confirm the importance of how work is seen. Inglehart concludes: "Intrinsic motivations for work are positively linked with progress. Societies that emphasize work as a means to live show low levels of progress."[20]

10. Frugality

The economic "miracles" of Japan, South Korea, Taiwan, Hong Kong, Singapore, and now China are in important measure driven by extremely high levels of savings. In 2001 Singapore saved 44.8 percent of gross national income, China 40.1 percent.[21] High savings, combined with the Confucian virtues of education, merit, and achievement, and an outward looking set of economic policies, go a long way toward explaining the miracles. Yet frugality is not always an economic virtue— Japan's recent prolonged economic stagnation is in part attributable to low levels of domestic consumption. Nor is frugality a permanent value, witness the low levels of saving in the United States—17 percent of gross national income in 2001—so contrary to a fundament of the Protestant ethic. A rich country may be able to afford low levels of saving, although this may not be true in the long run. However, it is a luxury that a poor country cannot afford if it seeks rapid economic development.

11. Entrepreneurship

The Austrian-born American economist Joseph Schumpeter identified the entrepreneurial function as the engine of development. It was not enough to save and invest, he argued. Human creativity must be injected into the formula: "the function of entrepreneurs is to reform or revolutionize the pattern of production by exploiting an invention or . . . an untried technological possibility for producing a new commodity or producing an old one in a new way, by opening up a new source of supply of materials or a new outlet for products, by reorganizing industry and so on. . . ."[22]

Schumpeter viewed entrepreneurship as requiring "aptitudes that are present in only a small fraction of the population."[23] He was, I think, wrong about this. For one thing, the proportion of entrepreneurs in a society varies with culture: Sweden's progress-prone culture produces proportionally many more entrepreneurs than does Argentina's progress-resistant culture.[24] For another thing, in a progress-prone culture, entrepreneurship is much less elitist than Schumpeter supposed: the surge of industrialization and commerce in the United States and Japan was driven by literally millions of entrepreneurs, some creating large businesses, many more creating small ones. Moreover, entrepreneurship is not confined to the private sector—public-administration innovators can play a crucial role in the progress of a society through wise policies imaginatively conceived and implemented.

That the proportion of entrepreneurs in Haiti is low challenges the utility of Peruvian author Hernando DeSoto's solution to underdevelopment, articulated in *The Mystery of Capital*.[25] DeSoto is surely right that there are many potential benefits from registering official property of poor people, which they can then collateralize for loans, for example their houses, shops, and small farms. The problem is, what will happen to the loan monies if the entrepreneurial drive isn't nurtured by the culture—not to mention, in the case of Haiti, one of the countries on which De Soto has focused, the absence of a favorable investment climate. Some Haitians are likely to use the additional resources to emigrate.

The contrast between the Anglo-Protestant and Ibero-Catholic dispositions to entrepreneurship and the depth of their divergent roots is captured in the diary of the American scholar-diplomat John L. Stephens, who visited Central America in 1839–40 and observed, after viewing the Masaya volcano in Nicaragua: "I could not but reflect, what a waste of the bounties of Providence in this favoured but miserable land! At home this volcano would be a fortune; with a good hotel on top, a railing round to keep children from falling in, a zigzag staircase down the sides, and a glass of iced lemonade at the bottom."[26]

12. Risk propensity

Risk propensity is intimately linked to entrepreneurship. Both are derivative of the worldview, particularly the view of one's possibilities of influencing destiny and one's view of knowledge. In fatalistic cultures, risks are likely to be seen as incalculable, since mysterious forces are at work. The incalculability may also encourage adventuresome behavior. In the progress-prone culture, a sense of control over one's destiny combined with the inclination to confront facts nurtures the capacity to estimate probabilities, to calculate the degree of risk.

13. Competition

Grondona's words in *Culture Matters* are apt:

> The necessity of competing to achieve wealth and excellence characterizes the societies favorable to development. Competition is central to the success of the enterprise, the politician, the intellectual, the professional. In resistant societies . . . what is supposed to substitute for it is solidarity, loyalty, and cooperation. . . . In resistant societies, negative views of competition reflect the legitimation of envy and utopian equality. Although such societies criticize competition and praise cooperation, the latter is often less common in them than in "competitive" societies. In fact, it can be argued that competition is a form of cooperation in which both competitors benefit from being forced to do their best, as in sports. Competition nurtures democracy, capitalism, and dissent.[27]

14. Innovation

Innovation is conceptually close to entrepreneurship and risk propensity. Like them, it is powerfully influenced by one's worldview, and particularly by the degree to which people believe they can control their destiny.

Openness to innovation is a key factor in many of the success-story case studies that follow. It was, for example, central to the early success of Islam, which revived the wisdom, knowledge, and skills of ancient Greece, and to the transformation of Japan by the Meiji leadership, which widely adopted or adapted the advances of the West in education, technology, organization, administration, military science, and numerous other fields.

With respect to Islam, Tibi sees an unwillingness to learn from others as a huge obstacle to the progress of Islamic countries in general, Arab countries in particular. So do the authors of the UNDP *Arab Human Development Reports*: "The truth is that Arab culture has no choice but to engage again in a new global experiment. It cannot enclose itself, contented with living on history, the past, and inherited culture alone in a world whose victorious powers reach into all corners of the earth, dominating all forms of knowledge, behavior, life, manufactured goods, and innovation."[28]

15. Advancement

The society that places the most able, best qualified people into jobs, whether in the public or private sector, is the society that is going to perform best, to progress most rapidly. To be sure, in all human societies, subjective factors enter into personnel decisions. It is a question of degree: in progress-resistant societies, where trust and identification with others is typically low, subjective factors, particularly family connections, are often dominant in personnel decisions; nepotism is common, and merit is sacrificed. In progress-prone societies, merit is usually the principal determinant of selection. Merit is one of the central emphases of Confucianism, and it is comparably salient in Protestantism and Judaism.

Social Behavior

16. Rule of law, corruption

The degree to which a society is respectful of the rule of law is directly linked to the rigor of its ethical code, for example, the extent to which honesty, fair play, and a sense of social responsibility are a reality in a society. With Weber's comparison of the two religions in mind, which contrasts the unrelenting Protestant insistence on daily good deeds with the Catholic cycle of sin, confession, absolution, and renewed sin— one would expect Protestant countries to be less corrupt than Catholic ones. That is the case, according to Transparency International's 2003 Corruption Perceptions Index, which ranks 133 countries according to the degree of perceived corruption: of the 10 least corrupt countries,

9 are predominantly Protestant, including the 5 Nordic countries, New Zealand, the Netherlands, Australia, and Switzerland; 1 (Singapore) is Confucian. [29] Predominantly Catholic countries do not do as well: for example, Spain is number 23, Italy is number 35, and Argentina is number 92. Interestingly, Chile, a country in which the Catholic Church is particularly influential, is a respectable number 20, an anomaly we shall pursue later in the book.

Inglehart concludes: "The Transparency International measure of corruption . . . shows a remarkably strong . . . correlation with human progress (indicating that human progress goes with *low* levels of corruption)."[30] He also recognizes that cause and effect move in both directions with respect to corruption: "It could be argued that governmental corruption is like a cancer that strangles economic development, effective administration of education and human services, and virtually every other element of a healthy society. But it might also be argued that, in a prosperous and effectively run society, corruption is less tempting. Although I think the relationship primarily functions in the former fashion, I would concede that there probably is some truth in the latter claim."[31]

The 10 least corrupt countries are strikingly similar in composition to the top 10 in the competitiveness index cited above and to another relevant index. In 1998 a group of economists produced a report for the National Bureau of Economic research on good government around the world, which focused on efficiency, personal freedom, and the degree to which government interferes in the private sector.[32] The top ten were all predominantly Protestant:

1. New Zealand
2. Switzerland
3. Norway
4. United Kingdom
5. Canada
6. Iceland
7. United States
8. Finland
9. Sweden
10. Australia

17. Radius of identification and trust

Also linked to the rigor of the ethical code is the extent to which people identify with and trust others beyond the family and circle of friends in a society. I have already stressed the key role that trust plays as a lubricant in an efficient economy. It is a comparably important factor for effective democracy. If mistrust is rife, as in many Islamic and Latin American societies, people will be reluctant to relinquish political power lest those who accede to power use that new power either to persecute those formerly in power and/or to deny them access to power in the future.

If one identifies with others in the society, one is more likely to pay taxes willingly; to engage in charitable and philanthropic activity; and to associate with others for common goals of a political, economic, social, or recreational nature. I am reminded of a comment by historian David Hackett Fischer about New England Puritanism that may well be relevant to the emergence of the town meeting as an expression of grassroots democracy in that region: "The Puritans believed that they were bound to one another in a Godly way. One leader told them that they should 'look upon themselves as being bound up in one *Bundle of Love*; and count themselves obliged, in very close and Strong Bonds, to be serviceable to one another' . . . Long after Puritans had become Yankees, and Yankee Trinitarians had become New England Unitarians (whom Whitehead defined as believers in one God at most) the long shadow of Puritan belief still lingered over the folkways of an American region."[33]

18. Family

In the progress-prone society, the idea of "family"—the radius of identification and trust—extends even to strangers within the society, along the lines of the passage just quoted. In the resistant culture, the radius of identification and trust is confined to the family, which becomes a fortress against the rest of the society. This view of family is prominent in Edward Banfield's classic *The Moral Basis of a Backward Society*, in which Banfield analyzes a village in the south of Italy where identification and trust are confined to the *nuclear* family, a phenomenon that he views as a major contributor to the relative poverty and institutional weaknesses of the region.[34]

Also highly relevant are the views of the Brazilian anthropologist Roberto DaMatta, who notes in *A Casa e a Rua* (*At Home and on the Street*): "If I am buying from or selling to a relative, I neither seek profit nor concern myself with money. . . . But if I am dealing with a stranger, then there are no rules, other than the one of exploiting him to the utmost."[35]

19. Association (social capital)

With Robert Putnam's emphasis on social capital in *Making Democracy Work* and *Bowling Alone*, and Francis Fukuyama's emphasis on it in *Trust*, "social capital" has entered the mainstream lexicon of the social sciences and the development community. James Coleman, who coined the concept, defined it as "the ability of people to work together for common purposes in groups and organizations."[36] Social capital is intimately linked to Putnam's "civic community" and to the "civil society" one hears referred to frequently in development institutions like the World Bank—sometimes as if civil society were a given and all one has to do is find it and nurture it.

But social capital is *not* equally distributed among societies, and some societies enjoy the benefits of civic community and civil society more than others. People sometimes forget that Putnam's earlier book was essentially a cultural explanation of the striking contrast between the north and the south of Italy, with respect to civic engagement specifically and the level of development generally. Putnam invokes Banfield's *The Moral Basis of a Backward Society* to help explain why Italians in the South are so bereft of trust, "an essential component of social capital."[37] He traces this condition to the higher authoritarian Norman presence there in the twelfth and thirteenth centuries. Similarly, Fukuyama argues in *Trust* that some societies engender "spontaneous association"—like Japan, the United States, and Germany—while others avoid association.

The key point here is that social capital is essentially a cultural phenomenon. In order to nurture it in a cultural environment of low trust, one must strengthen the cultural factors that build trust, for example the ethical code, the lesser virtues, the radius of identification. The Ecuador punctuality campaign is an example of an initiative to promote the lesser virtues. It has the additional benefit of bringing people into association for a common goal, in the process learning both the value of association and how to make it work.

20. The individual/the group

The issue here is a complicated one: individualism is the hallmark of the progressive West, while communitarianism is the hallmark of progressive Confucian Asia. The issue is further complicated by the extreme individualism of Latin America, which has impeded that region—and Spain as well, until the second half of the twentieth century—from consolidating democracy and producing equitably distributed prosperity. As José Ortega y Gasset observed about Spaniards: "The perfect Spaniard needs nothing. More than that, he needs nobody. This is why our race are such haters of novelty and innovation. To accept anything new from the outside world humiliates us. . . . To the true Spaniard, all innovation seems frankly a personal offense. . . ."[38]

Many communitarian societies, it is true, also resist progress, for example in Africa, where, in Daniel Etounga-Manguelle's view, emphasis on the group saps initiative and the sense of personal responsibility, and, through discouraging dissent and individual responsibility, among other obstacles, does not nurture democratic politics.[39] And as Fukuyama points out in *Trust*, strong patterns of association are sometimes found in individualistic societies like the United States and Germany. He argues that the Protestant/individualistic cultures of these two countries have generated substantially more social capital than has the Confucian/communitarian culture of China and Taiwan. (His third model of a high social-capital society, however, is Confucian Japan.) Further muddying the waters is the obvious drive for individual achievement, creativity, and entrepreneurship found in the Confucian countries, which has a lot to do with their economic success.

Obviously, the distinction between individualism and communitarianism in terms of their influence on progress is ambiguous and requires a high degree of case by case qualification. It is apparent that other cultural factors, such as work/achievement, frugality, entrepreneurship, and merit, can accentuate either the virtues or vices present in both individualism and communitarianism. China expert Tu Weiming calls for a synthesis of the virtuous aspects of both: "Surely, [Western] values such as instrumental rationality, liberty, rights-consciousness, due process of law, privacy, and individualism are all universalizable modern values, but, as the Confucian example suggests, 'Asian values,' such as sympathy, distributive justice, duty-consciousness, ritual, public-spiritedness, and group orientation are also universalizable modern values."[40]

It could be convincingly argued that such a synthesis has been substantially achieved in, for example, the Nordic countries and Japan. What is clear is that societies that are individualistic in the extreme, as in the traditional Iberian culture analyzed by Ortega y Gasset, and those that are communitarian in the extreme, as in the African societies analyzed by Daniel Etounga-Manguelle, confront major obstacles to modernization.

21. Authority

A society's view of authority is fundamental to cultural variation. It is substantially rooted in religion/ethical code and obviously has a profound influence on the way that societies organize their politics. I have already cited Tocqueville's observation about the strong egalitarian link between Protestantism and democracy in America. That Catholic societies have been generally slower to consolidate democracy than Protestant societies may be a reflection of the more authoritarian, hierarchical nature of Catholicism. Islam's administrative structure is closer to Protestant decentralization than to Catholic centralization, but its doctrines have promoted fatalism, absolutism, and intolerance, which in turn have nurtured authoritarianism. Confucian doctrine emphasizes filial piety above all and extends that deference to the ruler, which has a lot to do with the relatively slow evolution of democratic politics in Confucian societies.

22. Role of elites

The extent to which elites assume a responsibility for the well-being of non-elites—*noblesse oblige* captures the idea—is obviously related to the radius of identification within a society. The Nordic countries and Latin America make an interesting contrast, which has been the object of a study sponsored by the Inter-American Development Bank.[41] As Swedish political scientists Dag Blanck and Thorleif Pettersson write on Sweden: "During the mid-seventeenth century, iron foundries were established throughout central Sweden . . . The iron was produced in small communities called *bruk* where particular social and cultural relations developed, characterized by a paternalistic relationship between the foundry owners and the workers, but also by a sense of social and economic responsibility on the part of the owners."

It is not difficult to see that this paternalism and sense of responsibility, driven in part by Lutheran doctrine, may have evolved into Sweden's advanced welfare state of today. Contrast this with the enslavement of Indians and blacks throughout Latin America during the same period and the self-centered, self-aggrandizing conduct of many Latin American elites in subsequent centuries.

23. Church-state relations

In none of the advanced democracies does religion play a significant role in the civic sphere. This is above all true of Western Europe, where the link between church and state was broken long ago in most countries and where religiosity has declined notably. But it is also substantially true of the much more religious United States. To be sure, religion can exert influence through the religion-based values and views of politicians and media people, for example the anti-abortion, anti–stem cell research positions pursued by George Bush. But the wall of separation substantially prevents intrusion of religious *institutions* into the political process.

Michael Novak, a prominent lay Catholic, would modify the wording of the typology. In the progress-prone column, in lieu of "Secularized: wall between church and state," he would say, "Division of powers between religion and state; protection of individual conscience." And in the progress-resistant column, he would prefer, "Religious leaders perform political roles, and the state imposes religious mandates."

Robert Hefner adds: "It is the separation of authorities—and not the 'secularist' elimination or even privatization of religion—that is the key to social progress. As the U.S. shows, and as the Protestant reformation in Latin America also shows, a certain type of religious ethos can be very good for social progress."[42]

Alfred Stepan presents a helpful formulation of "twin tolerations" in the church-state relationship in a democratic society: "Freedom for democratically elected governments, and freedom for religious organizations in civil and political society . . . individuals and religious communities . . . must have complete freedom to worship privately. More: as individuals and groups, they should also be able to publicly advance their values in civil society, and to sponsor organizations and movements in political society, as long as their public advancement of these beliefs does not impinge negatively on the liberties of other citizens, or violate democracy and the law, by violence."[43]

In this context, it is relevant that the stunning transformations of Ireland, Italy, Quebec, and Spain have all been accompanied by a significant reduction in the role and influence of the Catholic Church. Also relevant is Turkey, in many respects the most modernized Islamic country in the world—and the most secular, even under the current Islamic government led by Tayyip Recip Erdogan. As Turkish political scientist Yilmaz Esmer writes, Erdogan and those around him "emphasized the fact that they were not 'political Islamists' and were at peace with secularism as well as the other founding principles of the Republic."[44]

24. Gender relationships

For several decades, development experts have recognized the important multifaceted role women play in development: as professionals, workers, teachers, politicians, and businesswomen, but also as mothers, with the responsibility for rearing children. As we shall see, child rearing is a key instrument of cultural transmission, and an educated mother is likely to do a better job of it than an uneducated mother. More than 90 percent of Japanese girls were in school in 1905, and atypically large numbers of women (for Latin America) were literate in Chile (30 percent) in the second half of the nineteenth century. In contrast, the rates of female literacy in some Islamic countries today are astonishingly low: in 2001, 29 percent of women were literate in Pakistan, 37 percent in Morocco, and 45 percent in Egypt.[45] Here is an instance—we shall encounter several others—where reforms and initiatives that make good development sense also offer a vehicle for promoting progressive values.

25. Fertility

In peasant societies, children are both a labor force and old-age social security, and these two practical considerations, added to religious injunctions to "go forth and multiply," have generally led to high fertility rates in poor countries.

But large, poor families are a recipe for the persistence of poverty and social pathologies, including high crime rates, common to Latin America and Africa. Pitifully small family budgets are stretched just to keep children fed, not to mention clothed, provided with pure water, and attending school. Harried parents, often single mothers, do not have the time necessary for adequate nurturing. These problems are explored in anthropologist Elisha Renne's CMRP essay on a Yoruba community in Nigeria.

The reduction of population growth through expanded contraceptive use is a reality in much of the world today. But fertility rates are also declining in most prosperous countries, particularly in Western Europe and Japan. Michael Novak points out that Europe's population is certain to decline by 2050 and goes on to remind us that low fertility may (thus) also be also a problem. I might note, in this connection, that the U.S. Census Bureau projects a population of 420 million in the United States in 2050, roughly a 50 percent increase over the population in 2000. The population growth is largely driven by immigration—about one million legal immigrants and perhaps five hundred thousand illegal immigrants arrive in the United States annually—and by the higher fertility rates of many immigrants. For example, fertility rates for Mexican immigrants are 3.5 per mother versus a national average of 2.0.[46]

The Essence of the Typology

AT THE HEART OF THE TYPOLOGY are two fundamental questions: (1) Does the culture encourage the belief that people can influence their destinies? (2) Does the culture promote the Golden Rule? If people believe that they can influence their destinies, they are likely to focus on the future; see the world in positive-sum terms; attach a high priority to education; believe in the work ethic; save; become entrepreneurial; and so forth. If the Golden Rule has real meaning for them, they are likely to live by a reasonably rigorous ethical code; honor the lesser virtues; abide by the laws; identify with the broader society; form social capital; and so forth. The Golden Rule is not just a Western idea. It is also central to Confucianism, although articulated in a negative construction: "Do not do unto others what you would not have others do unto you."

Universal Progress Culture

PROGRESS-PRONE CULTURE COMPRISES A SET OF VALUES that are substantially shared by the most successful societies on earth—the West and East

Asia—and, I might add, by high-achieving ethnic/religious minorities like the Jains and Sikhs in India, and the Chinese, Japanese, Koreans, and Jews wherever they migrate. I speak of a Universal Progress Culture that contrasts with the Universal Peasant Culture perceived by George Foster and others. Clearly, the West-East overlap is most apparent in economic as well as social development, for example, high levels of education and health and relatively equitable income distribution. There is an obvious divergence with respect to democracy: Confucian-style authoritarianism, stemming from its heavy emphasis on "filial piety," persists in China and Singapore. But the democratic evolution of Japan, South Korea, and Taiwan, and the nurturing of democracy by sustained high economic growth, suggest that the East-West synthesis of virtues that Tu Weiming calls for is fully realizable in East Asia. It is already a substantial reality in the West, above all in the Nordic countries.

If Tocqueville, Weber, and a long line of subsequent writers who believe that culture matters are right, the promotion of Universal Progress Culture values can accelerate progress in lagging societies. In the chapters that follow, we confront the central question of this book: How can those progressive values be strengthened?

3

Models and Instruments of Cultural Transmission / Change

HOW DOES CULTURE INFLUENCE BEHAVIOR? How does culture change? What are the instruments or institutions through which cultural values, beliefs, and attitudes are transmitted from generation to generation? To what extent can these instruments and institutions be modified to nurture progressive cultural change? These are the questions addressed in this chapter.

I will first look at two models designed to explain cultural change and then review the instruments and institutions through which cultural values and attitudes are transmitted. The first of the two models of cultural change, which operates at the macro level, was presented at the March 2004 CMRP conference by political scientist Harvey Nelsen of the University of South Florida. The second, which operates at the micro level, is the work of Harvard sociologist Orlando Patterson, which appears in his chapter "Taking Culture Seriously" in *Culture Matters*.

The Nelsen Model

AT THE OUTSET, Nelsen qualifies his model by stressing the difficulty of cultural change, noting that "the roots of culture are in language, religion, geography, climate, and shared historical heritage, none of which is easily changed." He goes on to point out that some core beliefs are so strong that they can be thought of as "cultural black holes which light can enter but never escape."[1] Individualism in the United States may be one such value. But much in culture is mutable, and Nelsen believes that the only way to effect change is through "development of a new consciousness . . . which . . . comes from cross-cultural fertilization . . . or internal dissidents." He cites the cultural impact of Elizabeth Cady Stanton's and Susan B. Anthony's campaign for women's suffrage in the United States. Martin Luther King's impact on attitudes about race is another example. Nelsen believes that internally generated change is easier than cross-fertilization from outside the society.

Nelsen perceives three modes of value and attitude change: through cataclysmic events, elite leadership, or social movements. His examples of cataclysmic events are the disastrous military defeats experienced by Japan and Germany, and the hugely disruptive consequences of Mao Zedong's Cultural Revolution. In the former cases, the military disaster fertilized the soil for democratic values and institutions. In the latter, the communist revolution was shattered. While clearly on a smaller scale, the abuses of the Pinochet dictatorship served to revive and fortify Chile's democratic tradition.

Nelsen uses China again as an example of elite leadership. Into the vacuum left by Mao's shattering of his own revolution entered Deng Xiaoping, who reversed centuries-old imperial and communist Chinese hostility to business activity with five words: "To get rich is glorious." Nelsen also mentions King Juan Carlos of Spain, Franklin Roosevelt, and Margaret Thatcher as examples of leaders whose policies and actions contributed to cultural change. I note, in passing, that each of these examples followed a crisis: the death of Franco in Spain followed by the unexpected, strong support of democracy by his handpicked successor, Juan Carlos; the onset of the Great Depression in the United States, which forced a fundamental reappraisal of the American experiment; and the sustained decline of the British economy as a result of the policies of Labor governments hostile to capitalism. Nelsen notes that democratic leaders are more often followers of public opinion than leaders: "In democracies, striking off in new directions—particularly where values are concerned—risks defeat in the next election."[2]

Social movements, for example feminism and environmentalism, are the third mode of politically driven cultural change. In authoritarian societies, social movements can lead to revolution; an example is the Solidarity movement in Poland, which contributed to the demise of communism in that country. In democratic societies, the effects may be to alter the political balance: the growth of the labor movement in the United States strengthened the Democratic Party, particularly during Franklin Roosevelt's presidency.

Nelsen concludes, "These three modes of political influence on cultures are not mutually exclusive. Most change comes about through a combination of factors, but internal or external comparisons resulting in consciousness-raising almost always serve as the foundation."[3]

The Patterson Model

PATTERSON EMPLOYS AFRICAN-AMERICAN HISTORY to illustrate how his model works. In this scenario, the behavioral outcome he focuses on is the current high rate of paternal abandonment of children by African-American males.

Point A, the Transmitted Cultural Model, is the condition of slave male-female relationships in slavery. Those relationships discouraged

Figure 3.1
The Patterson Model

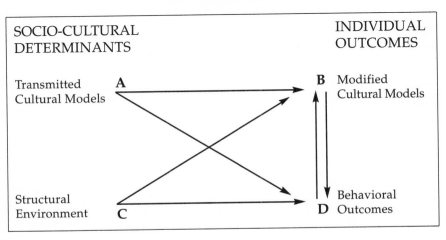

the sense of paternal responsibility because "most men did not live regularly with their partners." Many such relationships were formed between partners who lived on different plantations, "and a third [of the male slaves] had no stable unions."[4] Paternal responsibility was further undermined by the African tradition of "matrifocality," which placed higher value on the mother-child relationship than the father-child one, and which persisted through slavery. Paternal responsibility was also undermined by the related tradition of female independence, which also persisted through slavery. Finally, in Patterson's words, "slave men lacked the one thing that all other men primarily relied on for their domination of women: control of property."[5]

The pattern of male irresponsibility with respect to children was perpetuated (Point B) during the Jim Crow period when vast numbers of former male slaves became sharecroppers. Their income depended on the amount of labor they could apply to their land, and virtually their sole source of labor was the children they sired. Viewing children as an economic resource did not enhance the paternal instinct. Moreover, Patterson believes that the demeaning treatment of black males—at the extreme, castration and lynching—established a psychological environment in which the only way that African-American males could "prove their worth" was through sexual conquest. One result was the strengthening of bonds among African-American women, and between the women and their children.

Point C in the diagram is the structural environment: "unemployment, low income, and the neighborhood effects of segregated habitats, as well as ethnic and gender discrimination in employment."[6] Patterson also mentions the impact of welfare programs; the profound influence of successful black athletes on the value system of African-American males; and the influx of low-skilled immigrants as contributing structural factors.

Patterson concludes: "Thus we have A and C leading to . . . variants of B, leading to a . . . model of sexuality of and paternity among young men, expressed in D, which in turn encourages attitudes toward mainstream society and work (DB) and a ghetto lifestyle that reinforces . . . predatory sexuality and unsecured paternity. In this context of opposition to mainstream norms, the likelihood of the modified sexual and paternal models being actualized in D is even greater. . . . It is reasonable to conclude that among a large number of urban, Afro-American lower-class young men, these models are now fully normative and that men act in accordance with them whenever they can."[7]

Instruments and Institutions

A SOCIETY MAINTAINS CULTURAL CONTINUITY through a variety of instruments and institutions that transmit its values and attitudes from generation to generation, and which presumably are available for modification of those values and attitudes. The principal instruments and institutions are grouped under the following headings: child rearing, education, the media, and leadership. The fifth grouping, religion, is so salient in its impact on cultural values and attitudes, and so varied, that I devote a separate chapter to it, following this one.

Child Rearing

Jerome Kagan

Harvard University development psychologist Jerome Kagan has been deeply involved in the Culture Matters Research Project since it began in 2002 and is the co-editor of *Developing Cultures: Essays on Cultural Change*. His essay in the volume explores the link between child-rearing practices and progress toward the three CMRP goals—democratic governance, social justice, and prosperity—rooted in the UN Universal Declaration of Human Rights. What follows is drawn directly from his essay, "Moral Values and Culture."

DEMOCRACY

Anthropologists suspect that most early humans were communitarian, concerned with the opinions of their neighbors, empathic toward those in need of help, and loyal to the ethical requirements of the social categories to which they belonged. Early humans were neither democratic nor egalitarian during the first 80–90 millennia of human existence. This fact suggests that the three values promoted by the Culture Matters project do not have an obvious priority in human biology.

In order to promote the ethic of democracy, the family must encourage a sense of personal agency in children by providing experiences that allow sons and daughters to feel they have some power to affect the family. Put simply, consulting the child, asking her opinions, and when appropriate taking the child's preferences into account, should strengthen the child's sense of agency. Psychologists call parents who adopt these practices authoritatively democratic. Research indicates that in Europe and North America, such families are more common in homes where parents have attended college. This does not mean that parents who have less education cannot promote this standard, only that it is a bit more difficult for such families, many of whom feel less agency themselves, to believe that children should have a deep faith in their potency.

The belief that all members of a community should have equal power to decide on the future of the community is harder to promote than a sense of agency because the former requires the child to understand the difference between economic gain and symbolic signs of status, on the one hand, and political privilege, on the other. Unlike a sense of agency, which can emerge before age seven, this more abstract idea has to wait until the years before puberty, when the maturing cognitive abilities make it possible for youth to understand that the vitality of the community should sometimes take priority over the desires of the individual. Promotion of this goal requires conversation and discussion between parents and children and is accomplished less easily through parental rewards and punishments. Parents have to be clever and detect when a context is appropriate to teach this lesson.

One class of opportunities occurs when a member of the extended family who lives some distance away is ill or lonely. By insisting that the visit include the child, even though he may have had a different plan for the day, families teach the child that the psychological state of the larger family unit can take precedence over personal wishes. By emphasizing the social categories of family, clan, ethnicity, and religion, to which the child belongs, and explaining why the requirements of these groups deserve priority, parents prepare youth to award this privilege to the state.

SOCIAL JUSTICE

The task of persuading children that impoverished or disenfranchised members of the society deserve empathy confronts the same difficulties that accompanied teaching them that all should have an equal political voice. Families do have an ally as they try to meet this assignment. Nature awarded all children, save a very small proportion, with a special biology, the ability to empathize with those in physical or psychic distress. An empathic concern over a whining puppy or a crying infant comes easily to all children. This sentiment, which Hume assumed was the foundation of human morality, represents a significant foundation on which the teaching of social justice rests.

If children are reminded regularly of the deprivation experienced by disenfranchised citizens, they should, by adolescence, create a concern for strangers in need. It helps, of course, if the parents not only promote this ethic in conversation but also display it in their behavior. Because most children identify with their parents, they are more likely to believe in the validity of an attitude if they see it practiced by their role models. Words alone, without support in the daily behavior of role models, are often too weak to maintain a strong empathic concern for the less privileged.

ECONOMIC PROSPERITY

The attainment of economic prosperity requires an ethic that celebrates the intrinsic value of personal accomplishment; that is, a work ethic in which individual accomplishment brings virtue. Many have noted that this view, inherent in Luther's sermons, is one basis for the economic prosperity of Protestant societies. This standard, common in North America and parts of Europe, requires suppressing worry over "being better than another."

The belief that economic gain requires a work ethic has, as a corollary, the conclusion that those who are poor failed to learn or to practice a work ethic. If they had done so, they would not be economically distressed. Hence, empathy for their state is not a moral imperative because their condition is their fault. As with the abstract idea of the community taking precedence over the individual, parents have to explain to youth that some citizens are unable to improve their position because of structural conditions in the society rather than because of their moral failure.

WHAT SHOULD BE DONE?

The goal of the Culture Matters Research Project is to enable nations that do not enjoy the combination of political democracy, concern for the disadvantaged, and economic prosperity to implement changes that will allow them to command these goals if they choose. A society can possess any one feature of this trio without the others. Many Latin American and African nations have some of the defining features of political democracy without social justice or prosperity. The People's Republic of China during Mao's reign was concerned with the plight of peasants but was totalitarian. Attainment of all three features requires those with political power, whether a dictator or an elected assembly, to acknowledge the will of the majority and to allocate resources and legal protections to the less advantaged.

However, the values of the community are necessary for permanent change. Adoption of an ethic that combines democracy, social justice, and economic prosperity requires that youth be socialized by family, school, and media to believe in four propositions:

1. It is possible for every person to improve his or her economic and social position through education and the conscientious application of individual talents. Many in less developed societies hold a fatalistic belief that they are passive victims of social forces they are unable to change—often not without reason. As a result, improving one's talents in order to work toward a goal is unlikely to result in a better life; this attitude might be called the "helplessness ideology."

2. The political and judicial system is generally fair and just and, therefore, conformity to the law is expected and violations are punished.

3. Individuals who are members of a social category that has experienced prejudice are entitled to dignity, freedom from bigotry, and an opportunity to improve their lives. The belief that members of some social categories are inherently less talented or less virtuous than a majority, because of their historical origins or presumed biology, is a formidable obstacle to the goals being sought. That is, in part, why Rwanda, Guatemala, Nigeria, and Russia are less prosperous than Botswana, Costa Rica, Chile, and China.

Furthermore, identification with the nation must be stronger than identification with tribe, clan, or region. America's advantage, as Tocqueville appreciated almost 200 years ago, is that most Americans believe they are members of the same national category; hence they are receptive to the notion that all citizens have equal dignity and are entitled to equal opportunity and equal legal protection.

4. The accumulation of wealth, which usually brings status, is a virtue; it should not be assumed that a person has violated some ethical standard simply because he is more advantaged than a neighbor.

Persuading a majority to believe in and to adopt these ideas requires the cooperation of family, educational institutions, and the mass media. The family's responsibility is to praise perseverance, academic achievement, and autonomy in its children and to chastise the avoidance of responsibility, school failure, excessive dependence, and passivity. Parents, who are role models for their children, must display these desirable behaviors in their daily activities.

Luis Diego Herrera

The CMRP paper on child rearing was prepared by the Costa Rican child psychiatrist Luis Diego Herrera, who has also practiced in the United States. He examines parenting practices in Costa Rica, in his view a surrogate for Latin America more generally, and links them to behavioral patterns that impede progress for the society as a whole. Costa Rica is quite different from most other Latin American countries in the strength of its democratic institutions, and some may judge that Costa Rican child rearing is not representative of the entire region. Moreover, Herrera focuses on middle- and upper-middle-class parents, proportionally more numerous in Costa Rica than in most other Latin American countries; some may question whether the same child-rearing practices are common to the lower classes. While recognizing the possible distortions, Herrera believes that his conclusions are generalizable because of his extensive experience in other Latin American countries and the United States.

Many of Herrera's critiques may be applicable to child-rearing practices in other countries, including the United States. But he believes that there is a major difference of degree and sees Costa Rican child-rearing practices (and Latin American practice, more generally) as flawed in six respects:

1. Parents are excessively concerned and indulgent about the health of their children, with the result that adversity, stress, or anxiety is

converted into physical symptoms: "A prominent physician in Costa Rica once said that Costa Ricans can be easily divided into two categories: those who were tired and those who had a headache."[8]

2. Costa Rican child rearing undermines accountability and confuses honesty and smartness. To begin with, the idea of accountability is not highly developed in Hispanic culture, witness the absence of a Spanish word that fully captures the idea. In Herrera's words, "In fact, the need to position oneself as unaccountable permeates everyday language. In the Spanish language, if one breaks, loses, or damages something or makes a mistake, it is expressed in a passive, impersonal form: it was broken, it got lost, it got damaged, instead of I lost it or I broke it."[9]

Moreover, "children are taught many contradictory standards of behavior: they are supposed to abide by the rules, but if they break them, the important thing is to get away with it. Not being caught is a sign of competence that undermines the moral obligation to follow the rules. It is common to see parents comment with pride on how their small children were able to take a shortcut, lie cleverly, or cheat successfully, thereby transmitting confusion between being honest and being smart—a powerful message that rewards being shrewd more than that being truthful."

In his milestone book, *The Achieving Society*, psychologist David McClelland emphasized the impact of childhood stories on the values and attitudes that children internalize. Herrera notes: "There is a set of very popular children's bedtime stories, related to the character of *Tío Conejo* (Uncle Rabbit), whose core message to children is that being sly and cunning is better than being honest and truthful, if you want to get your way. It is a subtle validation in Costa Rica and other Latin American countries of what could become [dysfunctional] behaviors through cultural approval."[10]

3. Costa Rican parents are overprotective to the point of diminishing the child's sense of autonomy. Parents often do their children's homework, choose their friends, solve their day-to-day problems. (This may sound familiar with respect to parents in other countries, including the United States; but Herrera insists that the problem is far greater in Latin America.) They do not permit the child to develop a genuine sense of accomplishment or sense of self-esteem. "Even if overprotection does not damage self-esteem, it might have another harmful effect on children—it could foster an undue sense of being special, unique, and smart that is not the result of objective interaction with their environment but instead a reflection of their parents' over-involvement. [A sense of] entitlement follows as a consequence."[11]

4. Costa Rican parents encourage meandering styles of communication and fear of assertiveness. "A salient aspect of communication in Latin America is a meandering, verbose style. The style is one by which direct communication is avoided using all kinds of circumlocutions to evade commitment, clear-cut answers, interlocutor disappointment, or potential confrontations. This trait is more evident when dealing with conflicting or emotional issues."[12] The message is communicated to children that there are only two possible outcomes of assertiveness: acquiescence or violent confrontation. The idea of measured but effectual assertiveness is not fully developed in Latin American culture.

Herrera continues: "If you add to the meandering communication style and the fear of assertiveness the weak emphasis on accountability and the informal encouragement of short cuts and getting away with bad behavior, the stage is set for children to resort to 'illicit' strategies to affirm themselves and accomplish what is expected of them. These illicit strategies may well mold children's character and commitment and pave the way to corrupt behavior and disrespect for the rule of law during adult life."[13]

5. Costa Rican parents display authoritarian and inconsistent parenting styles.

> [Widely accepted] theories of how children internalize values support the idea that power-assertive discipline, particularly by itself, has detrimental effects in children's moral development, whereas affect withdrawal, reasoning, and warmth all [have] a positive correlation to values acquisition. According to these views, power assertion inhibits the development of moral reasoning, while a persuasive discussion allows children to entertain psychological scenarios different from their own and thus fosters the development of empathy and respect for others.
>
> Also pertinent to the analysis of how parents in Latin America exert authority are the contributions of Diana Baumrind[14] with respect to an authoritative (as opposed to authoritarian) parenting style. Authoritative parents use a democratic style of communication, which at the same time conveys high expectations and consistent limits and

firm rules. Children of authoritative parents displayed more adaptive behaviors, were more in charge, and showed more social competence and responsibility.[15]

In his practice, Herrera often encounters parents who are permissive in the child's early life and then become authoritarian. As he says, this "bipolar" parenting "may contribute to confusion in children's minds and weaken the internalization of a balanced, fair, and rational use of authority. . . . [T]he authoritarian style, by denying children the opportunity to negotiate rules of conducts and values, undermines their ability for moral reasoning. . . . When moral reasoning is insufficiently developed, children are rendered less competent to make decisions based upon adherence to principles and rules, and more likely to opt for self-centered and impulsively chosen alternatives with disregard to future consequences and considerations of the common good. In short, ruled-governed behavior is not internalized sufficiently."[16]

Herrera concludes that although inconsistent parenting is not unique to Latin America what happens there "is that this pattern, in concert with the other parenting styles described previously, determines an idiosyncrasy in our culture that may contribute to adaptations to living and working that sustain low perseverance, immature responsibility for one's actions, and great difficulties postponing satisfactions."[17]

6. Costa Rican parenting imparts deficient future awareness and diminished capacity for delayed gratification.

> Children in Costa Rica are socialized in ways that do not introduce them early in their development to the notions of planning, anticipation of alternative outcomes, and preparation for difficult times. Developmentally, this is related to intolerance for delayed gratification, which our child-rearing practices seem to encourage. One likely outcome of the cultural trait of limited future awareness is an indisposition to saving and to developing a well-thought-out strategy of allocation of limited resources. . . . Procrastination is widespread in our culture, maybe more than in other Western cultures. Children learn that if they have not planned their tasks and done their homework or chores they may give perfunctory excuses, or simply do nothing, and the system will not *consistently* respond with negative consequences. . . . All this weakens the possibility of visualization of the importance of behavior in relationship to prospective outcomes and, consequently, future awareness."[18]

INTERESTINGLY, the UNDP's *Arab Human Development Report 2003* also focuses on the need to change child-rearing practices: "Studies indicate that the most widespread style of child rearing in Arab families is the authoritarian mode accompanied by the overprotective. This reduces children's independence, social confidence and social efficiency, and fosters passive attitudes and hesitant decision-making skills. Most of all, it affects how the child thinks by suppressing questioning, exploration, and initiative."[19]

Herrera prescribes three remedies for the destructive aspects of child rearing in Latin America:

1. The preschool and school must develop curricula centered on values. A parent-school partnership needs to be incorporated so that parents participate actively in the identification of the values their children will be learning in the classroom. Moreover, children should work with their parents on projects or homework where active discussion of values is involved.
2. Private- and public-sector physicians, nurses, and social workers should combine their health-education and health-promotion campaigns with courses for parents on topics ranging from teaching children to tolerate frustration to setting limits and employing effective, non-coercive discipline techniques.
3. The mass media need to be approached and encouraged to promote an agenda of social responsibility that portrays corruption, disrespect for the rule of law, and lack of accountability as public and private problems relevant to all citizens.

There is yet another instrument available that could be of prime importance in modifying traditional approaches to child rearing: parenting education.

Education

Parenting education: Sharon Lynn Kagan and Amy Lowenstein

Sharon Lynn Kagan teaches at both Yale and Columbia Universities. Amy Lowenstein is a doctoral student at Georgetown University.

Formal parenting education has become increasingly popular in recent years, above all in the advanced democracies. But its focus has been parenting skills and behavioral change, and values have rarely been incorporated. The avoidance of values is partly explained by the presumption that values are the exclusive domain of the parents.

However, from the preceding discussions of parenting it is obvious that the way parents relate to their children has a lot to do with the values internalized by the children. It is not just a matter of introducing values into the education of prospective parents, although that is certainly desirable. But if a parent tries to transmit democratic values and yet behaves in an authoritarian manner, the message received by the child will be confusing. Interestingly, Kagan and Lowenstein also refer to Diana Baumrind's three types of parenting: authoritarian, authoritative, and permissive, with a strong preference for "authoritative."

With respect to the inclusion of values in parenting education, Kagan and Lowenstein conclude:

> The purposes of parenting education need to be re-examined with an eye toward its potency as an accelerator and inculcator of values, not only as a device for altering behaviors. The United Nations Human Rights agenda, with its broad goals and emphasis on social justice, is a good place to start. Consideration could be given to adopting social justice, democratic governance, and prosperity as ultimate goals. Interim goals that are correlated in the literature with these ultimate goals could be specified. For example, goals of trust and tolerance have been linked to democratic governance, social justice, and prosperity. Benjamin Franklin's 13 virtues (temperance, silence, order, resolution, frugality, industry, sincerity, justice, moderation, cleanliness, tranquility, chastity, and humility) could be individually examined for their relevance to a contemporary vision for parenting education. Also the 12 points of the Boy Scout Law: a Scout is trustworthy, loyal, helpful, friendly, courteous, kind, obedient, cheerful, thrifty, brave, clean, and reverent.
>
> Parenting education with value content should become a matter of priority for ministers of education and human services agencies worldwide. It can be appropriately incorporated into the curricula of high schools and universities. But special courses for prospective parents would also make a lot of sense.
>
> In summary, it is necessary to:

- Distinguish between efforts that explicitly promote behaviors only and those that explicitly promote behaviors and values;
- Delineate through an inclusive process the values to be promoted;
- Assure that the content of parenting education reflects the desired values;
- Align instructional strategies and pedagogy with the values;
- Establish a delivery system/systems that effectively promote values; and
- Develop the infrastructure to support parenting education adequately.[20]

Character Education: Thomas Lickona

Like parenting education and civic education, character education—emphasis on morality and ethics in the curricula of primary and secondary education—is receiving increased attention in the United States and elsewhere. Horace Mann, the father of American public education, considered that character was the highest goal of education. Columnist Carlos Alberto Montaner, a CMRP contributor, says: "Education has to do with character. It has to do with discipline, respect for norms of behavior, intellectual honesty, the quest for excellence, making good on commitments, punctuality, scientific curiosity, problem solving, and the rest of the virtues that characterize the most advanced peoples of the earth."[21]

In his CMRP essay on character education, Thomas Lickona, a development psychologist and professor of education at the State University of New York in Cortland, writes;

> Character matters. Character is needed not only for a society to survive but also to progress toward the dignity and development of all of its members. Progressive cultural change requires the widespread internalization of values such as democracy, social and economic justice, honesty, and individual initiative and responsibility. Such values must become virtues—habits of mind, heart, and conduct—in the character of large numbers of citizens. Just as character enables a culture to flourish, it also enables a person to lead a fulfilling life. . . .
>
> As the authors of *The Federalist Papers* emphasized, democracy is government by the people; the people themselves are responsible for ensuring a free and just society. That means the people—or at least a critical

mass of citizens—must in some basic sense be good. They must understand, and be committed to, the moral foundations of democracy: respect for the rights of individuals, voluntary compliance with the law,
participation in public life, and concern for the common good. Loyalty
to these democratic virtues, the Founders maintained, must be instilled
at an early age.[22]

What are the virtues that should be nurtured through character
education? This is a question that each society must decide for itself. But
the California-based Character Counts! Coalition has successfully promoted six "pillars" of character that should have universal relevance:
trustworthiness, respect, responsibility, fairness, caring, and citizenship.
Lickona offers another formulation: "Our character education center at
the State University of New York College at Cortland promotes 'ten essential virtues' that are affirmed by nearly all philosophical, religious,
and cultural traditions: wisdom, justice, fortitude, self-mastery, love,
positive attitude, hard work, integrity, gratitude, and humility."[23]

The link between improved child-rearing practices and character
education becomes apparent in an observation made by Luis Diego
Herrera in his paper, before he met Lickona at the first CMRP conference in March of 2003: "Thomas Lickona, in his landmark book *Educating for Character*, states that 'the long term success of the new values
education depends on forces outside the school—on the extent to which
families and communities join schools in a common effort to meet the
needs of children and foster their healthy development.'"[24]

Civic Education: Richard Niemi and Steven Finkel

Richard Niemi is a political scientist at the University of Rochester who
has studied the evolution of civic education in the United States. Steven
Finkel is a political scientist at the University of Virginia until recently
and now at the University of Pittsburgh who has studied the applica-
tions of civic education in other settings, including countries in Africa
and Latin America. They summarize their collaborative essay on civic
education as follows:

> For a generation or more, civic education [in the United States] has been
> considered old-fashioned, ineffective, and, by implication, unnecessary.
> Though alternative views were never fully articulated, it was as if it

were thought that young people automatically—perhaps from life's experiences, perhaps from parents or from non-civics course work—learned the knowledge and attitudes that are appropriate for democratic citizenship. Alternatively, it may have been thought that the kinds of knowledge and attitudes learned previously were no longer necessary (or were never needed in the first place). Now, however, in light of widespread disinterest, disengagement, and distrust, especially among the young, we have begun to turn our attention back to the topic of citizenship for democracy.

In the process, we have reinforced some long-standing conclusions and learned some new ones:

- Education is a major factor underlying civic and political participation *and the attitudes that support it*. Education is a strong correlate of interest in politics. Education promotes both following politics (passive participation) and active participation. Education generally increases political tolerance.
- Education encourages personal responsibility in the political life of the community and nation and the feeling that one can effectively participate (political efficacy).
- Civic education per se is an important component of education for democracy. Civic education should begin early in the life of the student. It should continue through the end of secondary schooling. It should infuse many aspects of the curriculum—not only the one or more courses devoted to training for citizenship but also history and other courses as well.
- The way in which the school and classroom ("classroom climate") are run is also an important component of civic education. Students should be encouraged to follow and to discuss current events. They should be encouraged to discuss controversial social and political issues, freely and openly. Students should be encouraged to think about school problems and about ways of solving them. Student councils are an excellent way of involving students in understanding how school problems can be solved and in actually solving them. Teachers and principals need to be protected from excessive criticism when raising controversial issues as long as they do it in a responsible, nonpartisan manner.
- Community service may be a significant way for young people to become involved in longer term, adult civic engagement, depending

on how it is approached. Sustained, long-term engagement has more enduring effects than episodic, short-term involvement. Service should involve projects that meet real needs rather than projects created simply for filling some minimum level of involvement. More uncertain is whether community service should be required; encouraging and facilitating participation seems to stimulate high levels of involvement; when students are forced to participate, they may rebel. Whether and how such service should be integrated into the curriculum is the subject of continued experimentation and evaluation research.

- The family remains a major contributor to all aspects of social and political development. Attitudes of young people are strongly influenced by their parents' attitudes, especially if parents have strong opinions and express them clearly. Adult voluntary and political participation is strongly influenced by parental behavior patterns. Parents are important indirectly as well, by their support of good civic education.

- Civic education is increasingly prevalent in the new democracies of Eastern Europe, Latin America, Asia and Africa. Civics programs funded by U.S. and other international donors are being widely implemented, not only in the formal school system but also in numerous community-based programs for adults. They attempt to inculcate the knowledge, values, skills, and participatory orientations that are thought to develop a supportive democratic political culture. Civic education conducted for adults by community-based organizations can have particularly powerful effects on political participation.

- The way in which civic education is delivered differs from one country to another, but the goals of an informed, active and thoughtful citizenry are widely shared, and many of the same principles govern instruction of new generations across a wide range of democratic settings.[25]

Educational Reform: Fernando Reimers and Eleonora Villegas-Reimers

Educational systems, in both their philosophy and structure, reflect a society's values and tend to perpetuate them. That is why educational reform can be a crucial element in cultural change.

Fernando Reimers of the Harvard Graduate School of Education, and Eleonora Villegas-Reimers of Wheelock College wrote about educational reform for the CMRP. While their focus was specifically on Latin America, their analysis and prescriptions have clear relevance for other lagging regions, starting with their opening statement: "Among the institutions in societies that promote the development of . . . shared values and dispositions, none—with the possible exception of families—is more powerful than schools, especially given the large proportion of time people spend in them during critical years, and their influence in shaping people's minds and hearts. . . . The meandering historical evolution of civil liberties and human rights in Latin America offers no guarantees about how open societies in the region will be in the future; any number of scenarios is possible, much depending on what habits of mind are passed on to the young."[26]

Reimers and Villegas-Reimers identify six major shortcomings of Latin American education. In their words:

1. Schools in Latin America do not provide equal learning opportunities to all. It is not just that individual children learn differently as a result of effort or ability; rather it is that most educational institutions in the region have been better at reproducing or increasing intergenerational social differences than at narrowing those gaps, as evidenced by the persistent problem of inequitable distribution of income, wealth, land, and opportunity in most Latin America countries. . . . Access to schools, particularly to secondary and tertiary education, is significantly more constrained for the children of poor families. This is partly because there are not sufficient public schools and universities to satisfy the demand for education; because there are not adequate financing mechanisms to enable low-income students to invest their time in their education; and because the basic preparation many low-income students receive is inadequate to allow them to pass college entrance examinations or to succeed academically in college. Second, the quality of basic education is segmented, with low-income students often receiving education of a lower quality.

The state of affairs in schools reflects a view of society as organized in two different groups, with little mobility between them, where social origin is also social destiny. Indeed, the purpose of educational institutions for most of the last several centuries in Latin America has been to perpetuate this set of feudal values and social practice. Partly because the idea that all people have the same basic human rights—including the right to be well educated—does not have widespread support in Latin America, blatant educational disparities persist, undermining the formation of social capital and perpetuating divided societies, poverty, and inequality.

2. Educational management and decision making in Latin America reflects an authoritarian culture where government officials often confuse their role as public servants with the private administration of their own affairs. "Arrogant [policy] elites tend to see little need to bother reading evaluation research or asking those who do for advice, believing they know the answers because their position confers authority on them. They also believe they know the problems and the questions that call for answers. Since they operate in a context where they are not held accountable for their actions, the systematic underperformance of the education systems of Latin America has little consequence for the perpetuation of their ineffective practices."[27] Deficiencies of school cultures with respect to developing trust, reciprocity, and social capital are apparent from the low levels of trust among school staff and students.

3. Reinforcing the deficiencies of schools as models for and promoters of democratic participation are the limited opportunities for parents to be engaged with schools. There is wide inequality among schools in the region in the extent to which parents participate in school management committees. This is because many schools do not have such councils and those that do involve typically only school staff. Opportunities for student participation in school management councils are even more limited. . . . But the limits of parental participation run deeper than the lack of input in school governance. Many parents do not visit their children's schools frequently.

4. The fact that students in Latin America are not learning at high levels . . . is also in part due to the fact that their teachers are not teaching students well, and in particular are not teaching students to think for themselves and to value the freedom to do so. Yet it would be unreasonable to place all the blame and responsibility for this failure on the teachers. There are many factors that contribute to the shortcomings of the schools, and many of these conditions result from cultures that do not foster trust, reciprocity, and freedom.

As in many other regions, teachers in Latin America could benefit from more and better professional preparation. Most teachers in the region come into teaching with very poor academic preparation; many do not choose the profession but land in it by default, after having been denied entry into other professional fields in higher education. Most of them come from low socio-economic backgrounds and have a hard time making ends meet with the extremely low salaries. Many teachers work two or more jobs, the other(s) often not in the education field.

The content of teacher-preparation courses and programs varies by country, but in almost all countries it does not include anything related to education for democracy or activities to promote democratic practices. Thus, even when the school curriculum may target the development of democratic skills, knowledge, and attitudes, as it does in an increasing number of countries, teachers have not been prepared to implement such goals effectively and simply require their students to memorize facts about the constitutions of their countries, without any emphasis on the development of critical thinking skills, logical reasoning, communication skills, or the civic values necessary to participate in a democratic society. And of course, the teachers' experiences in democracy are limited, as they are citizens of their societies and products of the existing cultures.

The emphasis in teacher preparation on rote learning and the limited opportunities for students to learn to think for themselves further limit the preparation of democratic citizens.

5. There is a clear need for a civic education curriculum. In recent years, several countries in the region have begun to develop curricula to promote values, including those necessary for democratic citizenship, such as respect, tolerance, and both personal and social responsibility. Although only a small piece in the larger system of influences through which schools develop democratic skills and dispositions, it is a move that should continue and be strengthened, as direct and explicit teaching of democratic knowledge, skills, attitudes, and values is necessary for democratic societies to exist and function, especially when the social climate of the society is not one that is conducive to learning and practicing these values and skills.

6. Students do not have adequate opportunities to develop independent thinking. To the extent instruction in the classroom provides students more opportunities for individual expression, to learn for themselves, and to work independently or in groups in solving problems, rather than merely to listen to the teachers, it will help students develop independence of mind and learn the most valuable lesson—that knowledge is a personal construction, that one can apply one's efforts to learn just about anything, and that anyone can learn.

The practice of instruction in many classrooms in Latin America, however, is diametrically opposed to what we describe here. Teachers talk most of the time, they provide students with low-order explanations and engage them in low-order cognitive tasks, copying from the board or taking notes from teacher lectures. Students have very limited opportunities to work on research projects that reflect their interests. In many instances, teachers disrespect and humiliate students. This kind of education is boring and mind-numbing, and is survived only by very resilient spirits.

Reimers and Villegas-Reimers conclude:

"In order for schools in Latin America to be successful in preparing democratic citizens who can actively participate in designing and implementing the destiny of their own countries in an informed and just manner, important changes are necessary in the culture of education. These changes include a curriculum that emphasizes the development of democratic knowledge, skills, values and dispositions; designed, taught and implemented by teachers who are professionals of the highest quality; who work in an educational system where participation and accountability is encouraged and expected; and where access is open to all. These changes are possible and should guide all education decision-making in the region, but will only occur when policymakers and other leaders in these societies face incentives and sanctions that commit them to change—to democracy and social justice."[28]

The Media

News and Opinion Media: Mariano Grondona and Carlos Alberto Montaner

Mariano Grondona is a columnist for *La Nación*, one of Buenos Aires's leading daily newspapers, and is also the host of the highly popular Argentine weekly public-affairs television talk show *Hora Clave* (Key

Hour). Carlos Alberto Montaner is the most widely read columnist in the Spanish language. He is a Cuban exile now living in Madrid. Grondona and Montaner write in their CMRP essay that "[they have] learned a sad lesson that has immunized them against any kind of triumphant temptation: columnists hardly ever really 'create' public opinion. Their task is to try to give an elegant and logical form to what many people suspect in a disorganized and fragmented way. Editorial writers do not even 'make' readers. What they do is find them. They collect them and keep them interested in the newspaper that these readers habitually buy."[29]

This means that in most cases, the opinion-piece writer is not influencing the public so much as preaching to the converted. "The reader does not look at all sections of the newspaper with the same attitude. . . . He wants to know what happened in Kosovo, the New York Stock Exchange, or the stadium of his favorite sport. The news can sadden or gladden him, but it is unlikely to trouble him seriously . . . his reaction to the information is rarely visceral. The opinion piece, however, is a different case. In the opinion pages, the reader seeks agreement, complicity. The pleasure in reading lies in being able to say, 'This is what I would have said or written about this topic.' And he feels annoyance for the opposite reason: 'How does this idiot dare come to these mistaken conclusions?'"[30]

The same is true of those dailies, like Madrid's *ABC* or Paris's *Le Figaro*, that highlight opinion pieces. They operate at a narrow margin of openness: most of their readers are looking for confirmation of their own values and attitudes.

Public-affairs television talk shows can have far more impact. Grondona and Montaner write:

As Walter Cronkite noted in his memoirs, the problem with TV journalists is that they often do not compete with each other, as happens in the press, but with highly popular situation comedies, law and order shows, sports events, and movies.

But those who succeed—for example Larry King in the United States—may become "institutions" with a powerful influence on an audience that is vastly larger than the audience of the print press. To be sure, this larger audience is more diverse. When a columnist writes, he addresses himself to a well-known universe of readers who by and large

coincide with his views. In contrast, the TV audience offers the opportunity to reach people ideologically and culturally distant from those
who address them, opening a wider scope for promotion of the values
of development, or whatever else may be the predilections of the host.[31]

Grondona and Montaner find a strong leftward bias in the news media
in Latin America. "The main reason must be sought in the psychology
of a great number of the young people who enter university journalism departments or the media. It is not true that these are people who
want to think objectively, who feel the pressing need to devote their
lives to the search for a truth they do not know. On the contrary, these
are idealistic young people who are convinced that there are many
things wrong with this vale of tears and that they know the best way to
fix them. They want to change the world, not report on it."[32]

To be sure, the reporters are not reporting on conditions in the Nordic countries. They are reporting on conditions in some of the most
inequitable societies in the world, societies in which political traditions
are largely authoritarian. Nevertheless, the universities they attend are
often regrettably politicized, and the search for the truth is subordinated to ideology. Commonly, reporters see the world through an ideological prism that reinforces popular views based not on objective
observation and fact but on emotion. The current renaissance of Dependency Theory in Latin American universities—the belief that Latin
America's ills are the result of its exploitation by the United States—is
a case in point. It is fed in part by the U.S. adventure in Iraq. But by
encouraging Latin Americans to return to economic statism, protectionism, discouragement of foreign investment, and even authoritarian governance, the renaissance of Dependency Theory flies in the face
of some of the most important lessons of the past half-century.

Grondona and Montaner conclude that it is only through the repeated
failure of experiments contrary to the lessons of history that Latin
American journalists will develop the objectivity that is indispensable
for a truly constructive role. In the meantime, the "bombardment" of
messages attacking capitalism and market economics is producing a
palpable impact on public opinion. As Grondona and Montaner note:
"In developed countries, journalism is 'liberal,' but its power is limited because it can modify but not undermine the momentum of the

prevailing capitalist consensus. In underdeveloped countries, in Latin America and elsewhere, journalism is 'populist' but powerful because it reinforces the prevailing anti-capitalist consensus. The inevitable failure of populism, however, pushes us toward the point where the inevitable link between capitalism and economic development will become apparent to all but the most fervent ideologues."[33]

Grondona and Montaner continue: "The recent Latinobarometro polls are unsettling with respect to Latin America's declining faith in democracy. But that decline is driven by the failure, in most but not all countries, of democratic electoral processes to produce vibrant economies. Before long, it will become apparent that the failure is not rooted in democratic processes and 'neo-liberal' economics but in the traditional cultural rejection of the capitalism and entrepreneurship that have driven the advanced democracies to prosperity. At that moment, our long years of minority dissent in the media will be vindicated. At that point, Latin America will be on the road to the First World that Spain has staked out for it."[34]

Entertainment Media: Reese Schonfeld

Reese Schonfeld was the founding president and CEO of the Cable News Network and is the founder of the Television Food Network. His provocative paper is titled: "The Entertainment Invasion—The Global Battle for Cultural Domination." In his introduction, Schonfeld quotes John Berger: "Propaganda requires a permanent network of communication so that it can systematically stifle reflection with emotive or utopian slogans."[35] Schonfield goes on to ask, "Has there been a more effective propaganda vehicle than a 24/7 satellite channel or streaming video network of one's own? We have reached a critical moment in human history: satellite communication and the Internet permit a free flow of information that cannot be dammed. Civilizations, nations, penetrate each other, delivering messages that can affect and may even infect targeted cultures. Just as democracies can subvert dictatorships, so can dictatorships subvert democracies. Theocracies can be converted to rationalism; secular societies can be transformed into theocracies."[36]

Schonfeld cites the view of Bernd Schiphorsst, former head of Bertelsmann television:

Knight Rider, an innocuous American police/adventure series, helped bring down the Berlin Wall. East German authorities had banned satellite reception. But East Germans who demanded more varied, particularly non-government controlled television, beat their trashcan covers into satellite dishes, built their own receivers, and spent hours watching Western entertainment programs.

Most East Berliners paid little attention to [official] news or documentaries because they regarded them as propaganda. They did, however, accept Western entertainment programs as accurate representations of life in the West. On the surface, the programs appeared mindless and trivial, but they carried a subtext: the standard of living enjoyed by most Americans and other Westerners was considerably higher than that of the East German.[37]

Of the Middle Eastern cultural wars, Schonfeld notes:

Fundamentalist Arabic networks are rigidly doctrinaire, but secular Arab networks, which have far more viewers than their fundamentalist competitors, model their entertainment programming formats on American television. "Reality shows" are the battleground over which the cultural war is raging. *The New York Times*'s Thomas Friedman takes great comfort in that trend: "Consider what was the most talked-about story in the Arab world in recent weeks. Iraq? No. Palestine? No. It was *Super-Star*, the Lebanese version of American Idol!"[38] Naturally, the Fundamentalist Islamic Action Front condemns *Super-Star*, claiming the show facilitates substitution of the culture of globalization, led by America, for the cultural identity of the Arab people.

As content, *Super-Star* seems innocuous—a talent contest produced by Future TV, in which viewers help choose the winner. The contestants are male and female, women do not wear veils, and perhaps most important, viewers are encouraged to vote. In August, 4.5 million Middle-Easterners chose, as most talented, a Jordanian singer over a Syrian performer. The vote was 52 percent for the Jordanian, 48 percent for the Syrian. Rami Khouri, editor of the *Beirut Daily Star* commented: "I do not recall in my happy adult life a national vote that resulted in a 52 to 48 percent victory." So democracy's first Middle Eastern success determines the victor in a talent contest.[39]

But the Middle East culture wars also involve an influential voice of Islamic extremism:

> Al Manar, the fundamentalist Muslim network funded by Hezbollah which features news, documentaries, historical dramas, kid shows, and religious programs. It produces two different program schedules—one, a Shiite broadcast signal for consumption in Lebanon and Iran; the other a pan-Islamic satellite network seen throughout the world. Both networks schedule news programs and documentaries that portray Americans in Iraq as murderers and terrorists. They claim that American soldiers violate Iraqi mosques and Iraqi women. Israelis are also portrayed as murderers and terrorists, while the suicide bombers who attack them are recruited and openly glorified as martyrs by Al Manar.
>
> Al Manar's most successful program to date is *Al-Shattat*, a Syrian dramatization of that classic myth of anti-Semitism, *The Protocols of the Elders of Zion*, a Czarist forgery accusing Jews of killing gentile babies and baking their blood into matzos as part of the Passover ritual, all depicted graphically and in full color.[40]

Schonfeld goes on to note another satellite television cultural war—in East Asia. "The Far East is in the midst of its own entertainment war—state-controlled Chinese broadcast (CCTV) and cable programming networks versus New Tang Dynasty Television (NTDT), a satellite service associated with the Falun Gong cult. China is officially atheistic while the Falun Gong preaches a unique mixture of Buddhism and Taoism."[41]

Schonfeld writes, "NTDT Primetime features Hollywood movies from the thirties through the fifties, partly because they are affordable but, more importantly, because they conform to NTDT's avowed intention to promote democratic cultural change [so that] 'more people can enjoy peace and freedom and live harmoniously among different races and beliefs.' Hollywood films of the Thirties and Forties promote a similar credo: democracy is applauded; religion is treated with reverence; good fights against evil and good always prevails. The message couldn't be more simple—black and white, no grays, a trip back to what [Falun Gong founder] Li Hon Zhi sees as a glorious past."[42]

The Chinese government has recently convinced Eutelsat, the satellite service that carries NTDT, to end the transmission of the network within China. Meanwhile CCTV, the government network, is responding with its own use of entertainment media to deliver important messages. Schonfeld writes:

> Over the past six years, PCI [Population Communications International, a non-profit U.S. group affiliated with the United Nations] and CCTV have developed a primetime serial, Bai Xiang (*Ordinary People*), set in rural China. The plotline is built around a strong woman named Luye who defies her husband and gives birth to a little girl. This is a brave decision, given the one-child regulation. (The Chinese government now supports one child per family with a stipend, free education, and free medical care. After one, the family bears all the costs.) After her daughter is born, Luye divorces her husband, remarries, and then divorces her second husband when he too demands that she bear him a son. Ultimately, Luye launches a successful business, and she and her daughter gain the respect of their fellow villagers. Despite, or perhaps because of, the introduction of controversial issues, *Ordinary People* has the highest ratings on CCTV in its time slot.[43]

The soap-opera-like *novelas* so popular in Latin America are being adapted by institutions including PCI, the Johns Hopkins Center for Communication Programs, and the BBC, to communicate value-laden messages about specific issues like birth control but also broader goals like reducing poverty and empowering citizens, particularly women, at grassroots levels.

Schonfeld, who is a great admirer of the BBC, has a preference for public television over private. "Commercial television, even when regulated, disregards program content as it tries to reach the largest audience possible. Since advertising is its only source of revenue, it has no choice: it sells its audience to its advertisers by the pound, and the mass audience weighs the most. In the world of commercial broadcasting, bad television drives out good."[44]

His conclusion is surprising, and sure to be controversial: "If I were now designing a media plan for an emerging nation, I would not grant commercial licenses for at least twenty years. Public broadcasting, which is better suited to introduce cultural values, must have a head start or it will fail. I would fund programming through television license fees or from government tax revenue. I would do my best to keep out foreign satellite broadcasts, and, following the Chinese example, I would begin to build a national cable network that could deliver a wide variety of cable programs so long as their cultural messages coincided with [the values that promote] democracy, social justice, and prosperity. News and discussion shows would not be censored."[45]

Leadership

RICHARD LAMM was the Democratic governor of Colorado for 12 years, from 1975 to 1987. One of his chief concerns was African-American and Hispanic underachievement, above all in education. His frustrations in trying to solve this problem subsequently led him to the conclusion that powerful cultural forces were in play.

Lamm later became interested in the role of leadership in cultural change, which he focuses on in his essay "Public Policy and Culture." In reviewing some cases where leadership played a clearly important role in cultural change, he makes a general statement that echoes Harvey Nelsen's model of cultural change: "When things are going well in a country, cultural change is a non-starter. It is when things are going poorly that visionary leaders may attribute adversity to cultural factors and seek to change them. Often, of course, leaders will take the easy way out and blame external factors, e.g., 'dependency' and 'colonialism.'"[46]

Lamm notes that cultural change sometimes occurs under the guise of political or ideological change: "One person's cultural change is another person's political change. Franklin Delano Roosevelt forever changed America and its political culture, reaching to the very essence of the ways Americans think about themselves individually and as a society. But the same national work ethic, desire for upward mobility, and propensity for freedom, cooperation, and wealth creation were present both at the beginning and end of his administration. The culture was modified but not transformed."[47]

Lamm poses the question, "How does one change a society in the absence of chaos and trauma?"[48] In response, he looks at Puerto Rico and its substantial transformation under Luis Muñoz Marín.

Muñoz Marín lived most of his early life in the United States and was consequently bicultural. As Puerto Rico's first elected governor, in 1948, he seized the opportunity to promote a cultural revolution aimed at modernizing the island.

He promoted economic development through Operation Bootstrap, which encouraged new investment from the United States. He provoked a revolution in the education system: religious instruction was ended in public schools; public education was made available to females; and boys and girls shared the same classroom. Rote memorization of catechistic questions and answers gave way to education that called for experimentation and pragmatic solving of problems.

During Muñoz Marín's 16 years as governor, Puerto Rico experienced transforming rates of economic growth. Today, it is the most affluent society in Latin America. Teodoro Moscoso, one of Muñoz Marín's principal aides and first U.S. Coordinator of the Alliance for Progress, wrote in 1988, ". . . the most fundamental cause of our economic takeoff was the political leadership of Muñoz Marín. He changed the state of mind of the Puerto Rican people. He changed the culture."[49]

Yet for all the achievements of Muñoz Marín and his successors, "Puerto Rico's transformation is far from complete. Per capita income on the island is half that of the poorest U.S. state. Unemployment rates and welfare usage are substantially above U.S. averages. And Puerto Ricans who migrate to the mainland do very poorly in education, income, and upward mobility. We do not appreciate how powerful the momentum of traditional values can be."[50]

Lamm also looks at the Meiji Restoration in Japan; Ataturk's vision of a modern, western Turkey; and Singapore's transformation under Lee Kuan Yew. Those countries are among the CMRP case studies addressed in chapters 5 and 6.

WE NOW TURN to an examination of the link between religion and culture, and of the evidence that some religions are more prone to progress than others.

4

Religions and Progress

PART OF OUR LIBERAL TRADITION is to accord equal respect to all religions. We generally try to avoid comparative value judgments when it comes to religions. This presumption—let's label it religious relativism—is arguably dominant in the West, and surely in our universities. However, when it comes to the relationship between religion and human progress, I find compelling evidence that some religions do better than others in promoting the goals of democratic politics, social justice, and prosperity.

As an example of a religion that is highly resistant to progress, consider again Voodoo, the dominant religion of Haiti and a surrogate for the many animist religions of Africa, the birthplace of Voodoo. Not only does Voodoo nurture irrationality; it also nurtures a sense of impotence and fatalism and discourages the entrepreneurial vocation. It focuses on the present, not the future. It is also essentially without ethical content, at least in the sense of the Golden Rule behaviors so central to the typology. I believe that Voodoo has made a major contribution to the sociopolitical pathology, including poverty and extremely low levels of trust, that has plagued Haiti's history. I also believe that, as Daniel Etounga-Manguelle argues in *Culture Matters*, animist religions have similarly impeded progress in many African countries.

Table 4.1

Religion Summary

Category/Country	Religion[a]	Population[b]	UN Index[c]	Literacy[d]	Female Lit.[e]
Total	Protestant	530			
Weighted Average	Protestant		9.2	99%	99%
Unweighted Average	Protestant		18.8	99%	99%
1st World Wtd. Avg.	Protestant		8.5	99%	99%
1st World Average	Protestant		9.2	99%	99%
Israel	Jewish	6	22	96%	94%
Total	Catholic	904			
Weighted Average	Catholic		58.3	86%	88%
Unweighted Average	Catholic		63	88%	86%
1st World Wtd. Avg.	Catholic		17.4	99%	99%
1st World Average	Catholic		17.3	98%	98%
Total	Orthodox	262			
Weighted Average	Orthodox		58.9	99%	99%
Unweighted Average	Orthodox		62.6	99%	99%
Total	Confucian	1491			
Weighted Average	Confucian		77.8	86%	79%
Unweighted Average	Confucian		34.6	93%	90%
1st World Wtd. Avg.	Confucian		14.5	99%	98%
1st World Average	Confucian		21.5	96%	94%
Total	Buddhist	146			
Weighted Average	Buddhist		92.2	86%	83%
Unweighted Average	Buddhist		42.2	70%	67%
Total	Islam	1122			
Weighted Average	Islam		111.9	65%	54%
Unweighted Average	Islam		105.5	66%	54%
Total	Arab countries	252			
Weighted Average	Arab countries		103.3	64%	51%
Unweighted Average	Arab countries		91.8	68%	58%
Total	Islam: non-Arab	870			
Weighted Average	Islam: non-Arab		114.8	65%	56%
Unweighted Average	Islam: non-Arab		116.6	64%	51%
Total	Hindu	1041			
Weighted Average	Hindu		115	57%	45%
Unweighted Average	Hindu		115	57%	45%

[a]50% or more of population; [b]In millions, source: World Bank, World Bank Development Report 2002; [c]UN Human Development Index 2001, most advanced is 1, least 162; [d]UN Human Development Report 2001; [e]UN Human Development Report 2001; [f]UNDP total fertility rate 1995–2000; [g]Freedom House 2001 Survey, assesses political rights and civil liberties, best = 2, worst = 14; [h]Date of start of democratic continuity; [i]IBRD, World

Fertility[f]	Freedom Total[g]	Dem. Date[h]	Per Cap. GDP[i]	GINI[j]	Trust[k]	Corruption[l]
1.8	2.3	1826	$29,784	36.8	42%	14.9
1.7	2.5	1877	$22,373	32.3	46%	14
1.8	2.3	1826	$30,062	36.8	42%	14.7
1.6	2.5	1852	$26,340	31.4	50%	9.1
2.9	4	1948	$19,320	35.5		16
2.6	5.5	1940	$ 9,358	45.6	16%	45.6
2.9	5.4	1969	$ 9,366	42	22%	45.7
1.4	2.7	1927	$22,890	30.4	24%	24.4
1.5	2.6	1934	$23,311	30.3	32%	22.3
1.3	8.6		$ 7,045	40.4	25%	75.7
1.4	7.2	1985	$ 6,038	34.3	25%	63.8
1.8	11.7		$ 6,691	38.5	51%	52.2
1.5	7.8	1976	$19,133	33.2	47%	27.6
1.4	3.4		$24,239	27.3	46%	25.8
1.4	5		$22,172	31.4	44%	20.3
2.9	8.9		$ 4,813	39.5		
3.8	9.7	1992	$ 2,625	37.3		61
4.1	9.7		$ 3,142	36.3	26%	78.6
4.4	10.7		$ 3,755	39.6	27%	65
4	12.1		$ 4,950	33.7	28%	50
4.3	11.8		$ 5,721	35.8	25%	40
4.3	8.9		$ 2,781	37.5	26%	82
4.5	9.8		$ 2,674	41.3	27%	73
3.3	5	1950	$ 2,390	37.8		71
2.8	5	1950	$ 2,390	37.8		71

Development Report 2002 (purchasing power parity); [i]IBRD 2002, lower is more equitable income distribution; [k]World Values Survey 1999–2002, percent who believe people can be trusted; [l]Transparency International Corruption Perceptions Index 2001, lower is cleaner.

I have examined the performance of 117 countries, each with a million or more people of whom a majority identify with one of six religions—Buddhism, Catholicism, Eastern Orthodox Christianity, Hinduism, Islam, and Protestantism—and one secular ethical code—Confucianism. Each religion or secular code is dominant in at least three countries with a combined population of at least 100 million. I also include one small country—Israel—that is predominantly Jewish.

I have located the ranking of each of the 117 countries with respect to ten indicators or indices and have then grouped these data by predominant religion (see Table 4.1: Religion Summary). The data are presented in both weighted (for population) and unweighted averages, with separate calculations for Protestant, Catholic, and Confucian countries in the First World. Within Islam, I have also grouped Arab countries separately. The ten indicators or indices are:

1. The UN's Human Development Index
2. UN data on literacy
3. UN data on female literacy
4. UN fertility data
5. Freedom House's Annual Survey of Freedom in the World
6. The chronology of democratic evolution
7. World Bank per capita income data[1]
8. World Bank income distribution data
9. World Values Survey data on trust
10. Transparency International's Corruption Perceptions Index

I acknowledge the considerable scientific limits to the analysis. The data derive from respectable sources, but some distortions are inevitable. For example, while I have generally held to the operating assumption that a majority of a country's people subscribe to the religion in which that country is grouped, there are obviously wide variations in the religious composition of many countries. Although India is predominantly Hindu, it has one of the largest Muslim populations in the world. Indonesia, by contrast, is overwhelmingly Muslim, but has a small Chinese, mostly Christian, minority. Although I regard South Korea as a Confucian country, many Koreans practice a religion, Christianity prominent among them. And the label "Confucian" is itself oversimplified: it would be more accurately described as Chinese culture, also embracing aspects of Buddhism, Taoism, and ancestor worship, among other sources. Finally, I have classified Germany, the Netherlands, and Switzerland as Protestant, although there may today be more practicing Catholics than Protestants in each country. I have done this on the same grounds as the World Values Survey: because, to quote Ronald Inglehart, "historically, Protestantism has shaped them."[2]

I want to reiterate an important point made earlier: within a given religion, there are divisions, cross-currents, and national variations that are not reflected in Table 4.1. For example, several of the generalizations that follow about Catholicism do not apply to the Basques, who have a centuries-old tradition of entrepreneurship, creativity, and cooperation, and who are very Catholic (the Society of Jesus was founded by a Basque). Islam is quite different in Indonesia and Saudi Arabia. And our analysis does not disaggregate Sunni, Shia, and Kurdish Muslims.

I also had to make some judgment calls. For example, I had to address the question, "When did democratic continuity start in Great Britain?" Some might argue that the appropriate year was 1215. Partly in recognition of the mathematical distortions that would have resulted had I chosen the year of the signing of the Magna Carta, I chose instead 1832, a year of sweeping political reforms.

I want to stress again that religion is not the only influence on a country's performance with respect to the indicators, nor on its culture. Geography, including climate, topography, and resource endowment, clearly plays a key role, as do the vagaries of history—for example, wars, colonial experiences, geopolitical forces, and economic models chosen or imposed. The level of prosperity powerfully influences performance, as is apparent from Table 4.1. Leadership matters: that Singapore is among the most affluent and least corrupt countries in the world surely reflects the vision and influence of its dominant political figure, Lee Kuan Yew.

But culture also matters, and culture is profoundly, although not exclusively, influenced by religion and/or an ethical code like Confucianism. While I am unable to quantify "profoundly" with any precision, the patterns in the data tend to confirm the conclusion that some religions are more conducive to modernization than others. But these patterns must be considered approximations. Narrow differences could too easily be explained away by shortcomings in the data or by the intrusion of non-cultural factors. So we must look for patterns that involve significant contrasts.

Seven broad conclusions emerge from the data:

1. Protestantism has been far more conducive to modernization than Catholicism, above all in the Western Hemisphere.

Predominantly Protestant countries do substantially better than predominantly Catholic countries on the UN's Human Development Index. The Index is the most comprehensive of the ten listed above, combining life expectancy, adult literacy, school enrollment, and GDP per capita. On a scale of 1 (best) to 162 (worst), the weighted average of Protestant countries is 9.2, that of Catholic countries is 58.3. To be sure, the majority of Protestant countries are developed—in the First World—while the majority of Catholic countries are not. But a significant difference is also found when comparing First World countries: the weighted average for Protestant countries is 8.5, for Catholic countries 17.4.

Differences in literacy rates between the two are distorted by the contrasting First World/Third World composition and don't merit elaboration. I note in passing that substantial adult illiteracy still exists in Latin America—10 percent or more in seven countries: Guatemala, Nicaragua, Honduras, Bolivia, Dominican Republic, Peru, and Brazil, not to mention Haiti, whose illiteracy level is more than 40 percent.

The Freedom House rankings on democracy do show a significant difference—weighted averages of 2.3 for Protestant countries and 5.5 for Catholic on a scale where 2 is best and 14 worst. This difference primarily reflects the fragile condition of democracy in Catholic Latin America. With democratic continuity being at best relatively recent in Latin America as well as in some African and former Soviet-bloc Catholic countries, it is the First World that offers the most meaningful grouping for testing Tocqueville's contention that Protestantism is more congenial to democracy than Catholicism. There is a sharp contrast in the longevity of democracy. The average date for the commencement of democratic continuity in the Protestant countries of the First World is 1852, of the Catholic countries 1934. When one weights the countries by population, the discrepancy becomes even wider, chiefly because the United States is so populous.[3]

Reflecting the difference in First World/Third World composition between the Protestant and Catholic countries, the former enjoy almost a 3-to-1 advantage over the latter in per capita GDP. This narrows substantially when only First World countries are considered, but there is still a substantial gap—about seven thousand dollars in the weighted average. I might add that Angus Maddison's data for the year 1900 show a substantial advantage for the Protestant countries over the Catholic countries in what is today the First World. The GDP data confirm Max Weber's thesis about the economic creativity of Protestantism.

Latin America may be the most inequitable region of the world in terms of income distribution, and that fact skews the income distribution substantially in favor of the Protestant countries overall. But when you focus on the First World, the Catholic countries do slightly better than the Protestant countries on average and a good deal better on weighted average—in large part because among the advanced democracies, income distribution in the populous and predominantly Protestant United States is the least equitable.

Trust, as measured by answers to the World Values Survey question, "Can people in general be trusted?" is much higher in Protestant countries than in Catholic countries generally. While the gap narrows when one considers only First World countries, it is still substantial: a weighted average of 42 percent trust others in the First World Protestant countries, a weighted average of 24 percent in the Catholic countries. The trust factor may be related to comparable levels of corruption. On Transparency International's scale where the least corrupt is number 1 and the most corrupt number 91, the weighted average for the Protestant countries is 14.9, for the Catholic countries 45.6. With respect to First World countries, the Protestant advantage is 14.7 to 24.4.

Of the ten least corrupt countries, eight are Protestant, one is Confucian (Singapore at number 4), and one (Luxembourg, with a population of fewer than five hundred thousand) is Catholic.

An article in *The Economist* highlights the disproportionate contribution of French Protestants to the progress of that country in which Catholicism has predominated: "the French tend to think that a Protestant background spells honesty, respect for one's word, hard work, a sense of responsibility, a modest way of life, tolerance, freedom of conscience—and a dour inflexibility. Protestants have been in the van of most of the great liberalizing ideas and reforms in French history: the Declaration of Human Rights, the abolition of slavery, the market economy, the devolution of power from the center, the spread of state education, the separation of church and state, advocacy of contraception and divorce."[4]

To be sure, the influence of the two religions on culture was a good deal greater prior to the twentieth century, and in most First World countries, a substantial homogenization has occurred in which the dominant ethical code is generally adopted by people of all religions— and agnostics and atheists as well. In this sense, we assimilated Americans, whether Protestant, Catholic, Jewish, Muslim, or non-believers, are all Anglo-Protestants (see the summary of Samuel Huntington's essay, later in this chapter).

2. The Nordic countries are the champions of progress.

The Nordic countries—Denmark, Finland, Iceland, Norway, and Sweden—all of whose evolution was profoundly influenced by Lutheranism and all of which are relatively homogeneous, get high marks across the board. They are all rated 2—the top—in political rights and civil liberties by Freedom House. Norway is number 1, Sweden number 4 on the UN's Human Development Index. Denmark, Finland, and Sweden are among the countries with the most equitable distribution of income. Norway and Denmark are at the top of the trust listing, with Sweden and Finland not far behind. Finland is the least corrupt country in the world; Denmark is second.

The same pattern of Nordic achievement appears in four other listings:

- In the National Bureau of Economic Research study of good government around the world mentioned in chapter 2, Norway was number 3 (New Zealand was 1, Switzerland 2), Iceland 6, Finland 8, and Sweden 9. All of the top ten countries were Protestant.[5]
- The World Economic Forum published a 2004 listing of countries ranked according to competitiveness. Finland was number 1, Sweden 3, Denmark 5, Norway 6, and Iceland 10. (The United States was ranked at number 2.) Nine of the top ten countries were Protestant; Japan was number 9.[6]
- A ranking of countries by scientific articles per billion dollars of GDP showed Sweden number 2, Finland number 4, Denmark number 5, and Iceland number 11. (Israel was number 1.)[7]
- A 2004 listing of rich countries according to their contribution to the progress of poor countries shows Denmark as number 2 (The Netherlands is number 1), Sweden 3, and Norway 9. Nine of the top ten countries are Protestant; France is number 10.[8]

Interestingly, a recent assessment of social capital in the United States (social capital is defined by writer Rodger Doyle as "a high level of trust and tolerance, an egalitarian spirit, volunteerism, an interest in keeping informed, and participation in public affairs") finds Americans of Scandinavian and British descent at the top.[9]

3. Confucianism has been far more conducive to modernization than Islam, Buddhism, or Hinduism.

The data for the Confucian countries are, of course, dominated by China, which drives all of the indicators down, particularly when we weight for population. The averages for the Confucian First World societies—Japan, South Korea, Taiwan, Hong Kong, and Singapore—are similar to the Catholic First World country averages in (1) the UN Human Development Index; (2) literacy, including female literacy; (3) per capita GDP; and (4) income distribution. The First World Catholic countries consolidated democratic institutions about a half century before the Confucian First World countries, reflecting in part the authoritarian current of Confucianism, and the First World Catholic countries do slightly better than their Confucian counterparts in the Freedom House Index. Trust is substantially greater in the Confucian countries than the Catholic countries, while corruption is about the same—with one noteworthy exception: in the 2001 Transparency listing, Singapore is tied with Iceland in fourth place.

4. The most advanced Orthodox Christian country, Greece, was the poorest of the European Union members prior to the 2004 accessions. There are some parallels between the Orthodox Christian and Catholic countries. But there are also some apparent residues in Orthodox countries from the Communist experience.

The Orthodox Christian and Catholic countries come out in the same position on the UN's Human Development Index with weighted averages of 58, and they are fairly close in per capita GDP and trust. Greece is the only First World country that is Orthodox. Reflecting the Communist emphasis on education, the Orthodox countries* enjoy First World literacy levels. And their poor showings on the Corruption Perceptions Index might be explained in part as the consequence of the widespread corruption nurtured by the Communist system.

---

*Listed by per capita GDP: Greece, Belarus, Russia, Romania, Bulgaria, Macedonia, Ukraine, Armenia, Georgia, Moldova.

5. Islam has fallen far behind the Western religions and Confucianism in virtually all respects. There are some significant differences between Arab and non-Arab Islamic countries.

The data for the Islamic countries reveal a strong resistance to modernization, in striking contrast to the vanguard role of Islam during its first several centuries. The Islamic countries are far behind the Confucian countries and even further behind the Christian First World countries on the UN Human Development Index; in literacy, particularly female literacy; in per capita GDP; in the World Values Survey data on trust (except the Catholic countries); and in the Corruption Perceptions Index.

Particularly noteworthy are the low levels of female literacy—below 50 percent in Egypt, Morocco, Pakistan, and Bangladesh, among others—reflecting the subordinated position of women in the Islamic religion.

Also noteworthy are the data on fertility. The Islamic countries had the highest fertility rates in the world, according to the UN 1995-2000 estimates. While Islamic countries continue to present the highest rates among the various religious groups, UN estimates for 2000–2005 show an across-the-board decline.[10]

Table 4.2
Total Fertility Rate (births per woman)

	1995–2000	2000–2005
Algeria	3.2	2.8
Indonesia	2.6	2.4
Iran	3.2	2.3
Morocco	3.4	2.7
Pakistan	5.5	5.1
Yemen	7.6	7.0

The Islamic countries are less free according to Freedom House than any other group except the Confucian countries, which are overwhelmed by China's authoritarianism. Only one predominantly Muslim country—Mali—is considered free. Trust is low in the Islamic countries, and corruption is high.

I have disaggregated the Arab and non-Arab Islamic countries to see if there are any significant divergences. The Arab countries do substantially better in per capita GDP, where their oil wealth is reflected, and with respect to corruption. They do marginally better with respect to income distribution. But the Arab countries do measurably worse than non-Arab Islamic countries on the Freedom House political rights and civil liberties scale.

6. Hindu India's democratic institutions have held up well, and it has experienced rapid economic growth during the past two decades. But it has been very slow to educate its people, particularly its women, and it does poorly in the Corruption Perceptions Index.

Hindu India scores better than any other religious grouping except the Protestant countries in the Freedom House rankings. This can be attributed to the fact that British political institutions have taken root.

According to World Bank data, the Indian economy averaged 5.3 percent growth in the 1980s and 6 percent growth in the 1990s, in the wake of the opening up of the economy. India's continuing economic surge is among the most encouraging development trends of the early years of the twenty-first century.

But literacy in India remains surprisingly low—more than half of Indian women are illiterate—reflecting the subordination of women in Hinduism, similar to that in the Islamic countries. And India does not do well on Transparency International's Corruption Perceptions Index.

7. It is difficult to generalize about Buddhism because of its extreme diversity, but the data suggest that it is not a powerful force for modernization.

The seven Table 4.1 countries where Buddhism has had predominant influence include, in order of population size, Thailand, Myanmar, Sri Lanka, Cambodia, Laos, Mongolia, and Bhutan. Mongolia is among the freest countries in the Third World; Myanmar is among the least free. The data for equitability of income distribution (the Gini scale) on Mongolia, Cambodia, and Thailand are typical for Third World countries, but Sri Lanka does much better, in fact better than the United Kingdom and the United States (once again, income distribution in the United States is the most inequitable among the advanced democracies). The only Buddhist country to have experienced sustained high rates of economic development is Thailand, but, as in Indonesia, Malaysia, and the Philippines, the Chinese minority has made a vastly disproportionate contribution to that growth.[11]

The problem of generalizing is complicated by the diversity of Buddhism: major divisions, numerous sects, and sectarian variations over time. What is clear, however, is that no predominantly Buddhist country has made it into the First World, which up until now includes only Protestant, Catholic, Jewish, and Confucian members.

The CMRP Papers on Religion

THE FOREGOING DISCUSSION of the 117-country analysis provides us with a backdrop for the papers that were written by experts on each of the religions and Confucianism for the CMRP. I summarize their highlights and add my own comments in the following sections. The religions appear as ordered by the UN's Human Development Index.

Protestantism

The mainstream Protestant churches derivative of the Reformation—Lutheranism, Calvinism/Presbyterianism, and Anglicanism/Episcopalianism prominently among them—powerfully influenced the cultural evolution of Northern Europe, Great Britain, and the British offshoots—Canada, the United States, Australia, and New Zealand. In the seventeenth, eighteenth, and nineteenth centuries, these Protestant countries displaced Italy, Spain, and Portugal, and then France in economic and military power. The Protestant ethic was closely linked with the industrial revolution. And the advantage the Protestant countries today enjoy over other countries is in large measure the consequence of the progressive values inculcated by Protestantism over the centuries—even in the case of the Nordic countries, where secularism has now substantially displaced religion.

In general, the mainline Protestant churches are in decline today, even in the United States, which is more religious than other First World countries. But Evangelical and Pentecostal Protestantism are very much on the rise, particularly in Latin America and Africa. These two branches are the most numerous of the Protestant denominations; and it is these dynamic branches of Protestantism to which we first turn. Next, we'll consider the role and condition of Anglo-Protestant culture in the United States.

EVANGELICAL AND PENTECOSTAL PROTESTANTISM
IN THE THIRD WORLD

David Martin is an English sociologist and theologian who has focused his attention in recent years on the rise of Evangelical and Pentecostal Protestantism, particularly in Africa and Latin America. Evangelicalism and Pentecostalism, he writes, are "two phases of a faith based on change of heart and thoroughgoing revision of life."[12] The principal distinction, often blurred, is the greater emotionalism of Pentecostalism, which may express itself in unintelligible utterances ("the gift of tongues") and faith healing.

Martin estimates the global number of the two branches at about 500 million, with about 200 million in Africa, 100 million in Asia, 100 million in North America, and 50 million in Latin America. And their numbers are growing. As many as one-third of Guatemalans now consider themselves Evangelical or Pentecostal Protestants, and the 10 percent or more of Brazilians who have converted already constitute a political force in that country.

At least in Latin America, Evangelical and Pentecostal Protestantism are seen by the poor, including many indigenous peoples, as avenues to family stability and upward mobility. They emphasize values along the lines of those trumpeted by Weber and Benjamin Franklin. Martin observes: "In discussing how these virtues work out in practice, one needs to remember that these men of God are mostly women. Pentecostalism is a movement of women determined with God's help to defend home and family against machismo and the seductions of the street and the weekend. They represent female nurture and order over male 'nature' and disorder."[13]

These Protestant churches also provide a social structure that eases the adaptation from life in small villages to life in the intimidating chaos of big cities. Martin believes that the values engendered by Evangelicalism and Pentecostalism will lead to better lives for the converts and that the demonstration effect will sustain the momentum of conversion. Anecdotal evidence, for example the image of Protestant honesty and reliability held by other Latin Americans, points in the same direction.

At the end of his CMRP paper on Protestantism, David Martin offers some counsels to both mainline and Evangelical/Pentecostal Protestants:

A note to mainstream Protestants

In principle, mainstream Protestants respect religious variety and seek to appreciate other ways of understanding the Christian message. Yet Pentecostals have been excluded from this charity, partly because of alleged cultural affiliations with the United States at a time of generalized anti-Americanism but also because they are seen as successful competitors who share neither the mainstream's ecumenicism nor its propensity for "victim" explanations of poverty and deprivation. As the standard-bearers for the old Protestant ethic, the Pentecostals are stereotyped for espousing the wrong virtues and opting for the wrong social models.

Yet the Pentecostals and similar Evangelical movements are peaceful people engaging positively with modernity, not rejecting it or blowing people up. They are primarily a movement of black women for dignity and self-help—and a challenge to macho culture.

These movements now undermining the mainstream, at least in the Third World, are like the movements that undermined what was then the mainstream in Britain's industrial revolution and on the American frontier. And those movements were the forbears of today's mainstream!

Elites around the world tend to feel a protective nostalgia for "traditional" communities, a nostalgia led by anthropologists committed to cultural relativism. But change is inevitable as the poor and dispossessed increasingly become aware that life can be longer, less burdensome, and happier and discover that Pentecostalism is a viable vehicle to that better life. It deserves better than metropolitan contempt.

A note to the Pentecostals

Pentecostals are noted for their practicality. Yet as you improve your standards of living, you will spend more time in school and encounter wider horizons. This will test the spirit that raised you up as you confront the enjoyment of affluence and culture. You will also have to deal critically but fairly with the ideologies of intellectuals, which diverge from your own. And you will have to face the challenge of social responsibility: how the mutuality and participation of your church can be realized in the wider society.

The elites believe that the economic virtues no longer matter. But you know better from hard experience in the struggle for survival and a better life. The elites see no need for radical spiritual change and hence cultural change because they believe that the better life can be achieved by structural changes initiated by the state. But again you know from experience that spiritual and cultural change go together—and how crucial they are.[14]

Anglo-Protestant Culture in the United States

In his book *Who Are We? The Challenges to America's National Identity*, Samuel Huntington devotes a chapter to Anglo-Protestant culture, of which he writes: "For almost four centuries this culture of the founding settlers has been the central and lasting component of American identity."[15] What is the essence of Anglo-Protestant culture? What are the principal features of this product of "the dissenting, evangelical nature of American Protestantism"?[16] Huntington points to the American Creed, a term popularized by Gunnar Myrdal in his 1944 book *The American Dilemma.* "Myrdal spoke of 'the essential dignity of the individual human being, of the fundamental equality of all men, and of certain inalienable rights to freedom, justice, and a fair opportunity.'"[17]

Work ethic and individual responsibility are also central to Anglo-Protestant culture, as is opposition to hierarchy. Huntington observes: "The work ethic is a central feature of Protestant culture, and from the beginning America's religion has been the religion of work. In other societies, heredity, class, social status, ethnicity, and family are the principal sources of status and legitimacy. In America, work is. Both aristocratic and socialist societies demean and discourage work. Bourgeois societies promote work. America, the quintessential bourgeois society, glorifies work."[18]

Also central are the "long-standing English ideas of natural and common law, the limits of government authority, and the rights of Englishmen going back to Magna Carta. To these the more radical Puritan sects of the English Revolution added equality and the responsiveness of government to the people."[19]

Anglo-Protestant "dissenting, evangelical" culture has profoundly influenced the course of American history, time and again driving reform initiatives, including: the Revolution itself; the movement to abolish slavery; the Progressive movement, beginning in the 1890s; the fight for racial equality, beginning in the late 1950s; and the more general challenging of American institutions in the 1960s.

Anglo-Protestant culture has also influenced foreign policy. "In conducting their foreign policy, most states give overwhelming priority to what are generally termed the 'realist' concerns of power, security, and wealth. When push comes to shove, the United States does this too. Americans also, however, feel the need to promote in their relations with other societies and within those societies the moralistic goals they pursue at home."[20]

Judaism

There is just one predominantly Jewish country—Israel, with a population of about six million. But the extraordinary impact of Jews over the course of human history raises a crucial question for this book: What is it in Jewish culture that explains the prodigious record of Jewish achievement? That achievement is symbolized by the fact that 15 to 20 percent of Nobel Prizes have been won by Jews, who represent two tenths of one percent of the world's population. Jewish achievement has been apparent not only in academic pursuits but also in the professions, politics, business, labor, the arts and music, and entertainment.

Jewish achievement is centuries-old. The first Jews arrived in what would become the United States in 1654. "Peter Stuyvesant wanted to keep New Amsterdam free of Jews, arguing in a 1655 letter to the West India Company that '[the Jews were] very detrimental, because the Christians cannot compete against them.' His ban was overturned."[21] In a footnote to *The Protestant Ethic and the Spirit of Capitalism*, Max Weber presents the data on family income and education for the Baden region of Germany that, in showing measurably higher levels of achievement for Protestants than for Catholics, contributed to his decision to write the book. But the same footnote records substantially higher levels of achievement for Jews than for Protestants.[22]

Jewish success and the resentments and envies that it engendered were a major, if not often mentioned, source of the anti-Semitism that Adolf Hitler mobilized in Germany and elsewhere in Europe.

In his CMRP paper on Judaism, Canadian journalist Jim Lederman provides us with the following insights into what in Jewish culture drives achievement. Many of his comments evoke the progress-prone column of the typology as well as similar aspects of Protestant and Confucian doctrine:

> Jewish tradition holds that life, and living in the world, is essentially an incomplete, individual and group, "work-in-progress." Death is not sought. . . . Final judgment is based on the sum of a life as it was lived.
>
> All human activities and policies must, therefore, be directed towards the living and the living-to-be—and thus must also be future and long-term oriented. This, in turn, demands continuous social entrepreneurship and social engineering that can only be halted with the coming of the Messiah. . . . Participatory activism by everyone to improve the world is, therefore, a human obligation.[23] The guide to what should be done, and the ways in which it should be done, are embodied in a code of laws to which everyone must adhere—especially the Jews themselves.
>
> The basic rules of ethical behavior are believed to be immutable. However, implementation is subject to conflicting views and interpretations, debate and change. Thus, among Jews, uniqueness or novelty is not automatically disdained—and appreciation for the potential value of invention is carried over into almost all aspects of human activity.
>
> Among Jews, there is a . . . tension between innovation based on rationalism, and protective orthodoxy; between the desires for group survival, and individual expression; and between regulation, and creative freedom and personal responsibility.
>
> Leadership is self-selected and devolves to those who exhibit continuing merit in belief and practice. Merit is assigned based on proof over time. It is an award that can be withdrawn. While Jewish law requires obedience and obeisance to the sovereign (in the case of democracies this includes the will of the majority), this does not preclude the idea that one can be a member of a loyal opposition without being treasonous.
>
> Central to Jewish beliefs is the concept of *Tikkun Olam*, "repairing the world" . . . [and central to *Tikkun Olam*] is . . . the need to establish a level playing field for all. Utopian egalitarianism is, in general, rejected as denying the God-given uniqueness and creativity present in each individual. Instead, the purpose of almost all Jewish Law that does not deal directly with behavior towards the Divine is to encourage fairness in human relations.
>
> Social status and social mobility [are] predicated on an individual's personal accomplishments and his pursuit of excellence. Scholarship

remains . . . the highest social value. However, skilled, knowledge-based employment [comes] a close second.

Activism to "repair" human-created law where it is faulty or inadequate is deemed to be an obligation. For the most part, behaviors are viewed as means that can be altered, not objectives in themselves. Individual and group self-criticism, self-assistance, and a willingness to battle corruption are perceived to be required traits and assets.

Notably, among Jews, in almost all matters, immediate responsibility for creativity and action lies with the individual; but long-term success belongs to the group that sets the norms that foster accomplishment.[24]

Catholicism

Michael Novak, the prominent and prolific lay Catholic scholar, has contributed a paper on Catholicism to the CMRP. He notes that there are now more than a billion Catholics around the world, with the largest contingent in Latin America. Moreover, the Church is growing, particularly in Africa, and he expects that the number of Catholics will increase to almost 1.5 billion by 2025.

Novak observes that the Church came late to the support and promotion of democracy, in part because political liberalization in Europe in the nineteenth and twentieth centuries was often accompanied by secularization and anti-clericalism. But in the second half of the twentieth century, the Church dropped its support of authoritarian governments in favor of a pro-democratic stance that contributed to the wave of democratization in Latin America in the last decades of the twentieth century.

In this trend toward democratization, one perceives echoes of an observation by Tocqueville: "I think that the Catholic religion has erroneously been regarded as the natural enemy of democracy. Among the various sects of Christians, Catholicism seems to me, on the contrary, to be one of the most favorable to equality of condition among men. In the Catholic Church, the religious community is composed of only two elements: the priest and the people. The priest alone rises above the rank of his flock, and all below him are equal . . . no sooner is the priesthood entirely separated from the government, as is the case in the United States, than it is found that no class of men is more naturally disposed than the Catholics to transfer the doctrine of the equality of condition into the political world."[25]

The changed posture of the Church with respect to democracy is particularly apparent in the case of Spain. The Vatican sent a congratulatory message to Francisco Franco on his victory over the Republicans in 1939. But a quarter-century later, Cardinal Vicente Enrique y Tarancón played a key role in Spain's transition to democracy after Franco's death.

In his CMRP paper and book *The Catholic Ethic and the Spirit of Capitalism*, Novak refers to a minority Catholic crosscurrent favorable to free-market economics. He strongly advocates reconsideration by the Church of its ambivalence with respect to capitalism.

AT THE BEGINNING of this chapter I presented data that make a compelling case for reform of Catholicism. In most of the dimensions of progress covered by the data, Protestant countries have outperformed Catholic countries:

- **Democracy**: Catholic countries generally have been slower to consolidate democratic institutions than Protestant countries, and democracy remains fragile in Latin America.
- **Prosperity**: Catholic countries, particularly those in Latin America, lag economically. The first Catholic country to appear on the World Economic Forum's Competitiveness Index is Austria at number 17. Rapid economic development in Italy, Spain, Ireland, and Quebec has been accompanied by processes of secularization that have led to labeling these societies "post-Catholic." An *Economist* article in 2003 announced: "It used to be spoken of as Catholic Spain. Not these days."[26] Subsequently, Marlise Simons noted in the *New York Times* that "of Spain's 43 million people, only one in five consider themselves practicing Catholics."[27]
- **Income distribution**: Some of the most inequitable income distribution in the world is found in Latin America. In 1998, the richest 10 percent in Brazil accounted for 48 percent of income, the poorest 10 percent for only 0.7 percent. By comparison, the richest 10 percent in the United States—the most inequitable of the advanced democracies—accounted for 30.5 percent of income in 1997, the poorest 10 percent for 1.8 percent.[28]

The highly inequitable income distribution found in Latin America is profoundly ironic: the Catholic Church has long championed the poor—remember Matthew's judgment that "it is easier for a camel to go through the eye of a needle than for a rich man to enter into the kingdom of God." The irony is compounded by Calvinist Protestantism's preference for the rich: the poor are proportionately fewer and less poor in Protestant countries than in Catholic countries.

- **Trust**: Trust is significantly lower in Catholic societies than in Protestant ones.
- **Corruption**: Corruption is significantly higher in Catholic societies than in Protestant ones.

Michael Novak signals a key reform goal for Catholicism: a whole-hearted commitment to market economics, coupled, of course, with democratic politics. Catholic doctrinal ambivalence about economics may be in part responsible for Latin America's dalliance with socialism/statism, the related chimera of dependency theory, and Marxist-Leninist-inspired Liberation Theology. Some Church representatives have advocated "Third Way" solutions to poverty and social injustice, presumably with the Nordic countries in mind. But the advanced Nordic welfare programs have been made possible by their essentially capitalist economies.

Another key reform goal concerns ethical standards in Catholic countries. I believe that there is truth in Weber's contrast of Protestantism's insistence on "a life of good deeds" with the "very human" Catholic cycle of sin/confession/absolution/renewed sin. The more flexible Catholic ethical code contributes to shorter radiuses of identification, lower levels of trust, and higher levels of corruption in Catholic countries.

The flexible ethical code probably also contributes to high levels of crime exemplified by the disconcertingly common incidence of kidnappings in Latin America today.

To be sure, the Church's influence, at least in Europe and Latin America, is not what it once was. The proportion of practicing Catholics has declined precipitously—a similar trend has occurred in the mainline Protestant denominations—and many tens of millions of Latin

American Catholics have converted to Evangelical and Pentecostal Protestantism. But the Church retains substantial influence, and through reform of its economic doctrine and a more aggressive stance on issues of morality and ethics, it could make a critical contribution to modifications in traditional values that would enhance the chances for greater progress in Catholic countries. Reform could also arrest and possibly even reverse the drift away from Catholicism in Latin America.

Orthodox Christianity

In his CMRP paper on Orthodox Christianity, expert on Eastern Europe Nikolas Gvosdev perceives a church that in its mainstream doctrine is supportive neither of democratic institutions nor of market economics. The circumstances of Orthodoxy are roughly comparable to the circumstances of Catholicism before the latter opted for full support of democracy in the second half of the twentieth century.

In his paper on the Republic of Georgia, former Georgian government official Irakli Chkonia lists the characteristics of Orthodoxy, strongly evoking the progress-resistant column of the typology and often contrasted with Western Christianity, especially Protestantism. They are as follows: "submission to authority, discouragement of dissent and initiative, discouragement of innovation and social change, submissive collectivism rather than individualism, emphasis on ethnic cohesion rather than supranational relationships, isolationism and particularism, spiritual determinism and fatalism. Also embraced in the pattern is the aversion of Orthodoxy to the non-Orthodox Christian West and the Islamic World, political rivals of the past and the present."[29]

With respect to the possibilities of change, in Gvosdev's judgment:

> Much depends . . . on two separate but interrelated processes. The first is whether the guardians of the Orthodox tradition—not simply the clergy but also its intellectuals and activists—are prepared to actively "re-imagine" the Orthodox tradition in ways that are more conducive to supporting democracy and free market institutions. The second is whether the bulk of the populations of the Orthodox world—especially the "unchurched"—will accept this re-imagination as a legitimate expression of their traditional culture. Again, the answer is unclear. The experience of the city of Novgorod [described in the next chapter] demonstrates that it is possible to engineer a broad consensus in favor of

reform and modernization while crafting a link to traditional culture and national identity, yet the experience of the Greeks in the modern era also points to the possibility of simultaneously maintaining a traditional, progress-resistant culture alongside a modern, Western, progress-prone culture.

The Novgorod experience suggests that it is possible. A successful re-engineering of the culture at the local level has produced tangible results. The gross regional product has grown on average by four percent every year since 1995. . . . While foreign direct investment (FDI) amounts for only five percent of all investment in Russia, in the Novgorod region FDI produces half of all investment. Novgorod ranks as one of the more "democratic" regions of Russia, and is in the top quarter of all Russian regions for the number of civic associations and non-governmental organizations. Meanwhile, the Orthodox Church has experienced a genuine revival, but not at the expense of denying religious freedom to others; outside observers call the Russian north the "most ecumenical region in the whole of Russia."

It remains to be seen, however, whether the revival that has occurred in Novgorod and other northern regions will be transferred to the national church as a whole.[30]

In a comment on Gvosdev's essay, expert on Greece Georges Prevelakis notes an Orthodox influence in Greece that diverges from Gvosdev's generalization:

The Greek case does not confirm the hypothesis of an Orthodox Christian family in respect to economic behavior. There are as many differences with other Orthodox Christians as there are similarities, and the Greeks can be successfully compared to populations of other religions. In the Greek case, to the extent that religious culture plays a role in the economy, it is generally positive.

The Greek Orthodox Church has a strong charitable function, a heritage from its Ottoman past. In order to maintain this role, the Church in diaspora depends on donations from its wealthy members. It is not surprising that it encourages economic achievement. Its message is clear: *enrichissez-vous*, get rich.

Inside the Greek State, Orthodoxy has sometimes functioned as a brake on modernization, but not always. Scholarly authors who defend "orthodox" Orthodoxy criticize the Church that is associated with the Greek State as too much influenced by Protestant values. Orthodox culture inside Greece is thus far from monolithic. Orthodoxy has, however, played another fundamental role: it has been the major element of the (modern) Greek national identity, and in that sense it has made an essential contribution in nation-building.[31]

With a few modifications, I here restate, *mutatis mutandis*, my concluding comments from the section on Catholicism. To be sure, the Orthodox Church's influence is not what it once was. But the Church retains substantial influence, and through reform of its political and economic doctrines and a more aggressive stance on issues of morality and ethics, it could make a critical contribution to modifications in traditional values that would enhance the chances for greater progress in Orthodox countries. Reform could also arrest and possibly even reverse the drift away from Orthodoxy.

Confucianism

Introducing the typology in chapter 2, I made frequent comments about the crosscurrents of Confucian culture, with many attributes falling in the progress-prone column, for example, the importance of education and achievement, the lesser virtues, merit, frugality (derivative of Taoism). But Confucianism also nurtures an authoritarian view of politics derivative of the overriding Confucian virtue of filial piety.

In *The Religion of China*, Max Weber made a case that dynamic capitalism was an unlikely outcome there because of the absence of the asceticism central to Calvinist doctrine, and also because of the low prestige that attached to economic activity. His failure to predict the Confucian economic miracles has been cited by a number of writers, mostly economists, as evidence that culture *doesn't* matter. But Weber did take note of some Protestant-ethic-like characteristics of Chinese culture, and he could not foresee that all of the Confucian societies would promote the prestige of economic activity to the highest levels by the second half of the twentieth century.

The anthropologist Robert Weller offers valuable insights into the complexity of change in a dynamic society and into how culture acts and is acted upon:

Culture always affects how policies develop and work on the ground, but we cannot always easily read those effects off broad descriptions of tradition. The complex and changing currents that make up culture demand careful local knowledge, properly placed in context. While culture is both malleable and multiple, it is never simply an artifact of broader social forces. For all its messiness and change, culture has deeply influenced how Chinese societies have developed, and will continue to do so. For example, the uniquely Chinese cultural resources for things like trust or individualism grew out of traditions very different from the ones that fostered those ideas in the West. Even though the global spread of Western ideas has had a profound effect on all Chinese societies over the past century and longer, the existence of those indigenous traditions should lead us to expect that Chinese will develop their own solutions to the problems of modernity. We can see the beginnings of this in the success of the kind of networked capital . . . or in the sorts of alternate civilities that helped Taiwan consolidate its democracy.

Culture and values are not passed down automatically, like genes. They must be reproduced in each new generation, which opens up the possibility for reworking culture in times of change. To some extent, this has already happened with the work ethic. When I was asked to consult about the massive unemployment that would result when a European firm took over a Chinese steel factory, the employees seemed to have little interest in diving into the sea of market risk, and much more interest in protecting their privileges as socialist workers. The laborer-elite of the planned economy was never a majority of the population, but it did show evidence of real cultural change away from a work ethic value. At least by anecdotal evidence, the most successful entrepreneurs in the market economy that has opened up are either well-connected officials or people who had been in marginal positions; they are much less likely to be the old privileged class of workers in state-owned enterprises.[32]

Buddhism

Christal Whelan, an anthropologist at Boston University, stresses the extreme diversity of Buddhism, arguably the most diverse of all the world's religions:

> Any discussion of "Buddhism" and its effects on economic, social, or political development in Asia is risky for a number of reasons. First of

all, so-called Buddhist countries are often in reality multi-cultural and multi-religious, and separating these streams is a most difficult task. Secondly, "Buddhism" comes in varieties—Theravada, Mahayana, Vajrayana—and an effervescence of newly arisen religious movements that are certainly "Buddhesque" if not Buddhist. The doctrinal and practical emphases of these diverse orientations lead in a number of directions. Thirdly, after centuries of culture-specific elaboration, the original "Buddhism" may be so totally transformed that Buddhism begins to resemble its own iconography—a bodhisattva with a multitude of faces, a thousand arms. In short, Buddhism is no monolith; yet some common ground does exist to warrant a discussion.[33]

Of the seven countries addressed in Whelan's analysis (in order of population: Thailand, Myanmar/Burma, Sri Lanka, Cambodia, Laos, Mongolia, and Bhutan), Thailand and Mongolia have made the most progress toward the goals of the UN Universal Declaration of Human Rights. Both are considered "free" by Freedom House, and Thailand is number 74 on the UNDP's Human Development Index, where Norway is 1 and Sierra Leone 175. Thailand is the only one of the seven to have experienced sustained high levels of economic growth, but much of that growth can be attributed to Thailand's Chinese minority.

A degree of compatibility exists between Buddhism and economic development, but many Buddhists stress the "small is beautiful" approach of E. F. Schumacher. In Whelan's words: "Buddhism need not retard progress since it neither condemns nor advocates the acquisition of wealth, but only the attachment to wealth. This suggests a significant potential for philanthropic enterprise. Indeed, the expansion of a global network of 'engaged Buddhists' is perhaps the most significant development within Buddhism in recent years."[34]

With respect to democracy and social justice, Whelan notes that "the original Buddhist community or *sangha* in India of the Buddha's time certainly suggests a democratic ideal—everyone is equal in the search for Enlightenment. However . . . Buddhism has since generated a multiplicity of complex and hierarchical institutions, both monastic and lay, wherever it has become indigenized."[35]

Gender equality presents another issue that underscores Buddhist diversity. Sirimavo Bandaranaike, who was prime minister of Sri Lanka from 1960 to 1965, 1970 to 1977, and 1994 to 2000, was the world's first female prime minister. Yet a misogynist current in Japan has been fed by the "Bloodbowl Sutra" transmitted from China to Japan centuries ago. Whelan continues, "Originally directed at those who had committed sins involving blood (i.e., violent crimes), it relegated such people to the Blood Pool of Hell. However, in Japan the sutra underwent a peculiarly misogynist transformation and was used to legitimate the inferiority of women on the basis of biology. Viewing women as contaminated by the blood from childbirth and menses, this new interpretation placed women categorically in the Blood Pool of Hell. . . . Furthermore, one of the most important [Japanese] sutras . . . states that a woman must be reincarnated as a man in order to achieve Enlightenment."[36]

To repeat my conclusion from earlier in this chapter: it is difficult to generalize about Buddhism, but the data suggest that it is not a powerful force for modernization.

Islam

Papers on Islam were written for the CMRP by Bassam Tibi, a Syrian Arab who teaches at the University of Göttingen in Germany, and Robert Hefner, an anthropologist at Boston University. Tibi confronts an Islam that resists progress and calls for sweeping reform, along the lines of the UNDP *Arab Human Development Reports 2002* and *2003*. Hefner views Islam through the prism of Indonesia, where the religion's crosscurrents vie with one another.

Tibi argues that conflicting currents in Islam have resulted in prolonged debate but have not significantly altered its steady decline as a force for progress. He concludes:

> There are various explanations for the cultural rigidity of contemporary Islam, prominently among them a cultural unwillingness to learn from others that also may have a psychological dimension: learning from others can be seen as wounding one's ego, one's sense of self-worth.* The rejection of innovation is a second major factor, and in addition to the cultural/religious explanation, the same psychology may also be operative. The third explanation is political. "The Revolt against the West" is a term coined by Hedley Bull in an essay in which he argues

---

*One is reminded of Ortega y Gasset's very similar observation about Spain before its opening up to the West and subsequent transformation.

that Islamic fundamentalism is not only directed against Western hegemony but also against Western values.[37]

The coincidence of globalization and cultural fragmentation is the fourth and final impediment. The processes of globalization change worldwide economic and political structures but not culture, because this is always local and persistent. People of different cultures may use the same techno-scientific means (for example, computer and the Internet) without sharing the same values. Cultural fragmentation stands in the way of universalizing the values on which peace and progress depend.

The gap between Islam and the West and simultaneously the intimacy between them has never been as intense as it is now. The prevailing view among the Islamists is that *Pax Americana* should be replaced through jihad by *Pax Islamica*. This resistance to coming to terms with the Western (and one might now add East Asian) values of progress and development is related not only to the cultural obstacles analyzed here but also to the anti-Western worldview that prevails in the world of Islam. We cannot reduce this sentiment to a protest against globalization because the values of progress and development are identified as Western and are rejected for so being.[38]

Hefner, who stresses that all cultures have "their own internal pluralism, variety, or rival 'streams,'"[39] injects a hopeful note: the evolution of Islam in Indonesia suggests to him an increasing compatibility with democracy, violent episodes like the Bali bombings notwithstanding, a judgment borne out by the successful national elections in Indonesia in 2004. He concludes:

> The long-term outcome of the struggle between [the anti-pluralist conservatives and the moderates] in Muslim political culture will depend on broader developments in society. A civic outcome will require, among other things, a more pluralist balance of power between state and society. This achievement will require in turn that religious scholars accept and legitimate the new social pluralism. If civility and pluralism prevail, however, they will do so, not because of the triumph of secularist modernism, but because a new generation understands what their classical predecessors acknowledged in practice if not always in word: that a separation of powers and a desacralization of the state is in the deepest interest of Islam itself. Certainly the fate of the Muslim world

in the twenty-first century is still far from clear. But there are grounds
for guarded optimism, because that future will depend on not just age-
old religious commentaries but on thoroughly contemporary cultural
matters.[40]

I want to insert at this point a comment by my colleague at the
Fletcher School, Adil Najam, a Pakistani political scientist. "On paper,
there is nothing in Islam that is against democracy, and one could argue that there is much in it that is very pro-democracy . . . the problem
comes more with jurisprudence and legislation—the presumption . . .
at least in Pakistan . . . that the laws are already complete in Islam and
therefore the function of government is not to create laws but merely
to implement the laws that have been given."[41]

The data in Table 4.1 present a somber picture of contemporary Islam.
With a few exceptions, most notably Turkey, those Islamic countries without oil are poor and authoritarian; and as their significantly lower female than male literacy rates demonstrate, they discriminate against
women. Those *with* oil are richer but, with the exception of Indonesia,
authoritarian, and they too discriminate against women. Fertility rates
are very high, although dropping; trust is low; corruption is high.

The current condition of Islamic countries contrasts starkly with
Islam's vanguard position during the last centuries of the first millen-
nium and the first centuries of the second, as well as with the power
and glory of the Ottoman Empire at its height in the sixteenth and
seventeenth centuries. Not only is the West far ahead of the Islamic
countries; so are the East Asian countries. The self-respect of Muslims
is assaulted by daily reminders of the wealth and power of East Asia
and the West, by their openness and democratic institutions, and by
the poverty, debility, and backwardness of most Islamic societies.

Osama bin Laden says that his acts of violence against innocent people,
above all Americans, are motivated by U.S. policies in the Middle East,
particularly with respect to Israel. But I suspect that what most motivates him is the extreme humiliation and bitterness that he and other
Muslims, particularly Arabs, must feel as they reflect on the decline of
Islam and are constantly reminded of how far behind it has fallen.

The reader will recall from chapter 2 Bernard Lewis's words: "When
people realize that things are going wrong, there are two questions
they can ask. One is 'What did we do wrong?' and the other is ' Who

did this to us? The latter leads to conspiracy theories and paranoia. The first question leads to another line of thinking: 'How do we put it right?'"[42]

In sharp contrast to Osama bin Laden, the authors of the UNDP *Arab Human Development Reports 2002* and *2003* have asked, "How do we put it right?" And as you will recall from the introduction to this book, they place heavy emphasis on culture and cultural change. The reports stress, among other goals:

- openness to and constructive engagement with the rest of the world, by strong implication the West;
- tolerance and respect for different cultures;
- respect for the rights and needs of women, young people, and children;
- reverence for knowledge and education.

The *Arab Human Development Reports* brings us back to the views of Bassam Tibi and Robert Hefner. The authors of the reports share Tibi's belief that the reform of Islam is indispensable to the progress of Arabs and by implication Muslims around the world. Tibi makes clear in his paper that substantial support for such reforms can be found in the Quran. The overriding problem is the one on which Hefner focuses: convincing the large numbers of Muslims around the world who are asking "Who did this to us?" (and answering "The Americans, the Jews, the West") that the only truly helpful question is "What can we do to put it right?"

Hinduism

Pratap Bhanu Mehta argues that Hinduism is too flexible in doctrine and too diffuse in structure to facilitate reform, particularly with respect to caste but also with respect to fatalism. He goes on to observe that if the state is disposed to reform, as has generally been true of India, "there are few religious sources of resistance to it."[43]

Mehta perceives a disconnect between Hinduism and modernization. "Hinduism's emphasis on the importance of coming to know and develop one's fullest potentialities, of realizing one's Highest Self . . . would seem to be a promising resource for the democratic imagination. Yet the history of Hindus records few attempts to create a social structure that might be mildly propitious for such an endeavor. The real point in such matters is not what a tradition teaches, but how and what its adherents think. Humans are not merely passive products of culture or religious doctrine, but agents who constantly and actively imagine and re-imagine their beliefs and social worlds."[44]

Hinduism was thought, by Gunnar Myrdal among others, to be uncongenial with democracy chiefly because of the caste system. Mehta observes:

> The invidious caste distinction . . . was itself a reminder of the compli-
> cated transformations that Hinduism has had to undergo in order to be-
> come compatible with democracy. The caste system with all its
> interdictions, exclusions, and regulations is one of the most elaborately
> and egregiously hierarchical social conceptions that humans have ever
> entertained. . . . A society preoccupied with caste would hardly seem to
> be a promising ground for democracy, individual freedom, or equality. . . .
> [T]he striking thing is that this most hierarchically ordered of societies
> should have so readily embraced, in principle at first and then increas-
> ingly in practice, the principles and the procedures of liberal democracy.
>
> The speed of the change in these millennia-old customs is also stun-
> ning. Universal suffrage first arose as a topic of discussion in the early
> 1890s. By the mid-1920s, the major movements representing Hinduism
> had accepted the principle. Since India's independence from Britain and
> partition from Pakistan in 1947, the overall direction of political change
> has been toward greater power for the numerically vast but long-down-
> trodden lower castes. They now occupy the political center of gravity in
> the world's largest democracy.[45]

Hinduism has been regarded as essentially hostile to economic de-velopment, by Max Weber and Gunnar Myrdal among others, because of its intrinsic fatalism symbolized by the doctrine of *karma*, and the rigidities and inefficiencies implicit in the caste system. But as Mehta observes:

> What anthropologists were identifying as the immutability of caste
> was simply a projection of a state of affairs that obtained under colonial
> rule and its immediate aftermath, into the past. Evidence of this is the

fact that caste relations have undergone an extraordinary transformation with the advent of democracy. Caste in urban settings has a very
different function from caste in conditions of rural scarcity. Second, there
is very little evidence that Hindu "beliefs" produced something akin to
a fatalistic acceptance of the world. There was no dearth of striving or
ambition.[46]

In fact, Mehta argues, caste barriers have been repeatedly and increasingly breached as economic development has advanced in India, particularly during the past two decades.

Hinduism has clearly contributed to the gender inequality symbolized by World Bank data on illiteracy: in 2001, 31 percent of adult males
and 54 percent of adult females were illiterate.[47] Mehta cites the Hindi
poet Maithli Sharan Gupta: "They call us goddesses and treat us like
slaves." Mehta observes:

> There is little doubt that most of the texts that discuss the ritual side
> of Hinduism and the rights of women often display streaks of misogyny,
> while the epic texts of the tradition show a good deal more recognition
> of women's agency. But there is no doubt that women were subordi-
> nated to an extraordinary degree and all kinds of practices that secured
> this subordination—child marriage, secluded widowhood, preference
> for a male child—were enforced in the name of religion.
>
> What is equally striking is the fact that under the force of reform move-
> ments it was easy to dislodge the ideological legitimacy of the subordina-
> tion of women. So formally, the Indian State, under a series of legislative
> enactments and judicial decisions, has been extremely progressive and
> even the last vestiges of discrimination are being removed. But the reality
> of women's lives remains one of appalling subordination.
>
> The conclusion to be drawn is that patriarchy has proved to be far
> more enduring and stubborn and has survived even religious reform.[48]

Mehta's overall conclusion is guardedly upbeat:

> It is one of Hinduism's virtues that it has at least given many of its
> adherents a way of transcending the confines of their own tradition
> without making that tradition despicable.[49]

Alfred Stepan's Views on the
World's Religious Systems and Democracy

IN *ARGUING COMPARATIVE POLITICS*, Columbia University political scientist Alfred Stepan asserts that Samuel Huntington's view in *The Clash of Civilizations* of Confucian, Islamic, and Orthodox Christian civilizations is excessively generalized.[50] He goes on to argue that all of the world's religious systems are—or at least can be—"politically compatible with democracy," a point with which Huntington in fact agrees, at least as it applies to the major religions.[51] I agree entirely with one point that Stepan makes: liberal and conservative crosscurrents—what he refers to as "multivocality"—are found in all religions. But in making the case for democracy as an "empirical democratic theorist," particularly with respect to Islam, Stepan ignores one salient empirical fact: the only predominantly Islamic country in the world that Freedom House considers "free" is Mali.

Moreover, Stepan's views are steeped in the "religious relativism" I mentioned at the outset of this chapter: he draws no significant distinctions between Protestant and Catholic countries, notwithstanding the evidence of Protestantism's earlier and greater success in nurturing democracy and the wide gaps in trust and corruption between Protestant and Catholic countries. And while he doesn't say it directly, one can infer that he might not perceive any insuperable obstacles to democracy in Voodoo and other animist religions.

Stepan argues that it is a fallacy "to confuse the conditions associated with the *invention* of a phenomenon with the possibilities of *replication*, or probably more accurately *reformulation*."[52] While I agree that latecomers have models to follow that should make it easier to replicate or reformulate democracy—the case of Spain comes to mind—his "fallacy" makes the democratization process sound a lot easier than it has proven to be in reality, for example, in Russia and Latin America. This confirms once more the wisdom of Alexis de Tocqueville: resources are helpful, good laws are helpful, but what really matters is the "habits, the customs, the mores" of a people. For example, it is difficult to make democracy work in societies where trust is low.

Stepan faces the same problem that Michael Novak faced in his book *The Catholic Ethic and the Spirit of Capitalism*—the progressive crosscurrent exists, but it has failed thus far to influence the mainstream. In an article in *Foreign Affairs* in 2005, Bernard Lewis stresses that "equality among believers was a basic principle of Islam from its foundation in the seventh century."[53] But that basic principle is not apparent today in the politics of most Islamic countries, above all in the Middle East. Until several Islamic countries consolidate enduring democracy, Huntington's more pessimistic views, and my own, will prevail. Of course, the purpose of this chapter is to encourage religious leaders to reflect on the mainstream currents that have led them away from democracy, justice, and prosperity; and to explore, in their own crosscurrents and the experiences of more advanced societies, the reforms that will lead them *toward* those goals.

Conclusion

LIKE CULTURES, RELIGIONS CHANGE—witness Islam's transformation from progress prone to progress resistant. Within Christianity, we note several dynamic currents, among them the decline of the mainline Protestant religions and the concurrent rise of Evangelical and Pentecostal churches, and the rapid growth of the latter in Latin America, Africa, and elsewhere.

I want to stress again that religion is not the only influence on culture. Basque culture has been progress prone for centuries, yet it is very Catholic. Chile's success since independence, relative to the rest of Latin America, almost surely reflects in part its population of Basque descent, proportionally the largest by far in Latin America.

Religion *has* played a highly influential role in shaping the value and attitude systems that influence the behavior of individuals and societies. Religious reform that moves away from traditional, progress-resistant values toward the values we associate with modernization may be crucial to accelerated progress in the several lagging regions of the world.

5

Culture in Action I

TO DEVELOP A BETTER UNDERSTANDING of the complicated cause and effect interplay of cultural and other factors in the evolution of societies and the factors that bring about cultural change, we commissioned 27 case studies, most of them of countries but also of a region (Eastern Europe), a province (Quebec), a city (Novgorod, Russia), a Yoruba town in Nigeria, and an ethno-racial minority (African Americans). The essays summarized in this chapter appear in a companion book *Developing Cultures: Case Studies*, published by Routledge.

The case studies break down by regional or civilizational grouping, or are ungrouped (India), as follows:

Africa
Botswana
South Africa
Yoruba community in Nigeria
Confucian countries
China
Japan
Singapore
Taiwan
India

Latin America
Argentina
Brazil
Chile
Mexico
Venezuela
Orthodox/Eastern Europe
Eastern Europe
Georgia
Novgorod
Russia

Islam	The West
Egypt	African Americans
Indonesia	Ireland
Pakistan	Italy
Turkey	Quebec
	Spain
	Sweden

The countries in the first column are addressed in this chapter, the countries in the second column in chapter 6.

The guidelines to the case study writers were very broad. We were looking for the answers to four questions:

1. How have cultural values and attitudes influenced the evolution of the society?

2. What other factors have influenced the evolution of the society?

3. How have other factors influenced cultural values and attitudes?

4. Is there evidence of cultural change? If so, to what can it be attributed?

Many of the case studies are success stories—striking political, social, and/or economic transformations. Others show some degree of transformation but also continuities with a traditional lagging past. Still others have experienced little change. My hope was that patterns would emerge from the case studies that would aid in the development of guidelines for cultural change—the ultimate goal of the Culture Matters Research Project.

Africa

CAMEROUNIAN ECONOMIST DANIEL ETOUNGA-MANGUELLE's work on Africa, particularly his chapter "Does Africa Need a Cultural Adjustment Program?" in *Culture Matters*, sets forth the following cultural obstacles to progress in most African countries:

- Traditional authoritarian, hierarchical mindsets and institutions; little social mobility.
- Present-time orientation, and little enthusiasm for work.
- Lack of concern with making efficient use of time.
- Subordination of the individual to the community.
- Excessive conviviality and avoidance of confrontation.
- Little saving, much conspicuous consumption.
- Belief in magic and witchcraft.
- Very short radius of identification and trust.
- Subordination and abuse of women.

Africa is the region where the optimism of the development experts of the 1950s and 1960s has proven to be least justified. East Asia has experienced several "miraculous" transformations, political as well as economic, capped by the surge of the Chinese economy during the past quarter-century. India's recent rapid economic growth if sustained could transform that huge democracy in another couple of decades. And while its progress toward the goals of the UN Universal Declaration of Human Rights has been disappointing, Latin America is more democratic, literate, and prosperous than it was 50 years ago—if still characterized by extremes of social injustice.

In his book *The Fate of Africa*, Martin Meredith concludes, "What is so striking about the 50-year period since independence is the extent to which African states have suffered so many of the same misfortunes . . . [by the end of the 1980s,] not a single African head of state had allowed himself to be voted out of office."[1] *New York Times* reviewer Janet Maslin adds, "almost all of [Meredith's] book involves copiously documented evidence of rampant graft and mind-boggling corruption."[2]

The plight of Africa is apparent to the world from the region's vast loss of life to civil wars, HIV/AIDS, and malnutrition. In the ten indicators of progress addressed in chapter 4, African countries occupy most of the lowest positions. Democratic governance, including political rights and civil liberties, is rare, and democratic continuity is even rarer. There is, however, a striking exception to this dismal pattern: Botswana.

Botswana

Botswana performs significantly better than other African countries on most development indicators. Freedom House ranks it as "free," with the same score as South Korea and Taiwan. It has sustained high economic growth rates for decades. It is the second least corrupt, after Chile, of the developing countries and is higher on that list than Japan, Spain, Belgium, Greece, and Italy. It suffers from a high incidence of HIV/AIDS, like so many other African countries, but in most other respects, it can be considered the African "miracle." Why is Botswana so different? Here are the answers adduced by economist and expert on Botswana Stephen Lewis:

- A long-standing tradition of consultation by leaders with the led, symbolized by the *kgotla*, "the traditional gathering place in the village which served as a judicial chamber, administrative body, or advisor to the chief, as the occasion demanded."[3]
- A constructive influence of British Protestant missionaries, particularly in education and health. The chiefs were the first converts.
- A tradition of peaceful conflict resolution.
- "Respect for others, integrity, modesty, lack of personal pride, and honesty were important virtues."[4]
- An enlightened, constructive colonial administrator, Peter Fawcus, during the decade prior to Botswana's independence in 1966.
- The discovery in 1967 of diamonds, and Botswana's success in negotiating favorable terms with the DeBeers company.
- Well-designed and well-administered economic and social policies.
- A strong civil service.
- Most important, the extraordinarily effective democratic leadership of the country's first three presidents, Seretse Khama, Quett Masire, and Festus Mogae. All had attended schools founded by Britons in South Africa and/or universities in Britain. All three leaders had a vision of a modern, democratic, prosperous Botswana and pursued policies and programs to that end. Unlike many other African leaders, the national interest, not questions of power, prestige, and personal wealth, topped their agenda.

South Africa

South Africa has moved from an apartheid society dominated by a white minority to a democratic society in which the black majority governs. In the process, South Africa has become a leader of African nations. But the shift has not been accompanied by transforming rates of economic growth. South Africa stood at number 119 (of 177 countries) in the 2004 UN Human Development Index. Nicaragua, among Latin America's poorest countries, was number 118.

In her paper on South Africa, Ann Bernstein, a policy analyst at the Centre for Development and Enterprise in Johannesburg, mentions a tradition black South Africans call *ubuntu*, roughly translated as "humanness." A traditional formulation is: "People become people through each other, and the king is king through the people."[5] *Ubuntu* served as a watchword for the anti-apartheid movement and is widely referred to today as an ethical pillar of the new multiracial South Africa, where the concept of community is paramount. It is far from clear, however, that *ubuntu* is much more than a romantic slogan. Bernstein points out that in a 1999 survey, only 3 percent of respondents mentioned *ubuntu* as an asset for South Africa's development.

President Thabo Mbeki is the architect of a framework for cultural change called "the African Renaissance." Its goals are as follows:

- Attack the notion that Africa is different and inferior.
- Argue that Africa can change and reclaim African dignity.
- Demonstrate Africans taking responsibility, acknowledging mistakes, and acting to correct them.
- Banish the shame of Africa, for example, the Rwanda horror.
- Recapture the African soul.
- Make the link between Africa and human rights a reality.
- Show pride in Africa's heritage but also in its capacity to modernize.[6]

As Bernstein notes, "the African Renaissance . . . is both a political tool and a deeply held set of beliefs for President Mbeki and members of his circle. However, survey evidence suggests that it has much less impact on people in general."[7]

Animism and sorcery are still pervasive and have been incorporated into some African Initiated (Christian) Churches. But there are also parallels with the Evangelicalism/Pentecostalism movements in Latin America: women play a major role in both continents, and the Protestant work ethic and wealth accumulation is promoted.

Other features of African culture that serve as obstacles to progress are noted by Etounga-Manguelle: extreme pressures to redistribute wealth to less fortunate family members to the point of impeding capital accumulation; subordination of women to men, the many manifestations of which include some that are conducive to transmission of HIV/AIDS; and a lack of concern about time—"time is a continuum without discrete segments."[8]

A Yoruba Community in Nigeria

Elisha Renne, an anthropologist at the University of Michigan, writes on changing cultural practices associated with fertility and local development in the Yoruba town of Itapa-Ekiti in southwestern Nigeria. "As Ekiti Yoruba, people have their own distinctive cultural practices and history, which relate the social ideal of raising children to adulthood with the development of their community. Indeed, the word for development, ìdàgbàsókè—literally, 'the fact of growing up (sí òkè) to become an elder (di àgbà),' supports this connection."[9]

The principal force for cultural change has been education—more-educated women are having fewer children. Renne links the expansion of education to the introduction of Protestant Christianity in the early decades of the twentieth century. Another agent of change was the construction of a road connecting the town to the rest of the country, which facilitated the migration of men seeking employment. (I am reminded of the modernizing impact of a new road in the case of Chiaromonte in Italy, the "Montegrano" of Edward Banfield's *Moral Basis of a Backward Society.*[10])

Once again we encounter an enlightened leader—Chief Samuel Ayoola Dada, who was educated in Methodist schools and went on to earn degrees from the University of Ibadan and the University of London. He taught, wrote math textbooks, worked in the state ministry of education, and became a leader in the national African Church, all the time retaining his ties to his hometown, where he became the first president of the Itapa Progressive Union. The Union was responsible for the construction of a secondary school and post office and the opening of a maternity clinic.

Renne traces the ups and downs of government support of development in Itapa-Ekiti and concludes: "While collaborative local development projects have contributed to improvement in the quality of their lives and a modest decline in fertility rates . . . the vital importance of maintaining social ties within the community—in the face of considerable political and economic uncertainty—has supported the continuing practice of child-fostering [adoption of children by family members or others] and relatively high fertility. Thus, while younger, educated townspeople are reassessing thinking about kinship relations—about who is the best parent, who should be considered 'close kin,' and child-fostering—the political and economic context are part of this picture as well."[11]

Renne's essay presents a society in which modernization and traditionalism vie with one another in a prolonged, indecisive competition. That cultural forces that resist modernization are in play in Nigeria is underscored by a front-page article in the August 11, 2005, *New York Times*, headlined "Entrenched Epidemic: Wife-Beatings in Africa." The article, by Sharon LaFraniere, was datelined "Lagos, Nigeria" and includes the following quote from the Nigerian Minister for Women's Affairs: "It is like it is a normal thing for women to be treated by their husbands as punching bags. The Nigerian man thinks that a woman is his inferior. Right from childhood, right from infancy, the boy is preferred to the girl. Even when they marry out of love, they still think the woman is below them, and they do whatever they want."

Confucian Countries

THE BACKDROP FOR OUR STUDIES of the Confucian countries is their "miraculous" economic performance during the second half of the twentieth century. The Japanese economic "miracle" after World War II was a reprise of its swift modernization following the overthrow of the Tokugawa Dynasty in 1868. South Korea, Taiwan, Hong Kong, and Singapore all experienced sustained high economic growth rates that vaulted them into the elite group of affluent nations. Today, after a quarter-century of sustained high growth, China's economy has become one of the most powerful in the world and there is even speculation that China may displace the United States as the world's dominant economy during the twenty-first century. What has been demonstrated beyond doubt is the explosive economic growth mixture of the Confucian value system and capitalist/market economics, and likewise the grave costs—in North Korea, Vietnam, and China itself until Deng Xiaoping—of the Marxist-Leninist model. We now have the answer to the old riddle: "Why do the Chinese do so well outside China and so poorly inside China?" In fact, with an economic policy environment at home that allows enterprise to be rewarded, the Chinese are doing very well indeed.

What remains to be seen is whether that economic dynamism, derivative of a pluralistic economic system, will drive China and Singapore to the same democratic political destination that Japan, South Korea, and Taiwan have reached. I believe that it will, because, as in the other East Asian success stories, the economic pluralism and middle class generated by high economic growth rates will inevitably produce irresistible pressures for political pluralism.

China

The paper on China by Harvard sinologist Tu Weiming focuses on the influence of intellectuals in recent Chinese history—a wholly appropriate emphasis, since intellectuals sit atop the Confucian social structure. He describes the crucial 1976 turning point—"the revival of Confucian humanism"—in these words:

> Deng's realistic pragmatism, sharply contrasting with Mao's revolutionary romanticism, recognized the necessity of the market economy for China's modernization. The marketplace of ideas, indirectly brought about by economic liberalization, was an unintended consequence of the "reform and opening" policy, but it was welcomed by the intellectual community like the spring after a long and bitter winter. The proposal "let a hundred flowers bloom," which in the 1950s turned out to be a ploy tricking the docile intellectuals into voicing strong criticisms against the authority of the party with devastating effects on their careers and lives, was put into practice by default, if not by design . . .[12]

In short, it was a thorough dismissal of Maoist radicalism in favor of a moderate, gradual, stable, and sustained program of development. Historically, what Deng Xiaoping advocated was a definitive departure from the dominant ideology of the PRC and a significant return to traditional cultural, specifically Confucian, norms.[13]

Suffice it to note that it took at least two generations of Confucian thinkers to thoroughly reformulate the tradition in response to the challenge of the modern West. They did not defend the tradition by stubbornly resisting corrosive foreign influences. Nor did they passively submit themselves to "cultural imperialism" derived from Western hegemonic power. Although they were critical of the aggressive anthropocentrism, callous rationalism, and possessive individualism of the modern Western mentality, they wholeheartedly embraced Enlightenment values, such as liberty, justice, rationality, due process of law, human rights, and the dignity of the individual.[14]

It is still open to debate whether China has already developed a viable civil society, but the trend toward pluralism is undeniable. In an increasingly pluralistic ethos, a marketplace of ideas flourishes. Competition for attention, power, influence, and financial rewards is keen and often vicious. . . . Corruption is rampant. Motivated by self-interest and private profits, the marketization of society seems imminent. Even in the academic community, civility and decency are relegated to the background.[15]

What Tu describes is the revival of the Confucian traditions, emphasis on education, achievement, and merit prominently among them, that contributed so much to China's earlier progress—at least comparable to that of Europe until the nineteenth century. Mao attempted, unsuccessfully, to suppress these traditions. The Chinese renaissance is a blend of Confucian and Western values that may lead to what was once considered an oxymoron: Confucian democracy.

Japan

Yoshihara Kunio is a Japanese economist, currently at the University of Kitakyushu, who has for several years explored the role of culture in economic development. Here is his fundamental conclusion with respect to Japan: "One reason why Japan developed is that it had a culture suitable for it. The Japanese attached importance to (1) materialistic pursuits; (2) hard work; (3) saving for the future; and (4) investment in education. These may have been influenced by income, prices, and other economic factors, but they were also influenced by the type of culture."[16] He goes on to mention "community values" as another cultural factor that has influenced how Japan has developed.

After reviewing the interplay of cultural and institutional factors in the Japanese post–World War II "miracle," Yoshihara reaches the following conclusions:

1. If Japan had a different culture (say, one more like the more passive, Buddhist-influenced Thai culture), it would not be a developed country today.
2. Institutions can be created and can change independently of culture, but we have to keep in mind that some of the institutions that are important for economic development reflect culture. Japanese politicians and bureaucrats have often pursued their own interests. But the question is to what extent they did. Yoshihara's judgment is that they did not do so as egregiously as their counterparts in the developing countries today. The reason is that Japan was more of an integrated national community than many other countries, and many politicians and high bureaucrats held altruism as an important element in their "utility functions."
3. Culture changes as income rises, and when people begin to enjoy a high standard of living, it ceases to be as much growth-promoting as when they were poorer. This is consistent with World Values Survey data that show increasing preference for leisure, the arts, and entertainment in "post-industrial" societies.
4. Community values, contrasted with "individualism," growth-promoting at an early stage, become a drag on the economy at a later stage, or at best, cease to be growth-promoting, because they may dilute entrepreneurship and saving. In order to revive its economy, Japan has to change the institutions in such a way as to make the system of reward and punishment more effective. But this is difficult because community values have been emphasized in Japanese society for a long time.

   One should not downgrade community values just because Japan is not doing well today. No country can discard community values and go all the way for individualistic values. All of them try to find a right balance between the two. The Japanese experience shows that what a right balance is depends on the stage of economic development.[17]

Singapore

The title of former Singaporean Prime Minister Lee Kuan Yew's 2000 book is, aptly, *From Third World to First*. Lee is the architect of the economic and social miracle that has propelled Singapore's transformation starting in 1965, when Singapore separated from Malaysia to become an independent country. Singapore has not yet experienced the transition to democracy that has accompanied sustained high growth in South Korea and Taiwan—Freedom House considers it "partly free." But it is number 25 on the UN's 2004 Human Development Index, ahead of Portugal and South Korea, and number 5 on Transparency International's 2004 Corruption Perceptions Index, ahead of Sweden, Switzerland, Norway, and Australia.

Chua Beng-Huat, a sociologist at the National University of Singapore, is the author of the CMRP paper on Singapore. In explaining the Singaporean miracle, Chua adduces three factors: (1) Singapore got a head start in attracting foreign investment, the key to its economic success, at a time when some of its regional competitors—China, the Indochinese countries, and India—were hostile to foreign investment, and Indonesia, awash in oil revenues, did not seek it; (2) "the integrity and sense of public responsibility of [Lee Kuan Yew's] leadership"[18] (I note Yoshihara's similar comment about Japanese leadership) and pragmatic, intelligent government policies; and (3) the Confucian values placed on education, merit, work, frugality, and the family. (Chua notes that the intensity of pressure parents place on children for educational achievement is comparable to that of Japan and Taiwan.) Of particular interest for cultural analysis is the role of government policies:

- Through both merit-based selection and salaries that are competitive with the private sector, the Singaporean civil service is highly competent and honest, as the 2004 Corruption Perceptions Index indicates.
- The government's housing policy has led to 90 percent home ownership. As Chua notes:

    Housing ownership is of particular interest because of the ways in which it blends public policy and private interest in a developing economy. At the household level, home-ownership is a focus of investment. Moreover, the desire of ownership and the need to

meet monthly mortgage payments serve to discipline wage earners to stay in employment in order to meet their financial obliga-
tions. This was and continues to be an essential process in the
transformation of the population from the informal economy and
unemployment into a disciplined industrial workforce. At the
macroeconomic level, construction and ownership of housing constitute a significant portion of national capital formation and wealth
accumulation.[19]

- English was chosen as the primary language of instruction in the
  schools as a common denominator for the Mandarin-speaking
  majority Chinese population and minority Malay and Tamil
  (South Asian) speakers. Singapore is now an English-speaking
  nation with all the advantages that attend proficiency in the
  principal global language. One is reminded of the advantage
  that English proficiency has conferred on countries as varied
  as India, Ireland, and the Nordic countries.

Chua concludes: "The Singapore case demonstrates that values matter. However, for values to play a significant role, the historical circumstances when the country embarks on the development process have
to be conducive, and the government has to provide exhortations and
institutional support to assure continuity, expression, and practical
effectiveness."[20]

Taiwan

Boston University anthropologist Robert Weller contributed the CMRP
paper on Confucianism as well as one on Taiwan. In the latter, he traces
the *two* Taiwanese miracles: sustained very high level of economic
growth ("Almost no experts in the 1950s expected much beyond poverty from Taiwan's economy . . ."[21]) and then the equally unexpected
political miracle of the transition to democracy. From 1949, when Chiang
Kai-Shek and the Chinese Nationalists fled to Taiwan after being de-
feated by Mao Zedong's Communists, to his death in 1975, Chiang
ruled Taiwan in a highly authoritarian manner. His son Chiang Ching-
Kuo, who succeeded his father and ruled until his death in 1988, earned
a reputation of comparable iron-fistedness. But Chiang Ching-Kuo
paved the way for the transition to democracy, encouraging a degree
of pluralism that his father would never have countenanced.

Weller says, "One reason the social sciences have had such a poor record anticipating these developments in Taiwan is an inadequate understanding of the role of culture. We have tended to err either by ignoring culture altogether, or by setting certain aspects of culture in stone to the extent that we have blinded ourselves to the potential for change. As one might expect from a place with most of its roots in China's long history and complex society, Taiwanese culture contains many strands."[22] The cultural factors Weller believes are most relevant are "individualism, a work ethic [including a propensity to save], a high valuation of education, civility, and trust with its associated social capital."[23] He disputes Francis Fukuyama's conclusions in *Trust* about the low level of social capital in Taiwan.

> While Taiwan may not provide a model, it does offer some important lessons. It shows, for instance, how "traditional" cultural features like local religion or personalistic ties can maintain reservoirs of social capital even under very authoritarian regimes. These are hardly the only cause of Taiwan's economic and political changes, but they played an important role in the successful implementation of both. Taiwan's experience also forces us to remember that cultures adjust in response to external conditions, in this case the highly international orientation of Taiwan's economy and the powerful influence of Taiwan's protector, the United States. We should not assume—as the early modernization theorists did—that cultures tied to earlier social and political systems cannot adjust very well to the new global economy. Taiwan's particular cultural path does not look entirely the same as anything in the West, but it too looks like a successful solution to modernity's challenges.[24]

India

THE BACKGROUND OF GURCHARAN DAS'S PAPER on India is the accelerated and sustained economic growth it has experienced since moving away from the socialist/dependency mindset that dominated the thinking of India's leaders from independence in 1947, to policies more friendly to the market and foreign investment. Das is a businessman who has written extensively about the changing Indian economy.

It will come as a surprise to many that, at least according to one study, India accounted for more than 20 percent of the world's GDP in the early eighteenth century, derived principally from textile and agricultural production.[25] But Das believes that even then, "India was significantly behind Western Europe in technology, institutions and ideas."[26] He argues that India's subsequent poverty is not the fault of the British colonizers. In fact, he counters, India would have benefited substantially if the British had invested as much in India in the nineteenth century as they did in the United States, Canada, and Argentina. "Although Britain could not lift Indians out of poverty, nor avert famines, it did give India the institutions of democracy—the rule of law, an independent judiciary, and a free press. It built railways, canals, and harbors. It gave India almost a hundred years of peace—the *Pax Britannica*. Although it gave modern values and institutions, it did not interfere with its ancient traditions and religion."[27] But the colonial experience had a major cost, in Das's view: the loss of Indian self-confidence.

Indian democracy continued and flourished following independence, but economic policies for the following four decades were based on import substitution, state intervention, and a general distrust of capitalism. Political pressures for redistribution were intense from the outset. But there wasn't much to distribute, given prolonged slow economic growth. In 1991 sweeping economic reforms were introduced that opened up the economy to both domestic entrepreneurship and foreign investment. Since then, GDP growth has averaged almost six percent annually. One consequence has been to raise the prestige of economic activity: in the caste system, it was close to the bottom, reminiscent of the Confucian social structure. This change has in turn broken down some of the rigidities of the caste system, as a more dynamic economy offers new opportunities. Das compares the Indian social revolution of today to the transformation of Japan under the Meiji leadership.

Simultaneously, English, the language of those who colonized India, lost its stigma. The surge of interest in English, which has become a major economic asset symbolized by the "outsourcing" to India now popular with so many American industries, symbolizes a "more relaxed and confident" India where "minds have become decolonized."[28]

Das looks first at economic factors to explain the ups and downs of India's development trajectory; if they are inadequate, he then turns to institutional and cultural factors. He notes, for example, that as mentioned above, "Indians have traditionally not accorded a high place to making money" and that the merchant has traditionally been viewed with disdain.[29] But he is skeptical of the emphasis that others, including Gunnar Myrdal and Deepak Lal, have placed on the adverse consequences of the social rigidities of the caste system, which he thinks is in the process of breaking down. He concludes:

> I find Deepak Lal's distinction between *material* and *cosmological* beliefs useful.[30] The material beliefs of a civilization are about ways of making a living and are the subject of economics; cosmological ones are about how to live and are in the realm of "culture." The rise of the West was accompanied by a change in both sets of beliefs, but East Asia's success has needed mainly a change in material beliefs—it has become prosperous without losing its soul. In other words, it is possible to modernize without Westernizing. Ever since the British Raj, material beliefs have been changing in India, unlike our cosmological beliefs. . . . The debate between modernization and Westernization . . . continues to rage in India. At the root is a fear of the loss of the Indian way of life. The older generation fears it more than the young, whose minds are more decolonized and who are more confident in adopting the West's material beliefs without fearing the loss in its cosmological ones.[31]

Islamic Countries

THERE IS A GOOD DEAL OF DIVERSITY IN ISLAM, both in religious doctrines and in the performance of Islamic countries. Turkey and Yemen are as different as Spain and Nicaragua. Yet as a group, the performance of the Islamic countries with respect to democracy, social justice, and prosperity lags far behind not only the West but also East Asia. The case studies of Egypt, Indonesia, Pakistan/Bangladesh, and Turkey offer insights into both the diversity and commonalities of Islam.

Egypt

Bassam Tibi contributed one of the two papers on Islam discussed in chapter 4. He also wrote a paper on Egypt, a country he calls "a textbook case for the encounter of Islamic civilization with the West."[32]

The starting point is Napoleon's conquest of Egypt in 1798, which Tibi equates with the U.S. invasion of Iraq in 2003. Despite the offer of freedom and a better life, the French met hostility. Why? "The answer is that the values of a progressive culture . . . cannot successfully be introduced from outside."[33]

The French were driven out of Egypt in 1801 by the Ottoman army officer Muhammad Ali, who initiated an ambitious program of modernization that failed, in Tibi's view, because European technological advances were superimposed on a traditional Islamic culture that rejected the values that nurture progress. Reforms were subsequently introduced by two Egyptians who had studied in Paris, Rifa'a al-Tahtawi and Mohammed Abduh. The latter became the head of al-Azhar University in Cairo, the most prestigious source of Islamic doctrinal interpretation in the world.

But the reform movement, and the liberal movement that followed it, failed. The movements, Nadav Safran writes, were unequal to "the need to develop a subjective, humanely oriented system of ideas, values and norms that would serve as a foundation for a political community under new conditions of life, to replace the traditional system based on objective divine revelation. In such an endeavor the leaders had eventually to come to grips with the problem of the possibility of conflict between reason and . . . divine revelation."[34]

What has resulted from this conflict has been control of Egypt since 1952 by military officers—Gamal Abdel Nasser, Anwar Sadat, and Hosni Mubarak—and the emergence of Islamist/Political Islam groups, foremost among them the Muslim Brotherhood, intellectual heirs to the Jihadist Sayyid Qutb.

Egypt today is something of a time bomb: its population of 70 million is growing rapidly and is expected to increase to 90 million by 2015; more than 40 percent of the population lives on two dollars or less per day; employment opportunities for educated young people are limited; more than 50 percent of women are illiterate; and the country is controlled by an authoritarian government.

Tibi concludes on a pessimistic note: "How one wishes to see a variety of Indonesian 'civil Islam' strike roots in Egypt, the hub of the Middle East. But . . . such a civil Islam is not in sight in Egypt. It continues to be the other way around. Muslims from all over the world come to Cairo to learn 'true Islam' at al-Azhar. But contemporary Egyptian Islam is neither liberal nor civil. One should not be deceived by the moderate institutional Islam of the Muslim Brothers nor by what is called the 'New Islamists.' Their jihadist offspring are a warning."[35]

Indonesia

Robert Hefner, who contributed the other paper on Islam reviewed in chapter 4, also wrote a paper on Indonesia, a country he has followed closely for several years. The following paragraphs form his conclusions, the guardedly optimistic tone of which is borne out by the successful 2004 elections:

> In 1967, Indonesia was one of the poorest and most tightly controlled countries in Asia. It was still just beginning its recovery from the devastation of the Great Depression, Japanese occupation, independence war, and chaos of the late Sukarno era. The legacy of these earlier periods was an ethnically fragmented and politically ineffectual private sector, a bloated and inefficient state sector, and a government that, despite some liberal ideals, was inclined to anything but real liberalization. In this context, the fact that the zigzags of state policy nonetheless managed to bring about a measure of economic development stands as a hopeful reminder that further progress may yet be possible.
>
> The Indonesian example also reminds, however, that there is nothing inevitable about economic growth bringing about political liberalization. Like Nigeria, Lebanon, South Africa, and many other countries, Indonesia is a deeply divided plural society. The impact of this pluralism on economic development can be seen in the fact that there has never been anything like a unified business community endowed with a shared economic culture. The business community remains divided by race, ethnicity, and religion, with the line between Chinese and Muslims the most severe. This [conflictive] pluralism has in turn fostered an often unhealthy variety of political opinions and actions. Although for a while it looked as if the Suharto regime had laid the foundation for a stable consensus over the country's future, the regime ultimately undermined its own efforts. Nowhere was this more apparent than in the final years of the Suharto regime, when, facing a growing pro-democracy movement, the regime played the Islamist and anti-Chinese card. The country has yet to recover from that reckless political adventure.

Indonesia remains a country of great social potential. Despite the fact that armed Islamists have recently captured international attention, the country has a large and courageous moderate Muslim leadership. The country is also blessed with an abundance of natural resources, and a population which, although not highly educated, is sufficiently skilled to respond to globalization. For these cultural resources to serve as social capital for progress, however, more will be required than their simple presence in society. If they are at last to realize their promise, the resources must be more effectively managed by leaders in state and society committed to a vision of a civic, pluralist, and democratic Indonesia.

An earlier generation of colonial and Indonesian leaders missed a critical chance when, rather than forging programs that would bring Chinese and Muslim business people together, they marginalized the Muslims and locked the Chinese in a cronyist and patrimonial cell. More recently, the Suharto regime made raids on the country's great reserves of Islamic moderation and tolerance, scaling up the social capital of extremist Muslims rather than Muslim democrats. Perhaps the greatest challenge facing Indonesia, then, lies in the realm of political culture. The challenge can only be met through an alliance of actors in state and society committed once and for all to working with rather than against the cultural endowments for civility and progress available in this great, but troubled, country.[36]

Both Egypt and Indonesia are predominantly Muslim. But at this point in history, they look very different from one another. Egypt is a time bomb, with daunting political, economic, and social problems. The solution of the Bush administration—to press for a democratic opening—may not be feasible so long as Hosni Mubarak is in power. U.S. governments, both Republican and Democrat, have after all been pressing for an opening of the Egyptian political system since the Carter administration, and without much success. But even if a political opening were to occur, the outcome could be anything but progressive democratic stability: Islamic radicalism or anarchy are two other possibilities, quite possibly followed by a return to authoritarianism.

Indonesia's future is more hopeful, particularly in the wake of the successful 2004 elections. The divergent prospects of these two Islamic countries—and the contrasting influences of Islam—are underscored by their stark differences in literacy, particularly female literacy: according to UN data, 88 percent of Indonesians were literate in 2002, compared with 56 percent of Egyptians. In that same year, 84 percent of Indonesian women were literate, compared with 44 percent of Egyptian women.[37]

Pakistan and Bangladesh

The CMRP paper on Pakistan and Bangladesh was prepared by F. S. Aijazuddin, Pakistani journalist and author, who examines the "bizarre political aberration [that] brought into being [in 1947] one country with two disparate wings, located a thousand miles apart with a hostile country, India, in between."[38] In 1971, the two wings separated. A common religion, Islam, had proven insufficient to overcome differences of culture, language, and history.

Since 1971, Pakistan and Bangladesh, with populations of about 150 and 145 million respectively, have followed similar development trajectories. Bangladesh stood at 139, Pakistan at 143 on the 2003 UNDP Human Development Index. Female adult literacy was 31 percent in Bangladesh in 2001, 29 percent in Pakistan. But there are also some significant differences. Freedom House rates Bangladesh as "partly free," Pakistan as "not free" in its 2004 report. And the totality fertility rate per woman in the period 2000–05 was 3.5 in Bangladesh, 5.1 in Pakistan.[39]

But, in Aijazuddin's words: "Perhaps the most telling statistic is the level of self-employment among women in the non-agricultural sector. Regionally, Pakistan is the lowest at 34%; India is higher at 41%; Bangladesh is highest at 83%. Much of this can be attributed to the small-borrower initiatives, the most prominent of which has been Grameen Bank, 94% of whose borrowers are women. Grameen Bank has a presence in almost 39,000 villages and targets the small borrower. Its average loans are $160 per borrower, with a 95% success rate in repayment."[40,41]

My colleague at the Fletcher School, Adil Najam, has appended some comments to this paper concerning the role of religion and the diverse histories of the two countries that elicited these further reflections by Aijazuddin:

> Obviously religion cannot be the only determinant of cultural development in any society. But to the extent that Pakistan was created in

1947 on the grounds of a religious distinction between the communities living in the Indian subcontinent, given that almost 98% of the population of the present residual Pakistan is Muslim by faith, and recognizing that a ritualistic observance of Islamic injunctions (in law, education, commerce, and in social customs) permeates almost every aspect of the ordinary Pakistani's life, it is justifiable to regard Islam as the key propellant or retardant to cultural change within Pakistan.

The differences between the East and the West wings of Pakistan were far too deep to be papered over by the simplicity of a common national name or the intangible unity of a common religion. These disparities were exacerbated by centuries of domination, by marauding foreigners such as the Tughlaqs, the Mughals, the Europeans, and then latterly by the British, and, within India throughout its history, by classes of local Indians over each other.

Perhaps the supple subservience of West Pakistanis, bending under the yoke of any form of dictatorial rule (particularly marked during the periods of military governance post-1947), may have something to do with a propensity to take orders rather than to formulate them. Similarly, its inability to have developed structures of community self-help may have much to do with the fact that at the local level . . . these were designed for community self-regulation rather than for self-help in the economic sense.

The critical issue remains one of population growth—its claims on resources, on education, on social infrastructure and on the national economy. What is clear is that the measure of success of the two former wings of an undivided Pakistan will be less a comparison between modern Pakistan and Bangladesh than a comparison with their own previous selves, of the centuries of their separate growth rather than the years they spent together temporarily as one nation.[42]

In the cases of Pakistan and Bangladesh, a common religion, Islam, and a similar colonial experience were not enough to bind together two societies separated not only by 1,000 miles but also by centuries of distinctive histories and identities. Yet in terms of their levels of development, they are quite similar. Islam was unable to fuse the two societies, but it may be an important part of the explanation of why the pace of progress in both has been so slow, in sharp contrast with democratic India's recent economic success.

Turkey

Yilmaz Esmer, a political scientist at Bogazici University in Istanbul, wrote the CMRP paper on Turkey. He focuses on the secular-religious division in Turkey, arguing that the Turkish model is probably not replicable in the rest of the Islamic world.

In addition to the major fault lines between groups of societies that Huntington refers to as civilizations, there are what we might call "minor fault lines" running within the same society that broadly correspond to the generally accepted global classifications of civilizations. . . . Turkey is one such society, where two civilizations (Western and Islamic) have existed together for a long time and continue to do so. This has not been a painless cohabitation, however; far from it. The situation has been uneasy at best and has resulted in open conflict on numerous occasions. The struggle for domination between the Western and the Islamic sets of values has been a major defining characteristic of the Turkish and earlier Ottoman society for at least two centuries. To be sure, these two cultures do have an intersection within Turkish society. However, the existence of some common ground does not necessarily mean that a happy harmonization of the two cultures has taken place.

Turkish women gained the right to vote and gain office in local elections in 1930, and in 1934 women's suffrage was extended to include all elected offices. French women had to wait for ten, Belgian women for fourteen, Greek women for eighteen, and Canadian women for twenty-six more years to gain unrestricted access to electoral politics. The process of Westernization in this Islamic society was, in a way, proceeding faster than the in the West itself.

A frequently asked question is whether Turkey can serve as an example for other Islamic societies in the transformation to a democratic and secular form of government. . . . The question is especially pertinent in view of the commonly voiced argument that Islam is not compatible with democracy.

It is possible—at least not totally impossible—that a number of Islamic societies will in time give in to the forces of democratization. . . . However, the Turkish experience does not seem to be very relevant to these societies and is unlikely to be relived.

First of all, the Turkish revolution is the product of a radical modernizing elite that came to power under exceptional circumstances. Led by a charismatic war hero determined to steer the country's course towards the West, these elites imposed their reforms on the society—one fails to observe a realistic prospect for such leadership coming to power in [other] Islamic countries.

Second, the Turkish revolution was entirely uncompromising on two issues about which Islamic publics and even elites are very sensitive: secularization and gender equality. The Turkish version of secularization certainly does not enjoy much support among Islamic publics or elites. . . . If there is one value dimension that sets Islamic populations apart from others, it is the attitudes towards sex and women.

Finally, the Turkish army has played a pivotal role as the vanguard of the Republican reforms and in particular of secularism.

If Arab societies, for example, succeed in establishing relatively democratic and mildly secular regimes, this will not come about by repeating the Turkish experience. The route they will take will have to be a very different one.[43]

Yet Turkey's success relative to the rest of the Islamic world cannot be ignored by Islamic reformers who seek to modernize their societies, especially as the moderate Islamic government of Recep Tayyip Erdogan leads Turkey towards the European Union. The Turkish model may in the long run prove to be more compelling than Esmer judges.

6

Culture in Action II

Latin America

Argentina

Mariano Grondona, principal architect of the CMRP typology, is the author of the paper on Argentina. He discusses six political values related to democratic development: (1) tolerance; (2) the republican spirit; (3) law versus power; (4) the state above the government; (5) overcoming "cultural restriction"; and (6) the primacy of "vespertine" ("evening") culture over "matutinal" ("morning") culture.

1. **Tolerance.** Grondona sees tolerance as the offspring of intolerance, in the sense that the consequences of intolerance, like murder or war, can be so grave that having experienced them, people are likely to shy away from a repetition. Post–Civil War Spain is a case in point (see section on Spain in this chapter). Tolerance is, in Grondona's view, the precursor of pluralism.
2. **The republican spirit**, which assures minorities the protection of their basic rights, is an extension of tolerance. Argentina has experienced authoritarian, authoritarian democratic, and democratic governments during its almost two centuries as an independent country.

3. **Law versus power.** A continuing tension has existed in Argentine history between law and the power of leaders. A recent example of disrespect for the law was President Carlos Saúl Menem's decision in 1994 to seek an extra term, which he managed by engineering an amendment to the constitution.

4. **State above government.** Grondona emphasizes the crucial role played by the state—the career bureaucracies—in the advanced democracies (see discussion of Sweden later in this chapter). These bureaucracies symbolize the fundamental consensus that binds the polity together. In authoritarian democracies, the government often usurps the state through, for example, nepotistic appointments.

5. **Cultural restriction.** Grondona perceives Argentina as a society whose politics, lacking a pragmatic foundation, seeks ideal, utopian solutions to problems—solutions that, in the long run, aggravate rather than ameliorate the problems. Recognition of repeated failure, for example of economic policies that ignore market forces, is the only way that such "cultural restriction" can be overcome democratically.

6. **Vespertine versus matutinal cultures.** "Vespertine" (evening) cultures are, in Grondona's lexicon, focused on the long term. They are patient. "Matutinal" (morning) cultures are focused on the short term. They are impatient. A big question for Argentina is whether its culture can be transformed from matutinal to vespertine, from a culture that expects significant change to take place in a few years to one that measures change in decades. This change in orientation characterizes Spain's transformation—over thirty years.

Brazil

The Brazilian sociologist Maria Lucia Victor Barbosa traces the roots of contemporary Brazilian culture back to four sources:

1. The patriarchal, authoritarian, patron/client administration of the Portuguese colony in the early years.
2. Catholicism, with intimate links to political power and two contradictory orientations: (a) the intolerance of the Inquisition and

the Counter-Reformation, and (b) a highly flexible ethical code that tolerated greed, corruption, and the pursuit of the pleasures of the flesh, even on the part of priests. The Church in Brazil also has a history of enmity to capitalism.

3. Slavery, above all in its reinforcement of authoritarianism and dependency, its depreciation of work (for both slave and master), and its tendency to force attention to the present and past rather than the future. Note, by the way, that slavery continued in Brazil until 1888.

4. The recreation of the centralized, authoritarian, corrupt structure of Portuguese governance and society after Brazil's independence in 1822.

The resulting culture is characterized by extremely low levels of trust—among the lowest in the World Values Survey—as well as extremely inequitable income distribution; authoritarianism/dependency; belief that a combination of luck and cunning is necessary for success; an underdeveloped sense of social responsibility; corruption and nepotism; disrespect for the law; a propensity for violence (reflected in Brazil's extremely high crime rates); and a tendency to blame others for one's own misfortunes.

Barbosa sees hope in an Evangelical/Pentecostal movement in Brazil that wields considerable political power, with 20 percent of the population participating. Echoing David Martin, she observes that the ethical code of these new Protestants is "based on the . . . values of the Protestant ethic . . . an austere life [without] alcoholic beverages, promiscuity, drugs . . . [a life of] material success."[1]

She concludes with a listing of Brazil's "cultural deformities" by the economist and statesman Roberto Campos:

The cultural deformities can be encapsulated in what I call the "disease of isms": temperamental nationalism, which undermines the positive effects of foreign technology and investment; populism, which is the project of distributing wealth before it exists; structuralism, which underestimates the role that monetary indiscipline plays in inflation: statism, which leads the state to do more than it can in economics and less than it should in social development; and protectionism, which punishes the consumer without requiring efficiency from the producer.[2]

Those who are apprehensive about the consequences of Evangelicalism for freedom of thought and expression in the United States—I count myself among them—should be reassured by the Evangelical/Pentecostal phenomenon in Latin America and elsewhere in the Third World. In Brazil, for example, the growing influence of Protestantism is likely to strengthen the values, trust prominently among them in that highly mistrustful society, that nurture democracy.

Chile

Chile is the only country in Latin America that has sustained relatively high economic growth rates following the regional shift two decades ago from protection/import substitution to tariff reduction/export promotion policies and that has also embraced fiscal responsibility. Its democratic institutions, prior to the Pinochet dictatorship among the most secure in Latin America, are today once again in the Latin American vanguard. It is number 20 on the Corruption Perceptions Index, ahead of France, Spain, and Japan.

While stressing that Chilean culture is highly complex, "plagued by ambiguities, inconsistencies, and contradictions," University of Liverpool economist David Hojman notes several features of Chilean history that diverge from the Latin American mainstream: an early tendency toward compromise that is atypical for Hispanic societies; a relatively high level of female literacy (about 30 percent at the end of the nineteenth century); the link between the opening up of the economy and progressive cultural change starting with Pinochet (reminiscent of the transformation of Spain late in Franco's rule); proportionally the largest Basque population in Latin America; and substantial conversion to Protestantism, perhaps as much as 20 percent of the population.[3]

Chile's history presents several parallels with that of Costa Rica, Latin America's longest-standing democracy and by far the most prosperous country in Central America. Both were remote colonial backwaters; neither was endowed with significant precious metal deposits; and neither offered large numbers of Indians for forced labor, Costa Rica because relatively few Indians lived there, Chile because the Indians, who *were* numerous, were bellicose, and many successfully resisted subjugation. Thus, the Spaniards who migrated to Costa Rica and Chile did so with little expectation of rapid enrichment and often with the expectation of making a living in agriculture, the resources for which were rich in both countries.

Many of those who migrated to Chile were Basques. Historian Arnold J. Bauer notes:

> Between 1701 and 1810, some 24,000 immigrants arrived in Chile from Spain [about doubling the number of Spaniards] and forty-five percent of these came from Navarre [a province just east of the Basque Country whose people share many Basque traditions] and the Basque provinces. Everyone agrees on the extraordinary impact these . . . groups had, including [the renowned Basque writer] Miguel de Unamuno who called Chile along with the Jesuit order the two great creations of the Basque people. Their road to economic success and social prominence ran from commerce to the countryside to office. . . . Luis Thayer Ojeda, one of the most accomplished of many Chilean genealogists, thought that "three-fourths of the distinguished personages of nineteenth-century Chile were of Basque descent."[4]

Substantial numbers of Basques also migrated to Costa Rica, evidenced today by the numerous Basque surnames like Echeverría and Chavarría. But the proportion of Basques in Costa Rica was small by comparison with Chile, and the fact that Costa Rica is so far ahead of its Central American neighbors is sometimes attributed to other early immigrants, including Jews (or Jewish converts to Catholicism).[5]

The Basque factor is one of several that can be adduced for Chile's success. The country's geography, including ample mineral deposits, above all copper, but also rich agricultural resources and a geographic position that is highly advantageous for winter markets in North America and Europe, is another. Its uniquely democratic, by South American standards, political evolution—it was referred to as "the model republic" in the nineteenth century—has created a degree of stability that has nurtured economic development.[6] And atypical for Latin America, Chile has a well-developed entrepreneurial tradition going back to the nineteenth century. Although the mining and export of nitrate and copper were principally in the hands of the British and Americans, Chileans were noted for their entrepreneurship in the

Southern Cone—Argentina, Chile, Paraguay, and Ururguay—and they provided a considerable impetus to the growth of the Argentine economy as well as their own.[7]

Chile's political and economic successes, and its early advances in education, reflect the profound Basque influence on the country. This conclusion is consistent with the analysis of the role of the Basques in early-nineteenth-century Venezuela by the French writer François Depons: "As proof of the advantages agriculture would reap if the owners lived on the estates, suffice it to observe the farms which prosper, those which sustain themselves . . . it will be noted that [they] are managed by their owners, who channel all their ambition into increasing their income and take pride in being farmers; in general those who act in this way are Basques."[8] Depons also notes a parallel pattern in the city, including the success of a large company "due to their effective administrators, who always came from the Basque provinces, which seems to be the refuge for good customs."[9]

WITH RESPECT TO THE LESSONS of Chile's success, David Hojman concludes:

> Chile's recent experience of cultural change and fast economic growth offers some lessons for other countries. It makes sense to ask: "What has worked in practice?" The answer is sound economic policies, institutional development, and education.
>
> Politicians and policymakers who wish to introduce new policies favorable to cultural change, economic growth, or institution building may need external support. This is particularly true for economic policies that need time for their positive effects to become apparent. Democratic practices and anti-corruption activities may also benefit substantially from international support.
>
> Education helps to increase human capital stocks, to enhance entrepreneurship, and to diminish inequality. Rapid economic growth will take many people out of poverty, but it will not be sufficient to improve income distribution, which will require its own specific policies.
>
> Open attitudes towards foreign trade, foreign investment, foreign views and values, and new technologies seem to have worked for Chile and should work for others. The Chilean experience over hundreds of years demonstrates that compromise may be slow, but without it true democracy cannot work.[10]

Mexico

Mexican political scientist Miguel Basáñez attributes the vast gap in progress between Mexico and its two NAFTA partners, Canada and the United States, as largely the result of the contrasting effects of Ibero-Catholic and Anglo-Protestant culture:

> Mexico was in the 1930s a highly traditional society built on three cultural pillars: Spanish Catholicism [notwithstanding a current of anti-clericalism in both the nineteenth and twentieth centuries], deep nationalism (anti-Spain and anti-U.S.), and a revolutionary ideology (pro-state and anti-business). Private enterprise, competition, and initiative were anti-values that challenged and disturbed status, hierarchy, and obedience. Children were taught, as the Church insisted, that it was "easier for a camel to pass through the eye of a needle than for a rich man to enter the kingdom of God." This metaphor symbolizes and synthesizes a culture. Government ownership and monopolies were acceptable, whereas private ownership and entrepreneurship were looked upon with suspicion, a mindset that still pervades the society today.[11]
>
> Mexico experienced . . . modernization from 1933 to 1982, which led to a deep shift in values from traditional to modern.[12] The stagnation of real GNP per capita since 1982 paradoxically propelled an acceleration of the trend toward modernization. The acceleration is a by-product of (1) an increase of legal and illegal migration to and trade with the United States, which brought an enormous influx of revenues, a development that was incompatible with the old anti-U.S. ideology; (2) the feminization of the labor force, which propelled gender equality, and in turn pushed changes in family structure and values; and (3) the explosion of the informal economy. The rapid change in cultural values has resulted in a strong convergence of values among Mexico, Canada and the United States. The process of constructing the prevailing Mexican system of values . . . took four centuries up to the 1930s, and its deconstruction is taking less than four decades. What were the traditional values that were constructed so slowly and what are the new ones that are changing so rapidly? . . . The new ones are still in formation. However, they seem to be moving toward a more tolerant, global, market-oriented, democratic society.[13]

Mexico today is a society more comfortable with democratic politics and market economics than it has been at any other time in its history. But the democratic experiment initiated by Vicente Fox with his victory in 2000 that ended 71 years of domination of Mexico by the Partido Revolucionario Institucional is far from consolidated; poverty and social injustice are widespread; crime is rampant; and something like 10 million Mexicans—10 percent of Mexico's population—have left their homeland in recent decades to seek their fortune in the United States, a considerable majority of them entering illegally.[14]

Venezuela

Luis Ugalde, rector of the Catholic University of Caracas, is convinced that culture matters, in part because of his Basque antecedence. And indeed, the Basques played a highly constructive early role in the development of what would become Venezuela, as noted in the discussion of Chile. But Ugalde and his team of researchers, who focused their work on economic performance, also note a powerful tradition of government favors and corruption starting in the colonial period and continuing to the present, a culture that discourages work and innovation and mirrors the mercantilistic, gold-and-silver-driven economic culture of *la madre patria*, Spain, the same culture that became dominant throughout Latin America.

The discovery of oil—the twentieth century's gold and silver—in Venezuela reinforced this rent-seeking tradition and has served as a major disincentive to the evolution of a culture focused on production since the easy way to wealth was to gain access to the oil bonanza through government connections and employment. Oil has also contributed to high levels of corruption: Venezuela is number 114 of 145 on the 2004 Corruption Perceptions Index of Transparency International.

Ugalde and his team conclude that economic reform and the reform of economic culture depend on: educational reform; reforms in the workplace, including transferring large numbers of people from the informal to the formal sector; the promotion of association, both political and nonpolitical; and efficient, just, and accountable public-sector institutions. These prescriptions also apply to Venezuelan culture more broadly—that is, the political and social dimensions of progress—particularly at a moment in history when the propensity of Ibero-Catholic culture for authoritarian governance has reappeared in the form of President Hugo Chávez.

Orthodox/Eastern Europe

Eastern Europe

Eastern European expert Janos Matyas Kovacs's discussion of the Soviet impact on the economic culture of Eastern Europe is of particular interest because of "the precession phenomenon"—illustrated by a spinning gyroscope, which moves not in the direction you push but at a right angle. As Kovacs explains:

> This culture had been Janus-faced under Communism, and its legacy became even more complex in the period of transformation. State paternalism and informal markets, public ownership and private redistribution, central commands and decentralised bargaining, over-regulation and free-riding, collectivist economic institutions and individual (or family-based) coping strategies, apparatchik and technocratic mentality, learned helplessness and forced creativity—one could go on listing the contrasting features of economic culture in Eastern Europe prior to 1989. To a varying degree country by country, it combined the command economy with elements of a rather diluted market socialism, and all this with pre-capitalist traditions and a dynamism/aggressiveness reminiscent of early capitalism. In a sense, it was not double- but quadruple-faced.
>
> It sounds paradoxical but it is true: even if in a distorted manner, Communism was not only a modernizer but also a school of capitalism. . . . Calculative behavior, risk taking, competitive attitudes, etc. were also obligatory subjects to learn—to be sure, by default, not by design. Communism conserved or reproduced a sort of capitalist ethos, rooted, for example, in trust rather than formal rules, personal rather than institutional transactions, small rather than large organizations, that in the meantime eroded in the West. Ironically, this ethos rooted in the reaction to communism may grant a comparative advantage to the Eastern Europeans today.[15]

On the other hand, it is clear that the Communist experience had negative consequences for East Germany:

> A recent survey by the Allensbach Institute shows how different mentalities in the two parts of the country remain. To most western Germans, freedom (49%) matters more than equality (35%). To eastern

Germans, it is the other way around (36% and 51%, respectively). In the west, 41% are happy with Germany's political system; in the east, only 27%. Other polls suggest that eastern Germans still feel like "second-class citizens. . . ."[16]

The East German experience is instructive with respect to the malleability of culture. East Germany was the most prosperous of the Soviet Bloc countries, reflecting the entrepreneurship and workmanship that have characterized German culture. But after the reabsorption of East Germany into contemporary Germany, East Germany lags far behind the former West Germany. Communist politics had changed— or at least modified—German culture in an enduring way.

Georgia

Former Georgian government official Irakli Chkonia explains why and how the Georgians resisted the ideological/cultural impositions of the Soviets. A part of the "why" has to do with Georgia's strong national/cultural identity. While Orthodox Christianity is part of this identity, it is, in his view, a uniquely Georgian Orthodoxy that has been reshaped by the more progressive Georgian culture.

Chkonia's conclusions are highly relevant to the central theme of University of Rhode Island political scientist Nicolai Petro's paper on Novgorod, the discussion of which follows:

1. Successful and cost-effective modernizing cultural change is possible through the legitimation of the proposed change within the authentic cultural system of the society. Change will be supported and carried on if its appeal is to the continuity of the core aspects of the collective being. This was true of Georgia's resistance to the imposition of Communism and Russian nationalism; it is also true of the overthrow of the corrupt Shevardnadze regime. In each case intellectual and political leaders appealed to the best elements of "Georgianness."

2. Societies with strong attachment to their cultural identity and the internalized experience of defying hegemonies are likely to resist even the most intensive and skillful assimilation attempts.

3. Identity reconstruction for the needs of a particular political project is doomed to failure unless it ensures continuity with the implicit,

historically transcendent themes of collective identity, as in the resistance to the imposition of Communism.

4. Paradoxically, the sense of national pride nourished by shared cultural identity can propel, or pave the way, to such *globalist* and *universalist* political projects as the struggle for Western liberal democracy.[17] [The "Rose Revolution" of 2003, led by Mikheil Saakashvili, is a case in point.]

Novgorod

Nicolai Petro has tracked the post-1989 development of the Russian region of Novgorod, near St. Petersburg, which has been atypically successful both in consolidating democratic institutions and promoting economic development, in contrast with the neighboring Pskov region, where the Communists remain influential.

Petro attaches overriding importance to the decision of Novgorod's leaders to emphasize the positive aspects of the city's past. "By systematically highlighting Novgorod's heritage as a medieval trade center and cradle of Russian democracy, local elites re-defined reform as a return to the values of a more prosperous Russian past, rather than as something imposed from outside."[18]

Other factors that have contributed to the transformation of Novgorod include enlightened leadership committed to democratic capitalism; active encouragement of foreign investment, particularly from the West; and help from foreign donors. But Petro is convinced that it was the elite decision to revive the progressive myths of Novgorod that was the indispensable foundation for Novgorod's success.

He goes beyond the Novgorod case to argue that cultural change is not viable because people are so bound to their value system and identity that the only feasible approach is to adapt modernization to traditional cultural attributes. "Studies of democratic transition in regions as widely disparate as Spain, Poland, Turkey, Taiwan, and Slovakia all show that the evocation of local symbols and myths played a crucial role in the early phases of democratic transition."[19]

But what if there are no salient features of a society's history that lend themselves to modernization? Spain is a case in point. A few of Spain's ethnic regions can legitimately point to progressive traditions of long standing, particularly the Basques and the Catalans. But when it came to the modernization of the country as a whole in the second half of the twentieth century, the new leaders evoked not the Spanish Golden Age but the contemporary Golden Age that was Western Europe.

Russia

Oxford University expert on Russia Archie Brown emphasizes the dual cause-and-effect relationship between culture and institutions in his chapter on Russia, which focuses on the period after the dissolution of the Soviet Union. In words that evoke Daniel Patrick Moynihan, Brown argues that culture limits the extent to which institutional change can be effective, though institutional change can also modify culture.

After reviewing the ups and downs of Russia's political evolution since the mid-1980s, Brown concludes:

> The liberalization and democratization introduced in the Gorbachev era . . . both facilitated and produced substantial belief change. Citizens were given the opportunity to hear a wide range of unfamiliar analyses, to listen to and engage in serious political debate, and to vote in contested elections. . . . The society was . . . far more ready to respond to an invitation to awaken than it would have been a generation earlier. There were several million more people with a higher education, and while knowledge of the outside world was still poor, it was much greater than at the time of Stalin's death.
>
> It was crucially important that the Soviet system placed great power in the hands of the top leader, and that when a reformer attained the post of general secretary, a combination of strongly innovative leadership and institutional power made possible systemic changes that were accompanied by cultural change. The presence of well-educated specialists in research institutes, and even in some sections of the central party-state apparatus, provided a reservoir of ideas that could be drawn upon, although it turned out to be easier to liberalize and democratize the political system than to move from an economic system based on one set of principles to a system operating under a different logic.
>
> The lesson is that democratic institution-building and a rule of law must be pursued for their own sakes. It is not enough to assume that they will emerge as by-products of something else, even a market economy, especially given the nature of "capitalism Russian-style."[20]

There are, indeed, cultural continuities to be discerned in post-Communist Russia as well as indications that changes of outlook evident in the last years of the Soviet Union have by no means disappeared. The development and consolidation of a democratic political culture may once again depend on a leader or leaders committed to a process of democratization. It will depend also on the construction of a civil society, which remains weak in contemporary Russia, and on conscious democratic institution-building. The task is essentially one for citizens of Russia themselves, but the West can help by not describing arbitrariness, when it occurs, as democracy and by taking at least as much interest in the building of democratic institutions in post-Communist countries as in the marketization of their economies or their recruitment in the "war against terror."[21]

The West

African Americans

John McWhorter is a black American who formerly taught linguistics at the University of California and is now a senior fellow at the Manhattan Institute. In his controversial book *Losing the Race*, he argues that African Americans are pursuing a self-destructive strategy by promoting a "victim" self-image, racial separatism, and the view that education doesn't matter. His paper starts in a fast-food restaurant in New York City, where he observed a group of African-American boys, around 14 years old, apparently skipping school and misbehaving, to the consternation of the manager, a black woman. "They seemed to consider themselves inherently exempt from observing public norms of behavior. They gave a sense of having begun checking out of mainstream society."[22]

McWhorter continues:

Since the 1960s, Black America has been infected by an equation, sometimes explicit but usually tacit, that the core of black identity is rebellion and disaffection. . . . Misbehavior and criminality are not the only ways this is expressed. Even the most educated blacks with the most assimilated demeanors get their "black authenticity" stripes to the extent that they subscribe to the notion that being black remains a battle forty years after the Civil Rights Act. . . .

The development of black identity among teens often entails learning to process mainstream America as an alien realm, deserving of contempt rather than engagement.[23]

He concludes:

The boys at the restaurant were victims indeed—not of "racism" but of an ideological detour that the sociological history of black America has conditioned. That detour would perplex the black Americans who worked so hard before the 1960s to pave the way for blacks to make the best of themselves in an imperfect world. Realizing that culture is the main problem now rather than racism or societal inequity, our task is to pull black America out of that detour, freeing us from the self-fulfilling prophecies of recreational indignation and returning us to a clear-eyed, proactive race leadership that will allow us to truly "get past race" for good.[24]

Ireland

In 1952, Ireland could have been considered an underdeveloped country, with widespread, persistent poverty; low levels of education, particularly at the secondary and university levels; high fertility rates; and a longstanding pattern of emigration. Fifty years later, in 2002, Ireland is number 10 on the UN Human Development Index, ahead of Switzerland, the United Kingdom, Finland, France, and Denmark, among others.

Former Irish Deputy Prime Minister Dick Spring explains the Irish economic "miracle" as a consequence of the following:

- The liberalization of economic policy in the late 1950s—at about the same time that Spain opened up its economy.
- Creation of the Industrial Development Authority in 1959, which was charged with attracting foreign investment; the subsequent reduction of the corporate tax rate to 10 percent enhanced Ireland's attractiveness to foreign investors.
- Ireland's joining the European Economic Community in 1973, which enhanced Ireland's foreign investment promotion and brought substantial flows of development assistance from Europe.
- An English-speaking labor pool.

- Budgetary discipline.
- High priority for education, dedicating more of its budget to education than any other European country. In 1968, Ireland introduced free public secondary schools. Until that time, the Catholic Church had a virtual monopoly on secondary education and charged fees that deterred many Irish parents from enrolling their children.

As in Spain and Quebec, the Irish transformation was accompanied by a diminution of the Catholic Church's influence to the point that today one hears references to "post-Catholic Ireland."

Spring stresses that Ireland is not Eden. Its economy is heavily dependent on foreign, above all U.S., investment, and should the investors chose to move their operations to lower-cost countries like China and India, the consequences for Ireland could be grave. He also notes social problems that were far less acute before the transformation: soaring crime rates, homelessness, marriage breakdown, and alcohol-related violence. Despite these challenges, Ireland, for so long a country of massive emigration, now attracts immigrants.

Italy

Matteo Marini is an economist who teaches at the University of Calabria. He focuses on three longstanding aspects of Italian culture: conformism, rebellion, and opportunism. Conformism is the preference of a majority of Italians not to rock the boat, but to take things as they come. This attitude is reflected in the fact that major reforms in political institutions in Italy have been introduced by outside forces, during the Napoleonic Wars and after World War II.

The passivity of conformism contrasts with the tradition of rebellion represented by elite dissenters, often committed to radical ideologies, most recently Fascism and Communism.

Opportunism is, as Marini observes, "the art of 'changing everything in order to change nothing,' according to a famous sentence from Lampedusa's *The Leopard*, a novel that describes the strategy conceived by Sicilian landlords when the Kingdom of Piedmont was unifying the country under its flag. The feudal landlords, afraid to lose their privileges after the coming unification, transformed themselves into fervent patriots in order to be co-opted into the winning elite and to be able to maintain their rent-seeking strategy based on the exploitation of local peasants."[25]

While Francesco Guicciardini (1483–1540) is not as well known as his contemporary Nicolò Machiavelli, his insights into Italian culture were more important. Marini continues, "In his diaries, he urges a cynical approach to life because every human being is motivated above all by his own interest. This 'amoral particularism' evokes the 'amoral familism' of Edward Banfield's seminal 1958 book about a southern Italian village, *The Moral Basis of a Backward Society*."[26] Marini also notes the longstanding divide between the north and the south that was the focus of Robert Putnam's *Making Democracy Work*, in which Putnam made extensive reference to Banfield.

Marini believes that Italy's long-term well-being depends on cultural change that will promote greater individual autonomy, social responsibility, and trust.

> In the polarized Italy of today, any call for unity and national cohesiveness is destined to fail. If the problem lies chiefly in a deep sense of distrust, as I believe it does, the only way to overcome it is to go directly to the core of the problem, through the analysis of the prevailing cultural system.
>
> What usually happens in contemporary Italy is that . . . public opinion is against competition and permissive with those who break the rules. Italians have to learn to *accept* competition and to *punish* those who break the rules.
>
> Cultural change does not happen easily, since ordinary people in their everyday lives are caught in the dilemma: why act properly if everybody else *expects* others to act unfairly? But cultural change is possible if political, intellectual, religious, business, labor, and other leaders recognize that a better future for their people depends on it and if the institutions in charge of early socialization—families, schools, churches, and mass media—promote progressive values.[27]

Quebec

Until the Quiet Revolution of the 1960s, French-Catholic Quebec lagged far behind the Anglo-Protestant provinces, and Anglo-Quebeckers, constituting about 20 percent of the province's population, did much better than the French-Catholic majority:

- In 1950, Quebec workers earned 60 percent of what Ontario workers earned;
- Between 1901 and 1950, Quebec had the highest birth rate in Canada (in 1921 it reached 5.3 children per woman);
- Mandatory schooling to age 14 was established in Quebec in 1943, twenty years later, on average, than the rest of Canada;
- In 1959, less than 50 percent of the 14-17 year olds were in school in Quebec, compared to more than 80 percent in Ontario.[28]

Some Quebec intellectuals had arrived at a conclusion similar to the one that many Latin American intellectuals had reached about "Yankee imperialism": Quebec was backward because it had been exploited, chiefly by Anglo-Canadians.

In 1960, Jean Lesage of the Liberal Party became premier, serving until 1966. He and his colleagues and their successors engineered Quebec's Quiet Revolution—a classic case of politics changing a culture and saving it from itself. Major reforms included: a heavy emphasis on education with a new Ministry of Education substantially displacing the Church's dominance; a new labor code that facilitated the formation of unions; and a transfer of management of many programs from the federal to the provincial government. Today, the indicators of progress in Quebec are comparable to those in the rest of Canada, and in some respects, for example, the high school dropout rate, are the best in the country. What happened?

Canadian political scientist Daniel Latouche's catalogue of the cultural factors responsible for Quebec's earlier backwardness evokes the "progress-resistant" column of the CMRP typology. Many of the features he cites flow from the French cultural inheritance, absorbed prior to the French Revolution, including authoritarianism and a rigid social structure.[29] But the most powerful of the influences was traditional Catholicism, which not only reinforced the hierarchical French tradition but also discouraged education, entrepreneurship, and dissent.

Latouche introduces his analysis of the causes of Quebec's transformation with the wise observation: "There can be no cultural transformation without the widely-accepted belief that there is indeed something 'wrong' with the [culture] and without a systematic effort to discuss ways to fix it. For culture to matter, there must [first be] a realization that it needs fixing."[30]

Among the factors contributing to Quebec's transformation in Latouche's view:

- A selective reinterpretation of the traditional culture, in political rhetoric and the media, emphasizing progressive features, for example, tolerance (we are reminded of the Novgorod case).
- The use of an inclusive nationalism by political leaders to promote unity, effort, and sacrifice.
- A process of "declericalization" in which the Church's influence was drastically reduced by the political leadership, above all in education. Like Ireland and Spain, Quebec is sometimes referred to today as "post-Catholic."
- Massive resource allocation to education.
- Promotion by the political leaders of gender equality, particularly in the workplace.
- A "corporatist" approach bringing business, labor, the professions, and other groups together with government for policy discussions has been generally successful.
- State-led efforts to reduce inequality through education, employment creation, and social services.
- Enforced preference for the French language, which forced some Anglophones out of Quebec and opened the field to Québecois entrepreneurs. By the same token, Quebec's very substantial English-language resources, particularly in Montreal, have facilitated business relationships with Anglophone Canada and the United States.

Spain

Cuban-exile columnist Carlos Alberto Montaner has resided in Madrid since 1970. In part because of its potential relevance to Latin America, Montaner has taken special interest in the "Spanish miracle." In 1950 Spain was poorer than several Latin American countries; its government was a dictatorship; and the distribution of wealth, income, and opportunity was highly inequitable. Today, Spain is a prosperous advanced democracy and a member of the European Union; its income distribution is substantially more equitable than that of the United States.

Montaner explains the transformation as chiefly the consequence of a fundamental change in the thinking of the Spanish elites, beginning with the traumatic bloodletting of the Civil War of the 1930s, followed in 1945 by the defeat of the Axis, with whom General Franco identified and whom he had assisted.

In the late 1950s, as Montaner notes, "Franco's elite supporters and advisers began to appreciate Spain's backwardness in comparison with other countries of the Mediterranean basin, and they pressed for an opening to the outside world that quickly showed results. . . . In essence, Spain began to look toward Europe and copy its model for managing the economy."[31] Sustained high rates of economic growth resulted. So did extremely high rates of home ownership, aiding and reflecting the decline of poverty and the growth of the middle class. The Marxist economics that had driven left-wing politics were discredited.

But economic liberalization was not accompanied by political liberalization, and the elites, including the outlawed Communist, Socialist, and Liberal parties, became increasingly aware that their aspirations to become "European" were thwarted by Spain's authoritarian government. Montaner observes, "Jose Ortega y Gasset had written prophetically about it in 1910: 'Spain is the problem, Europe the solution.'"[32]

The intimate relationship between the Church and Franco ended in 1969 when the Vatican, liberalized by John XXIII and Paul VI, named the comparatively liberal Enrique Tarancón as head of the Spanish hierarchy. Actors as diverse as Tarancón and Santiago Carrillo, head of the Spanish Communist party, played a constructive role in Spain's transition to democracy after Franco's death in 1975. At that crucial moment, Franco's hand-picked successor, King Juan Carlos, revealed his own commitment to democracy as well as, subsequently, considerable skill and purposefulness in pursuing it.

Montaner continues, "It may thus be argued that the elite, right and left, had experienced a cultural transformation in the wake of the traumatically destructive civil war and the opening up of their country to the rest of the world after 1959, a transformation that they disseminated throughout the broader society. . . . [P]ossibly for the first time in Spain's history, most Spaniards felt that the government . . . was *their* government, created and voted into existence to serve the people, and that the laws . . . were *their* laws. Experience and practice had become deeply-rooted convictions, beliefs, and values. They were already a part of the culture. It is from this moment that one can speak of a truly consolidated democracy."[33]

Sweden

Sweden is, for our purposes, a surrogate for the "champions of progress," the Nordic countries. In the middle of the nineteenth century, Sweden was among the poorest of the European countries. That was, of course, a time when large numbers of Swedes (and Norwegians and Finns) immigrated to the United States—particularly, in the case of the Swedes and Norwegians, to Wisconsin and Minnesota, two of the most progressive states.[34] Today, the Nordic countries attract immigrants.

The economic boom that started in the 1860s was accompanied by advances in democratic governance that culminated in 1921 with full and equal suffrage. But the roots of Sweden's advanced welfare system go deeper, at least back to the seventeenth century when iron production took place in small communities in which the foundry owners, while paternalistic in their dealings with their employees, also felt responsible for their well-being. Over the centuries, this social responsibility has been transferred to a strong state and a strong, independent civil service, the roots of which go back even further, to the sixteenth century.

But one must ask why this kind of socially responsible management, atypical for the times, occurred in Sweden? And why were the peasants given a political voice as far back as the sixteenth century? The authors of the paper on Sweden, historian Dag Blanck and political scientist Thorleif Pettersson, note the consolidation of Lutheranism in Sweden during the sixteenth century. They quote Swedish author Nils Ekedahl: "Through the true, Lutheran faith and through obedience to the theocratic monarchy, the Swedish people were bound together into one community which united the subjects of the realm into one soul."[35] We are reminded of David Hackett Fischer's observation (see chapter 2) that "the Puritans [of Massachusetts] believed that they were bound to one another in a Godly way. One leader told them that they should 'look upon themselves as being bound up in one *Bundle of Love*; and count themselves obliged, in very close and Strong Bonds, to be serviceable to one another.'"

Blanck and Pettersson also note the profound influence of Lutheranism on education. Fewer than 10 percent of all Swedes were illiterate in the 1850s, perhaps the lowest rate in the world at that time, reflecting, as in the case of Scotland, the Protestant emphasis on ability to read the Bible. But they also note that most Swedes no longer attend church. (We are once again reminded of John Wesley's prophecy.)

The idea of social justice was translated into a metaphor for "the home" by Per Albin Hansson, Sweden's prime minister form 1932 to 1946. I quote it here for its relevance and eloquence:

> The basis of the home is togetherness and common feeling. The good home does not consider anyone as either privileged or unappreciated; it knows no special favorites and no stepchildren. There no one looks down on anyone else, there no one tries to gain advantage at another's expense, and the stronger do not plunder or suppress the weaker. In the good home, equality, consideration, co-operation, and helpfulness prevail. Applied to a home for all the citizens, this would mean the breaking down of all the social and economic barriers that now divide citizens into the privileged and the unfortunate, into rulers and subjects, into rich and poor, the glutted and the destitute, the plunderers and the plundered.[36]

Blanck and Pettersson conclude by stressing two key civic virtues of the Swedes: willingness to follow the society's rules and regulations, and readiness to participate in creating them.

7

Patterns of Cultural Change

WHAT DO THE EXPERIENCES of the countries discussed in chapters 5 and 6 tell us about the nature of cultural change? First, there is no magic wand. Values are deeply rooted and are bound up with personal identity. We easily get emotional about our values, and anything that challenges them is likely to evoke a strong response. For example: many Muslim males have been acculturated to the value of male superiority from earliest childhood. They have found reinforcement of that value in portions of the Quran and have ignored other portions that may suggest gender equality. They have been taught that they are responsible for the behavior of their mothers, sisters, and wives, and that the behavior of "their" females reflects directly on them. The idea of gender equality is not merely alien; it is a fundamental threat to the Muslim male's identity. He will not easily part with that value, that identity.

Beliefs and attitudes are less deeply rooted, but they also form part of our identity. We relinquish them with great reluctance and sometimes with emotional distress. Many of us who were socialists in our youth can remember how difficult it was to announce, to ourselves and to others, that we had concluded that socialism didn't work. After all, not only was an intellectual/ideological issue in play; having vigorously defended socialism before skeptical parents, relatives, and friends, we had to disinvest emotionally and confront some shame in the process.

The process of cultural change is even more difficult when what drives it is the realization of debilities in one's culture, brought home by the strengths of other cultures that have achieved higher levels of progress. Culture and ego are fused in these circumstances, and it is easier on both to explain the progress gap as a consequence of others' malevolent actions than one's own shortcomings. Nevertheless, cultural change *has* occurred in a number of different settings—often slowly, but sometimes in less than a generation, as in the transformation of Ireland and Quebec.

As we search for patterns of cultural change, and particularly for interventions to promote it, it becomes apparent that cultural change and "development," or "modernization," as they have come to be defined over the past half-century, are tightly bound up with one another. Initiatives to promote progressive cultural change are likely to promote political, economic, or social development; and initiatives designed to promote development in the traditional sense of economic growth cum democracy may also promote progressive cultural change. Examples, which we shall discuss subsequently in some detail, include education and economic policy.

The Key Role of Leadership

CULTURAL CHANGE USUALLY OCCURS when two factors coincide: (1) leaders with a progressive vision, and (2) a time of crisis or unique opportunity. This applies, with some variation, to most of the CMRP success stories:

- Botswana under Seretse Khama's enlightened leadership at the moment of independence.
- Deng Xiaoping's reversal of the Confucian—and Maoist—order of things by promoting private enterprise in the wake of the disaster of Mao's Cultural Revolution;
- The young Meiji leaders' response to compelling evidence of how far behind the West Tokugawa Japan was in the second half of the nineteenth century.
- Lee Kwan Yew's vision of a modern, efficient, and affluent—if not democratic—Singapore, initiated at a moment of political crisis.

- The Taiwanese economic and then political "miracles" under the Chiangs, facing a military threat from the mainland.
- A strikingly similar "miracle," first economic and then political, in South Korea, also under military threat.
- Mustafa Kemal's Western-oriented cultural revolution after the collapse of the Ottoman Empire and the threat to Turkey's continued existence.
- Chile's return to democracy after the traumatic Pinochet dictatorship, but with a series of center/left-of-center leaders starting in 1989 with Patricio Aylwin perpetuating the free market policies of the dictator.
- The vision of Governor Mikhail Prusak and other leaders of a democratic, progressive Novgorod, rooted in a centuries-old mythical tradition, in the wake of the collapse of the Soviet Union.
- New leadership in Ireland, starting with Prime Minister Sean Lemass in 1959, committed to the modernization of a country that had fallen far behind much of the rest of Europe in both economic and social terms.
- Italy's rejection of long-standing protectionist economic policies following its disastrous World War II collaboration with Germany.
- New leadership in Quebec, beginning with the Liberal Party government of Jean Lesage in 1960, committed to the modernization of a province that had fallen far behind much of the rest of Canada in both economic and social terms.
- The key role of King Juan Carlos in Spain's transition to democracy following the death of Franco.

Mikhail Gorbachev's role in the dismantling of the Soviet empire, which has not yet led to the transformation of Russia but certainly made several transformations—to democracy and membership in the European Union—possible in Eastern Europe, is another case in point.

A success story where the leadership/crisis formula is not applicable is Sweden, which moved steadily toward democratic prosperity over a period that extends at least back to the mid-nineteenth century. While it may be premature to label India a success story, it certainly would qualify after another decade of high economic growth. This would be a case where the failure of a protectionist economic policy led to open policies that work, similar in some respects to Italy, Ireland, and Spain.

In *Development As Freedom*, Amartya Sen writes: "If a traditional way of life has to be sacrificed to escape grinding poverty . . . then it is the people directly involved who must have the opportunity to participate in what should be chosen. . . . [A]ny real conflict between the preservation of tradition and the advantages of modernity calls for a participatory resolution, not for a unilateral rejection of modernity in favor of tradition by political rulers, or religious authorities, or anthropological admirers of the legacy of the past."[1] Ideally, this would be true. But in most of the above cases, it has been the political, intellectual, and military elites that have led the way to significant change.

Exceptions to this generalization are broad social movements, many originating at the grassroots although usually identified with a leader, which can produce relatively rapid value and attitude change. The civil rights movement led by Martin Luther King, Jr., brought about a dramatic shift in American values and attitudes with respect to race relations, with repercussions in other parts of the world. In a generation, attitudes in the United States about race have been transformed, to the point where racial intermarriage is widely accepted and increasingly practiced. The fight against apartheid in South Africa, led by Nelson Mandela, also produced profound cultural change for both the white and black populations. Blacks now perceive that control of their destiny is largely in their own hands.

The women's movement of the past several decades has produced dramatic change in values and attitudes. Formerly, women were viewed and treated as inferior—slightly or grossly—and often with condescension by men around the world, including the advanced democracies of the West. While gender parity is far from a universal reality, above all in most Islamic countries, the gender gap is a good deal smaller today than it was fifty years ago in many countries.

Grassroots movements for more open, participatory politics and against corruption are growing stronger and more numerous in Third World countries. Many such movements or groups have received support from First World donors. This is a promising development both for more efficient, responsive government and for progressive cultural change.

Openness to New Ideas

IN SEVERAL OF THE SUCCESS STORIES, a willingness to learn from other, more advanced societies has been crucial. We might start with the early success of Islam in the several centuries following the death of Mohammed. Bernard Lewis observes, "It had achieved the highest level so far in human history in the arts and sciences of civilization. Inheriting the knowledge and skills of the ancient Middle East, of Greece, and of Persia [through translations into Arabic of their texts], it added to them several important innovations from outside, such as the use and manufacture of paper from China and decimal positional numbering from India."[2] This is in sharp contrast with the scant flow of translated books into the Arab world today.

The contrasting reactions of Japan and China to Western intrusiveness in the nineteenth century are highly relevant. The Chinese, complacent in their "Middle Kingdom" presumed to be at the center of the earth, chose to ignore the evidence of Western political, economic, administrative, and technological superiority. Japan's Meiji leaders took that evidence very seriously indeed and in 1868 initiated a sweeping modernization program, much of it along Western lines and with the participation of numerous Western experts, which converted Japan into a world economic and military power within two generations.

Reminiscent of the extended visit to the United States and Europe by several of the Meiji leaders, both Seretse Khama and his successor Quett Masire "traveled abroad to learn how electoral politics and policymaking were done in other countries. They sent other politicians and civil servants to other countries to learn as well. They encouraged people to bring back their observations about both successes and failures. As Masire noted in a speech to the first parliament in 1966, 'our progress has been so rapid because we have benefited from the experience and the mistakes of others.'"[3]

Mustafa Kemal, hero of the Gallipoli campaign and leader of the forces that averted the dismemberment of Turkey after the collapse of the Ottoman Empire, could understandably have tried to resurrect the Ottoman structure and make himself caliph. He chose instead to initiate a cultural revolution profoundly influenced by Western values and institutions.

Another kind of borrowing took place on a smaller scale, through the exposure of individual leaders to the West, for example: Seretse Khama's studies in missionary schools in Botswana and South Africa and at Oxford; Lee Kuan Yew's studies at British schools in Singapore and at Cambridge University; and King Juan Carlos's visits to Western countries before his accession to the Spanish throne in 1975.

Continuities

NOTE THAT CONTINUITIES play an important role in several of the success stories. Seretse Khama built on a long-standing tradition of popular consultation (*kgotla*) to consolidate democracy in Botswana. But other traditions also served Botswana well, particularly the modesty and frugality practiced even by chiefs.

Millennia-old "Confucian" values—education, work ethic, merit, frugality—have played a salient role in all the East Asian success stories. During the Meiji Restoration, Japan imported a host of social, institutional, and technological innovations from the West, many of which turned out to be quite compatible with the Japanese way of doing things, including sweeping changes in organization of government and education policy.

Chile was a success story long before the Allende-Pinochet detour—it was referred to as "the model republic" in the nineteenth century and was a showcase of the Alliance for Progress, John F. Kennedy's initiative to modernize Latin America, in the 1960s. That Chile does far better than other Latin American countries on Transparency International's Corruption Perceptions Index is evidence of a degree of institutional strength that is atypical in Latin America. On my first trip to Chile more than forty years ago, I remember being told by U.S. embassy officials in Santiago that Chile's national police force, the *Carabineros*, was a highly professional institution that evoked trust and respect in the citizenry, in sharp contrast to most other Latin American police forces.

In his CMRP paper, Nicolai Petro attributes much of Novgorod's success to the evocation by Novgorod's leaders of a centuries-old liberal ideal: "Local elites responded to the crisis of values caused by the collapse of communism by evoking the ancient image of the Novgorod

Republic . . . as a medieval trade center and cradle of Russian democracy . . . redefin[ing] reform as a return to the values of a more prosperous Russian past, rather than as something imposed from outside. This eased the shock of cultural discontinuity, broadened the social constituency in favor of reforms, and contributed to higher levels of confidence in local government."[4] (As we shall see in the next chapter, a similar evocation of civic mystique in the Ecuadoran city of Ambato has facilitated the practice of punctuality.) And Daniel Latouche, in his discussion of the transformation of Quebec, speaks of a cultural reconstruction process that "involves the creation of new mythologies based on selective memories" by Quebec's new political and intellectual leaders.[5]

Irakli Chkonia reaches a conclusion very similar to Petro's in the case of Georgia, where a centuries-old myth combines chivalry with intellectual and artistic achievement as central to national identity. "Successful . . . cultural change is possible through the legitimation of the proposed change within the authentic cultural system of the society. Change will be supported and carried on if its appeal is to the continuity of the core aspects of the collective being."[6]

But what if no such progressive myth or tradition exists? This is largely the case in Latin America, where the Iberian traditions of five hundred years offer not a foundation for democratic capitalist modernity but rather authoritarianism, corrupt mercantilism, and extreme injustice. Mexicans take pride in the organizational, architectural, and other achievements of the Aztecs, Mayas, and other pre-Colombian civilizations, and Peruvians take pride in the comparable achievements of the Incas. But these were ritual theocracies that offer few precedents for modern societies and were, in any event, virtually totally displaced by Hispanic civilization. When the nineteenth-century Argentine statesman, teacher, and writer Domingo Faustino Sarmiento exhorted his compatriots to make a better Argentina, he looked not to Spain but *al norte*: "We must *be* the United States."[7] As I argued in chapter 5, the same was largely true of the leaders of the Spanish transition to democracy and prosperity, who looked for inspiration not to some glorious Spanish past but rather *al norte*—in this case to Europe.

If, as anthropologist Robert Edgerton claims, some societies are *sick* in a cultural sense—one is reminded of David Landes's term "toxic cultures"—then there may be no alternative but to look outside for new models, as the Meiji leaders and Ataturk did.[8] So much the better, of course, if internal symbols and myths are plausible and available to buttress modernization with the appearance of continuity. But in many cases, such symbols and myths may be difficult to find.

The Crucial Role of Education

EDUCATION HAS BEEN A CENTRAL ITEM on the development agenda since the world became development-conscious after World War II. Its fortunes have ebbed and flowed as economists' assessment of its utility for economic development, including the opportunity costs of investments in education, have differed. Nobelist economist Amartya Sen mentions "the belief in some policy circles that human development is really a kind of luxury that only richer countries can afford." He counters this idea by citing the East Asian miracles: "These economies went comparatively early for massive expansion of education . . . in many cases *before* they broke the restraints of general poverty."[9]

The interest in political development during the past few decades has tended to reinforce education's priority: illiteracy is an obvious enemy of effective democracy. But when one views human progress thorough the prism of culture/cultural change, education becomes the highest priority for public policy. Several of the CMRP case studies reinforce this conclusion:

- Consistent with its Confucian heritage, the Meiji leadership placed heavy emphasis on education: by 1905, more than 90 percent of Japanese school-age children, both boys and girls, were in school—among the highest school attendance rates in the world at the time.[10] This investment in education was instrumental in Japan's surge into modernity as a formidable economic and military power. It also facilitated Japan's transition to democracy after World War II.
- Consistent with *its* Confucian heritage, the government of Singapore has accorded highest priority to education. Fortuitously for its economic development and social harmony, Singapore chose to solve its multilingual problem by establishing English as the primary language of instruction in schools.

We note again the value of English-language facility for economic development more generally today: the recent economic success of Ireland and India is in part attributable to the ease of communications that these countries enjoy at a time when English is the *lingua franca* of global economics. English-language facility has also served the Nordic countries well. And recently, the Socialist-led government of Chile has announced a program the goal of which is "to make all 15 million of Chile's people fluent in English within a generation," according to a recent *New York Times* report.[11] Chile's minister of education, Sergio Bitar, elaborates: "We know our lives are linked more than ever to an international presence, and if you can't speak English, you can't sell and you can't learn."[12]

- In his essay on Chile, David Hojman notes that female literacy in Chile approached 30 percent in 1895, extremely high for Latin America at that time, with important implications for progressive cultural change. "This new market of female readers not only raised the incomes of some writers and publishers; it also conveyed or transmitted new views and values that would eventually affect many of the new readers' perceptions."[13]

- Ireland's transformation since the 1950s has been achieved in large measure through huge investments in public education, facilitated by heavy aid flows from the European Union. Reflecting the absence of public secondary schools in 1960, only 35 percent of high school–age youngsters were in school in 1960.[14] "In 2001," Dick Spring notes in his CMRP essay, "from a population of 3.8 million, about one million people were engaged in full time education, and the expenditure on education at 13.5 percent of public expenditure was among the highest in Europe. Sixty percent of secondary school graduates now go on to third-level education."[15]

- Quebec's transformation parallels Ireland's with respect to education priority and reform. In both cases, public schools substantially displaced parochial schools, making education accessible to large number of children from families of limited means.

- In their essay on Sweden, Dag Blanck and Thorleif Pettersson point to the crucial role of Lutheranism in Sweden's development, above all in its encouragement of literacy. "Through systematic educational efforts by the Church, an unusually high literacy rate developed among Swedes. Even though general primary education was not introduced until 1842, less than 10 percent of the adult population was illiterate in the 1850s. In fact, at that time Sweden was one of the most literate countries in the world. The high degree of literacy became an important factor behind the empowerment of the people in their efforts to balance the strong state."[16]

The role of the church in Swedish experience was similar to that of Scotland, which owed its development largely to Presbyterianism. In *How the Scots Invented the Modern World*, Arthur Herman notes that "[John] Knox's original 1560 Book of Discipline had called for a national system of education. . . . Scotland's literacy rate would be higher than that of any other country by the end of the eighteenth century. . . . [D]espite its relative poverty and small population, Scottish culture had a built-in bias toward reading, learning, and education in general."[17]

There are two points that merit further discussion: (1) the putative link between educational underachievement and economic underdevelopment, and (2) the crucial importance of education of women.

A few years ago, I participated in a long-range planning session of Canada's Department of Foreign Affairs in Ottawa. One of the participants, an Indian (from India) who teaches at an American university, took umbrage when I pointed to the high rates of illiteracy, particularly among women, in India. (According to the UNDP Human Development Report of 2003, 53 percent of Indian women aged 15 and above were illiterate in 2001—illiteracy drops to 36 percent for women ages 15 to 24.) He dismissed my observation, insisting that illiteracy was an inevitable consequence of general poverty. But that is untrue, as the cases of Meiji Japan, eighteenth-century Scotland, and nineteenth-century Sweden demonstrate. All of them were poor at the time that they substantially eliminated illiteracy. If a society—or better, a society's leadership—believes that education is of the highest importance, it will find the resources to educate its people.

My CMRP colleague James Fox (see chapter 7) points out that my Indian interlocutor need not look as far as Japan, Scotland, or Sweden to appreciate the error of his theory. As Fox points out, "the Indian state of Kerala has achieved almost universal female literacy, despite having a per-capita income well below the all-India average."[18]

Discrimination in education against females is a widespread phenomenon. It is a particularly striking feature of most Islamic countries: the female adult illiteracy rate is about 70 percent in Pakistan and Bangladesh, 63 percent in Morocco, 55 percent in Egypt, and more than 30 percent in Saudi Arabia. (In Morocco, Egypt, and Saudi Arabia, the illiteracy levels for females ages 15 to 24 is significantly lower.) The costs of female illiteracy are huge. At a time when gainful employment by women is on the rise around the world, it denies fundamental tools to an important segment of the labor force. It handicaps women for commitment to and participation in democratic politics. In terms of cultural change, female illiteracy facilitates perpetuation of progress-resistant values, for example, by nurturing receptivity to animist religions like Voodoo.

The adverse consequences of female illiteracy for the individual and the society are compounded by the consequences for the family: since mothers bear the principal responsibility for child rearing in almost all cultures, an illiterate mother becomes the principal agent for the perpetuation of progress-resistant values generation after generation. Among other key values, an educated mother is more likely to cultivate respect for education in her children, along with the idea that they can influence their destiny.

I cautioned at the beginning of this chapter that there is no magic wand, either for development in general or for cultural change. While education, starting with literacy, is indispensable for any concerted effort to promote progressive values, it is not sufficient. Evidence of this is the high level of education achieved in the Soviet Union. Today, the former Soviet Socialist Republic of Uzbekistan enjoys full literacy, making it the most literate Islamic country in the world. Yet it is number 101 on the UN's Human Development Index for 2003. Nor have educational levels long comparable to those in the most advanced countries of the West and East Asia assured Russia of democracy, social justice, or prosperity.

This discussion brings us back to questions raised by the essays on education in chapter 3. What are children learning? How are they learning it? What is the relationship between the teacher and the pupil? Is education an instrument that transmits orthodoxy or one that promotes curiosity, dissent, innovation? Is education a force for progress-resistant or progress-prone values? The answers to these questions are closely bound up with culture. That is, the education system is likely to reflect broadly-shared values in the society, particularly among the elites who shape education policy.

Reform is, of course, easier to advocate than to accomplish. But when the leaders of a society conclude that cultural change is necessary, the education system offers one of the most powerful instruments available. The education system is relevant to another powerful instrument—child rearing—both through its general education of prospective parents, especially mothers, but also through the instrument of parenting education. To be sure, in some countries, particularly Islamic countries but also countries like Haiti, where animist religions predominate, religious reform may hold comparable power for beneficial change, as I suggested in chapter 4.

Economic Policy and Cultural Change

SEVERAL OF THE CULTURAL TRANSFORMATIONS were triggered by changes in economic policy. In most of the relevant cases, inward-looking, import substitution policies were replaced by outward-looking, export promotion policies. The impact on cultural values was two-pronged. First, the opening-up of the economy meant greater exposure to more modern, more efficient ways both of doing things and of thinking. Not only did new technologies get adopted—so too did new ways of seeing the world, life, social relations, politics, and opportunity. Second, the economic success of these policies meant increasingly higher levels of income for large numbers of people, many of whom never believed it possible that their circumstances would improve. In an environment of growing prosperity and optimism, eons-old assumptions and beliefs, for example, about one's ability to influence one's destiny or about the value of education, inevitably get reexamined and modified.

The experiences of Italy, Spain, and Ireland contain striking parallels. Before World War II, all three pursued inward-looking economic policies, characterized by high tariffs and discouragement of foreign investment. In the cases of Italy and Spain, the policies—extending in the case of Spain to a quest for self-sufficiency—were congenial with the worldview and philosophy of corporatist dictatorships. In all three cases, the policy was congenial with what Dick Spring describes as "the anti-materialist doctrine of the Church."[19]

The trigger for Italy's upward movement was the Marshall Plan, which had as one of its several successful features encouragement of trade among the recovering Western European nations. Trade, of course, gained momentum with the emergence of a European common market. With the advantage of its tradition of creativity and its relatively low-wage rates, Italy grew rapidly. Today, its per capita income, measured by purchasing power parity, is about equal to that of France and Germany. But the sharp contrast between Italy's north and south has been perpetuated even as the south has become more prosperous. Throughout the country, the influence of the Church has declined. The same may be true of the Mafia, though as this is being written, repeated *camorra* murders in Naples have once again sullied that city's image.

The trigger for Spain was forged by a group of young technicians, two members of Opus Dei prominent among them, who convinced Franco that the quest for autarchy had run into the stops and that the economy had to open up. To be sure, after the end of World War II, large numbers of Spanish workers had migrated over the Pyrenees, particularly to France and Germany. But with the economic *apertura* starting in 1959, ever larger numbers of tourists arrived, as did foreign investors, foreign managers, and foreign students. Spain, theretofore reclusive, rigid, highly nationalistic, even xenophobic, in a matter of a few years became *the* place to visit, *the* place to invest, and, year by year, more and more a *European* country.

The opening in Ireland took place almost simultaneously with that of Spain. But the trigger was new political leadership with a new vision, as Sean Lemass replaced Eamon DeValera in 1959. Ireland's cultural transformation has, like Spain's, been profoundly influenced by the investors, managers, and tourists who have come in the wake of the opening, as well as by Ireland's economic ties, first with the United Kingdom, and then with the European Community.

The "miracles" in East Asia were different. Japan had experienced high rates of economic growth with heavy emphasis on exports starting in the late nineteenth century and continuing up to World War II. The second Japanese economic miracle, after the country's catastrophic defeat in World War II, was also export-driven. The influence of economic policy on cultural change has been less direct than in the European cases. The Protestant-like values of education, achievement, merit, and saving were deeply rooted in Japanese culture, so powerfully influenced by Confucianism. The principal change in Japanese values and attitudes has probably been the result of affluence, although the continuities in Japanese culture are underscored by the persistence of high propensities to save, which contributed to the prolonged Japanese recession that began in the 1990s. Culture matters, but some values that promote rapid development may not be beneficial after an economy reaches high levels of prosperity. Moreover, the rise from poverty to prosperity may be accompanied by a shift in values away from those that produce wealth.

Like Japan, the sustained high levels of economic growth in South Korea, Taiwan, Hong Kong, Singapore, and China are cases of longstanding value systems congenial to economic development rather than, as in Spain and Ireland, of economic development driving cultural change. In East Asia, the economic progress-prone values were in place. What had been lacking before the "miracles" was government encouragement and support of economic development.

Foreign Investment

SEVERAL OF THE CMRP CASE STUDIES highlight the constructive role of foreign investment, in the first instance substituting for shortages in domestic capital, technology, organization, and marketing know-how, but subsequently cultivating entrepreneurial values, attitudes, and techniques. In some cases, foreign investment has propagated the idea of corporate responsibility to the broader society through enlightened labor relations and philanthropic activity. Yet there are also cases where foreign investment has ignored such responsibilities.

Foreign investment has played a prominent role in the success of Singapore, Spain, Ireland, Botswana, and Novgorod. It has also made a major contribution to economic growth in Eastern Europe, where the entrepreneurial spirit had been suppressed—at least for licit activities—during four decades of Soviet socialism. I might add that the collapse of Communism in Poland was facilitated by the numerous joint ventures with Western companies that the regime had countenanced.

My model for a foreign company that, through its enlightened labor relations and philanthropic activity, promoted change in the countries where it operated will come as a shock to many readers. It is the much-maligned United Fruit Company, which became a symbol of Yankee imperialism, particularly for many Latin American politicians and intellectuals including the Chilean poet Pablo Neruda, who wrote a caustic poem entitled "The United Fruit Co." During my first overseas assignment with the U.S. Agency for International Development, in Costa Rica in 1964–65, I received an invitation to visit the United Fruit banana operation in Golfito, on the Pacific coast. I accepted with some reluctance: like most liberals, I had a profoundly negative view of the United Fruit Company.

But what I saw in Golfito was astonishing. A banana operation is visually impressive because of its transformation of vast stretches of jungle into orderly, productive lands served by efficient transportation, packing, and port facilities. The visual impact was magnified by the tidiness of the company town itself. But what impressed me most was the way that United treated its Costa Rican workers. They lived in well-built houses; their children attended schools built and staffed by the company; and all had access to good health and recreation facilities. United's plantation workers were paid twice the going wage. And the company was increasingly bringing Costa Ricans into managerial positions. In sum, the United workers lived in conditions vastly superior to those of the average Costa Rican campesino, underscoring how much better United Fruit treated its employees than most Costa Rican employers did. And while it did so with reluctance, United Fruit enabled the fledgling Costa Rican labor movement to gain strength by negotiating with it. United Fruit's enlightened policies put pressure on national firms to treat their employees better.

The person largely responsible for these policies was Samuel Zemurray, a Jewish immigrant who came to the United States from Rumania as a boy, took over United Fruit in 1933, and ran it into the 1950s. An archetypical entrepreneur, he was also a liberal, an advisor to Franklin Roosevelt, and a philanthropist who, according to his daughter, whom I met some years later, gave half of his fortune to worthy institutions, among them the Child Guidance Clinic and a black women's clinic in New Orleans; Tulane University; Harvard University; and one of the most important tropical botanical gardens in the world, in Honduras. The Pan American Agricultural School in Zamorano, Honduras, which started operations in 1941 and of which more later in this book, was Zemurray's creation.

Those who may view Zemurray's policies as a cover for United Fruit's "exploitation" of Latin America should read the National Planning Association's 1958 assessment of United Fruit's impact on Ecuador, Costa Rica, Panama, Honduras, Colombia, and Guatemala.[20] The report, prepared by Galo Plaza, a highly-respected former president of Ecuador and OAS secretary general, and Stacy May, a Dartmouth economics professor and advisor to Nelson Rockefeller, concluded that United Fruit's operations had been "enormously advantageous" to the six countries.[21] Moreover, United Fruit's profits were lower than those of the average large U.S. corporation, and "far below the rates that are considered tenable for local business enterprises in [Latin America]."[22]

Home Ownership

HOME OWNERSHIP PLAYED A KEY ROLE in the transformations of Spain and Singapore. In both cases, housing policies were designed to give people a stake in the society and to create a middle class. This was facilitated by a rapidly expanding economy. As Carlos Alberto Montaner points out in his essay on Spain: "When Franco died, almost 80 percent of Spaniards were homeowners; the banks housed millions of private savings accounts; a broad middle class had emerged; there was almost no extreme poverty; and the country was enjoying the highest standard of living in its history. In other words, there were objective reasons to act with prudence and reject adventures."[23]

In Singapore, one of the government's central goals, consistent with its Confucian orientation, was to strengthen the family. Housing policy was a principal means to this end. An active housing market would increase family capital through capital gains, which could legally be realized after five years of ownership. "The result is that 90 percent of Singaporean households are home owners . . ."[24]

The rapid expansion of home ownership in Mexico in recent years was noted in an article in the *Economist* in 2004 that concludes that "Mexico is laying the foundations of a property-owning democracy. As this spreads, it will reduce the scope for the patronage politics of the past."[25]

Hernando de Soto's *The Mystery of Capital* is relevant to this discussion of housing. The central argument of that book is that by regularizing ownership of the enterprises of poor people, thereby converting those enterprises into capital against which banks can lend, governments can help mobilize vast quantities of new capital and the entrepreneurship necessary to translate that capital into economic development. This policy is supposed to have almost magical effects: by regularizing property ownership and assuring adequate credit facilities, governments can assure sustained rapid development. The vulnerability of this "single bullet" theory of development is apparent in the case of Haiti, one of the countries on which de Soto has focused.[26] When I described de Soto's approach to him, my Haitian son-in-law observed that the principal consequence of lending to poor Haitians would be to accelerate the flow of emigrants from that dysfunctional society.

Culture Matters and *The Mystery of Capital* were both published by Basic Books in 2000 and were reviewed together by both Robert Samuelson in *Foreign Affairs* and Michael Novak in *The Weekly Standard*.[27] De Soto is contemptuous of culture as a factor in development—an irony in light of his presenting the keynote speech at a conference in Costa Rica in 1996 on the role of culture in Latin America. Still, the kinds of initiatives he proposes may very well produce constructive changes in traditional values, beliefs, and attitudes. For example, fatalism born of endless generations of poverty may be displaced by a sense of empowerment and optimism when someone goes to a financial institution for the first time and receives a non-usurious loan. And the belief of many poor people throughout the Third World that government responds only to the needs and aspirations of the rich will be challenged.

The Key Role of a Professional Civil Service

THIRTY-FIVE YEARS AGO, the first article I wrote on development, "Some Hidden Costs of the Public Investment Fixation," appeared in *International Development Review*, a publication of the Society for International

Development. The article stressed the need to attract high-quality personnel into public service. "Professional work . . . in the public sector, be it of a policy or operational nature, presents opportunities for contributions to national . . . well-being of a magnitude rarely known in the private sector." Low public-sector salaries are the norm in poor countries, contributing to a "popular stereotype [in rich countries as well] of the government worker: inefficient, unrealistic, incompetent; a buck-passer, a clock-watcher, an empire builder who has never met a payroll; in sum, a second-rater who is feeding at the public trough."[28]

Low salaries and incompetence in the public sector, as well as inefficiency, nepotism, and corruption in government programs, burden development. For example, how can one institute sweeping educational reforms of the kind advocated by Fernando Reimers and Eleonora Villegas-Reimers in their CMRP paper on education with unqualified or barely-qualified teachers and administrators?

There is also a cultural cost of government inefficiency and corruption, as Mariano Grondona notes in his CMRP paper on Argentina. Trust is scarce in poor countries, and trust in government is in particularly short supply. In most poor countries, the radius of identification and trust rarely extends beyond family and friends, which undermines any larger sense of responsibility for the broader society. This aggravates the general human antipathy toward paying taxes. But when one adds widespread intense disrespect for and distrust of the public sector, it is easy to understand why tax evasion is rampant in so many poor countries. Think, for example, of popular attitudes about government in Nicaragua, the second poorest country in Latin America (Haiti is the poorest), after it became apparent that former President Arnoldo Alemán had illicitly acquired more than one hundred million dollars during his term in office.

The role of a professional civil service in extending the radius of identification and trust—in government and in the broader society—is central, in Grondona's view. It is particularly prominent in the case of Sweden. Dag Blanck and Thorleif Pettersson observe: "One very important feature of the legacy of the strong state of the seventeenth century is the centralized, relatively efficient, and at times quite independent civil service, simultaneously showing fairness and professionalism in its relations to the people, and loyalty and allegiance to the legal system and state superiors. . . . It is very likely that the Swedish model of the twentieth century would have become less successful had there not been a traditionally strong state and efficient bureaucracy to build on."[29]

Blanck and Pettersson go on to speak of "a strong state, good governance, a vital, open and trustful civil society, and a competent and efficient civil service, where the options for a career were primarily based on merit, rather than on family connections."[30] In Sweden, the civil service has not only provided government services efficiently; it has also enhanced the prestige of government and strengthened the bond of common identity—of community—among Swedes. And it has reinforced the cultural values of honesty and responsibility.

The civil service has also played a central role in Botswana's "miracle." Stephen Lewis makes clear how important that role has been and how Presidents Khama and Masire went far out of their way "to attract and retain the top people in the civil service":

> The government starved the private and parastatal sectors for new graduates for years, so the government had a virtual monopoly on anyone who had gone to university [with government financial help]. They . . . insisted that one of government's responsibilities was to be sure that it could efficiently implement development programs and provide services for the whole population, not to ensure employment for citizens. There was a very large allocation of budget to education, including [financial support] for students to go overseas for courses such as medicine and veterinary school and law for which the local university did not have the expertise. President Masire refers to the "talent spotting" he and Seretse Khama did in looking for high fliers among the younger citizens, promoting able people ahead of ones who were more senior in service but less able overall.
>
> There was also a conscious decision to have a minimum number of political appointees at the top, and to rely on a professional civil service.
>
> In fact, the civil service has at times been so good . . . that there were complaints in Parliament and even Cabinet that the civil service was too powerful and was usurping the responsibilities of politicians. It's also been pretty free of corruption. In one famous case in the late 1970s, a cousin of Seretse Khama, who was still president, was promoted to

acting permanent secretary in the ministry of agriculture. People (myself included) wondered why he had not been made the substantive permanent secretary. Then one day the police arrested him for misappropriating government property (if I recall, he was using government trucks to do things on his farm). He went to jail and was dismissed from the service. The offense was pretty mild by world standards, but they took these things very seriously.

A colleague in the technical assistance field said to me when I first worked in Botswana in 1975, "Botswana is the only country in the world where the ablest 20 people are in the 20 most important jobs [all in the public sector]."[31]

Chile is also noteworthy for the quality of its public servants, a characteristic reflected in Chile's impressive ranking (number 20) in Transparency International's Corruption Perceptions Index. Costa Rica is the next cleanest Latin American country at number 41. (As this is written, two recent Costa Rican presidents have been indicted on charges of corruption, and a third is being investigated.[32]) I recently asked David Hojman, who was raised in Chile and who wrote the CMRP Chile case study, about the role of the civil service in Chile's evolution. His response: "Yes, I agree. . . . Support for this is not only theoretical. In recent weeks, we either directly experienced, or were told by reliable sources, about different encounters, most of them positive, with civil servants in newly created primary care health units, the inland revenue, several utilities, airport police, and so on."[33] As mentioned above, the excellent reputation long enjoyed by Chile's national police force, the *Carabineros*, is another example that contrasts sharply with the generally unsavory reputation of Latin American police forces, a contrast underscored by a front page *New York Times* article (August 4, 2004) headlined "Corruption in Police Plagues Argentines and Their President."

A similar phenomenon may be found in the Confucian countries, consistent with the Confucian prestige hierarchy that places at the top of the ladder those who govern. In Confucian societies, the civil service is more highly respected than in many other countries. This is partly because of the power of the Confucian bureaucracy but also because merit is usually the basis for selection of civil servants. In an extreme example, the Singaporean government has increased public-sector salaries to make them fully competitive with private sector salaries—not without considerable grumbling from the citizenry, whose taxes pay the high salaries. (Note that Singapore is number 5 in the 2004 Corruption Perceptions Index.) But the Singapore miracle is in part due to the high quality of the country's civil servants, and the same may be said of the extraordinary success of Japan and South Korea. As in Sweden, the civil service in the Confucian countries helps bind together the national community.

8

Success and Failure

THIS CHAPTER REVIEWS eight development activities, most in Latin America, that may produce cultural change in order to learn about patterns of success and failure. The principal objective of the first four activities is cultural change: (1) Peru's Institute of Human Development (the Spanish acronym is INDEHU); (2) the programs of the National Strategy Information Center in Washington, D.C., to promote a culture of lawfulness in several countries; (3) a project to promote political participation in Bolivia; and (4) a campaign to promote punctuality in Ecuador.

In the second group of four, cultural change may be a byproduct: (1) U.S. government programs to strengthen democratic institutions in Latin America; (2) innovative investments by the city government of Bogotá, Colombia, focused on the needs of poor people; (3) promotion of philanthropy in Latin America; and (4) American and other schools and universities abroad.

The chapter concludes with an assessment of the impact on culture of six types of traditional development assistance.

Cultural Change as the Principal Objective

Peru's Institute of Human Development

Octavio Mavila was the Honda distributor in Peru from the 1960s through the 1990s. Mavila had been a motorcycle champion in his youth, and he was quick to appreciate the market potential for inexpensive, reliable motorcycles in Peru, which led him to Honda. After several visits to Japan over the years, he came to the conclusion that the only really significant difference between Japan and Peru was that Japanese children learned progressive values while Peruvian children didn't. "Over 32 years working with the Japanese, I have developed an appreciation of the wisdom of the focus of the United Nations on man as the true engine of development. Japan has only water and Japanese people. Peru has a rich endowment of natural resources. Japan dedicated itself to the development of its people. Peru fooled itself with the idea that it was rich because of its natural resources."[1]

In 1990, Mavila established INDEHU in Lima to promote "the Ten Commandments of Development." These commandments are based on Mavila's perception of the values that had made Japan a rich and powerful country: order, cleanliness, punctuality, responsibility, achievement, honesty, respect for the rights of others, respect for the law, work ethic, and frugality. INDEHU's goal was to inculcate the Ten Commandments of Development in half of Peru's population by the year 2000.

Mavila achieved international notoriety in December 1996 when he, along with other guests, was taken hostage at the residence of the Japanese ambassador to Peru in Lima by left-wing revolutionaries. From the moment he became a hostage, he gave sermon after sermon to the revolutionaries on the Ten Commandments of Development. He was among the first hostages released.

INDEHU focused on two target groups: the youth of Peru and business leaders. In the 1990s, more than two million Peruvian students participated in courses sponsored by INDEHU, which mobilized virtually all of its resources within Peru. With respect to business leaders, Mavila hoped that a combination of efforts to improve working conditions and to instill in employees the Ten Commandments of Development would lead to higher productivity, higher salaries, and greater creativity in the participating enterprises.

Mavila enlisted the support of three private universities as well as the government of Peruvian president Alberto Fujimori, including the armed forces. But the government never fully committed itself to the INDEHU program. Much of INDEHU's financing depended on support by private enterprise, and that support declined sharply during the economic crisis of 1998. Because of INDEHU's focus on cultural change, which was highly controversial in the development community, Mavila was unable to obtain external financial support.

The Ten Commandments of Development were preached outside of Peru, too. Humberto Belli, Nicaragua's minister of education in two administrations, viewed the Ten Commandments as central to his program of educational reform. Ramón de la Peña, rector of the Monterrey campus of Mexico's prestigious Monterrey Institute of Technology and Higher Studies (the Spanish acronym is ITESM), has promoted use of the Ten Commandments throughout the far-flung ITESM system. INDEHU's program was also adopted in Colombia.

In late 2004, the CMRP commissioned the Peruvian sociologist María Rocio Romero to do an evaluation of INDEHU.[2] She found that INDEHU was essentially defunct. Mavila's long-standing relationship with Honda had been severed, and he had encountered several years of adversity in his business activities. Several things besides financial problems contributed to INDEHU's demise in her judgment:

- INDEHU's goals were unrealistic.
- INDEHU had acquired a conservative and authoritarian image over the years, partly because of Mavila's emphasis on business and his own ideology as a self-made man, and partly because he selected two retired admirals who "directed" the program rather than leading it.
- Mavila failed to build bridges to people and institutions on the left. [To be sure, many people on the left would have rejected his program in any case, preferring to blame external forces, particularly the United States, for Peru's stunted development.]
- INDEHU did not have sufficient understanding of the complex cultural realities of Peru, with its large indigenous population and highly stratified society. He failed to conduct research (1) to illuminate existing value and attitude patterns, and (2) to identify obstacles to his project of cultural change.

- While individual members of the clergy participated in INDEHU programs, INDEHU failed to involve either the Catholic or Protestant churches as participating institutions.
- The message of INDEHU was particularly difficult to digest in the context of the scandals/corruption of the Fujimori and successor Toledo governments.

I would add to Dr. Romero's findings what may be the most important lesson of the INDEHU experience: *a single instrument like the INDEHU program cannot by itself deflect the powerful momentum of culture.* What is necessary is an all-out, coordinated program that involves child rearing, religion and religious reform, education and education reform, the media, civic groups, and above all, strong political leadership committed to the democratic-capitalist model.

The reader should not conclude that INDEHU has left no positive residue. The current Peruvian Ministry of Education is promoting similar programs, and the INDEHU approach still has its supporters in other Latin American countries. INDEHU's greatest success story, however, is a private Peruvian enterprise, the Furukawa Corporation, created by a Japanese immigrant. Romero reports a conversation with a former INDEHU staffer:

> In Furukawa, we started by dealing with their family problems: family planning, responsible parenthood, relationships between parents and children. . . . Then came instruction in the Ten Commandments of Development, which lasted 14 months. Then we focused on quality in the workplace through "circles of quality." . . . As a result, the workers learned to contribute their ideas, to show creativity.[3]

Romero notes that the INDEHU program continues in Furukawa ten years after it was initiated. But this is the only case she knows of where that is true.

Anti-Corruption Campaigns

The U.S. National Strategy Information Center (NSIC), which was founded in 1962, is dedicated to cultural change that promotes respect for the rule of law. NSIC has mounted projects to promote a culture of lawfulness in Mexico, Colombia, El Salvador, Peru, Lebanon, and the

Republic of Georgia. These projects build on successful experiences in Sicily and Hong Kong in the 1980s and 1990s to strengthen societal support for the rule of law and combat corruption and crime.

Georgetown University political scientist Roy Godson, the head of the NSIC, talked about the role of civil society in countering crime at a symposium in Palermo, Sicily, in December 2000:

> Bolstered by a sympathetic culture—a culture of lawfulness—law enforcement and regulatory systems function more effectively in myriad ways. Those who transgress the rules find themselves targeted not only by law enforcement but also by many sectors of society. Community support and involvement can also focus on preventing and on rooting out criminal and corrupt practices without the need for expenditures for a massive law enforcement and punitive establishment. This involvement also reduces the risk of intrusive government surveillance and regulatory practices harmful to individual liberties and creative economic, social, and political initiatives. In other words, law enforcement, as the mayor of Palermo has put it, is but one wheel of a two-wheeled coach.[4]

Godson restates my principal conclusion with respect to INDEHU:

> Various sectors of society and their institutions influence popular culture and foster a culture of lawfulness. Mobilizing each of them is necessary. However, only when these sectors operate synergistically and reinforce one another is it reasonable to expect major changes in culture.[5]

He goes on to list the following three key sources of social mobilization:

1. Civic and school-based education, including "formal, and less formal education programs in schools, professional associations, trade unions, and the workplace, as well as religious institutions."[6]
2. Centers of moral authority, including both religious and secular leaders and institutions. Godson cites the courageous stand against the Mafia taken by Cardinal Salvatore Pappalardo in Sicily in 1982. Until then, the Church had not publicly recognized the existence of the Mafia. He also extols the leadership

of Palermo mayor Leoluca Orlando, who spearheaded the effort to change Sicilian culture.

3. Media and popular culture. "The mass media in modern society is a powerful institution that can expose crime and corruption and reinforce the culture of lawfulness as well."[7] Godson cites the role of the major Sicilian daily *Giornali Di Sicilia*, which has encouraged children to write letters to the newspaper about rule-of-law issues in their communities. "Films, popular music, television, advertising," he adds, "both reflect and contribute to behavior."[8]

The promise of these programs can be appreciated from a June 2002 NSIC assessment of the impact of NSIC activities in Baja California, Mexico: "There is a growing recognition [in Mexico City] of the need to complement enhanced law enforcement with strengthening the rule of law and the culture of legality. The Executive Branch and important leaders of major political parties . . . maintain that formal democratic structures need to be accompanied by cultural change. The national education plan calls for the introduction of culture of legality education in all major cities by 2006."[9]

A more recent assessment conducted in the Mexican state of Sinaloa during 2003–2004 offered further encouraging results. Students who participated in just one year (60 hours) of intensive culture-of-lawfulness education showed significant improvement in knowledge and attitudes about the rule of law. They also showed reduced levels of fatalism, enhanced interest in upholding the rule of law, and a greater likelihood of feeling that their actions can affect the course of their lives.

Political Participation in Bolivia

Political scientist Mitchell Seligson of Vanderbilt University was involved in a USAID-financed project to increase citizen participation and social capital in Bolivia starting in 2002. Funds were provided to strengthen the services provided by local governments and to promote citizen participation. Data were collected on attitudes about democracy and association in participating and nonparticipating communities. Seligson summarizes the results: "Bolivians living in the regions where the [project] carried out its full program participated at significantly higher levels than those in the rest of the country. It shows a

27% increase in the [project] areas vs. the nation even when key control variables (urbanization, income and education) are introduced. How meaningful are these results? When [they] are placed in an international perspective, the [project] areas increase their participation to match the highest level reported in the Vanderbilt University Latin American Public Opinion Project data base."[10] While Seligson is encouraged by the data, he notes that it is too early to demonstrate that lasting results have been achieved.

Seligson served as a Peace Corps Volunteer in the remote Coto Brus region of Costa Rica in the late 1960s. He was involved with a USAID-financed project that provided mobile health services to the communities in the region if they organized themselves to receive the services and use the resources generated by them—small payments were required—for community development. When the project was restructured to require that prospective patients come to the regional capital rather than receive periodic visits in their communities, the success of the project was demonstrated by the political mobilization of the region against the change. Faced with this response, the minister of health then reversed the decision, and the visits to the community continued.

Seligson notes that this grassroots mobilization took place in a country with long-standing traditions of local responsibility atypical of Latin America. But he concludes: "Social capital is not merely a given, an inherent characteristic of a population that cannot be altered. Programs can be designed to increase social capital, just as they can be designed to reduce it (consider the impact of Stalinist terror on social capital). Most development programs, however, focus almost exclusively on the dependent variable of economic growth, without considering growth of social capital as an important additional or even primary goal."[11]

Ecuador's Punctuality Campaign

I lived and worked for thirteen years in five Latin American countries (actually four Latin American countries and Haiti, an African-American country) between 1964 and 1981. When I made appointments to meet with citizens of those countries, I was often asked whether the appointed hour was "*hora gringa* (American)" or "*hora local.*" If it were the latter, the presumption was that the person would arrive at least thirty minutes late.

The reader will recall that the CMRP typology includes the lesser virtues: a job well done, tidiness, courtesy, *punctuality*. The Latin American tradition of unpunctuality reflects in part the current of excessive individualism in Iberian culture that both Fernando Díaz-Plaja and José Ortega y Gasset have commented on. In his best-selling *El Español y los Siete Pecados Capitales (The Spaniard and the Seven Deadly Sins)*,[12] Díaz-Plaja refers to Spanish "superindividualism." Ortega y Gasset uses the word "particularism—that state of mind in which we believe that we need pay no attention to others. . . . Taking others into account implies at least an understanding of the state of mutual dependence and cooperation in which we live."[13] I hasten to add that the transformation of Spanish culture in recent decades has included a substantial diminution of this characteristic, as recent World Value Survey data confirm. But Spain still struggles with a concept of time in which "watches don't run; they walk."[14]

Toward the end of 2003, Participación Ciudadana, an Ecuadoran civic organization, one of several in Latin America created with help from U.S. public and private organizations, inaugurated a punctuality campaign throughout Ecuador. The reader will recall that *The Economist*, in reporting on the campaign, noted that "punctuality is not a Latin American comparative advantage," adding that, "even the president, Lucio Gutiérrez [ousted from office in April of 2005], turned up for the launch . . . at the last minute."[15]

There is a significant economic cost to unpunctuality. Participación Ciudadana estimates the annual cost of lateness in Ecuador at $724 million, or more than four percent of GDP, according to *The Economist*. Another study, cited in an article in the *New Yorker*, estimates annual losses at $2.5 billion.[16] "Government is the worst offender," asserts *The Economist*. "Two out of three appointments at the Ministry of Education . . . start late." James Surowiecki, author of the *New Yorker* article, agrees: "Lateness can be a way for the rich and powerful to assert themselves, to show how much more valuable their time is. In Ecuador, members of the military and the government are the most notorious offenders, and businessmen are far more likely to show up late than blue-collar workers are . . . in a country where everyone is always late, it becomes rational to be late. . . . Tardiness feeds on itself, creating a vicious cycle of *mañana, mañana*."[17]

Surowiecki goes on to make an observation highly relevant to this book: "What Ecuador really has to overcome is the idea that culture is destiny, that showing up late is just what Ecuadorans do. In the past two decades, great attention has been paid to the economic significance of cultural predispositions—to the role, for example, of trust and risk aversion in the old Soviet-bloc countries' fitful attempts to adapt to capitalism. Culture, we have discovered, matters more than many bondholders wish it did. But it is not immutable."[18]

Will the punctuality campaign work? I posed that question in October 2004 to Osvaldo Hurtado, who served as president of Ecuador from 1981 to 1984. Hurtado is another prominent Latin American who is convinced that culture matters. His comment:

> The punctuality campaign in Quito promoted by Participación Ciudadana has gradually lost momentum as often happens with initiatives that don't involve other sectors in promotion and follow-up. My impression is that even if the campaign hasn't produced tangible results, it has accomplished something by highlighting a cultural obstacle to progress the significance of which many Ecuadorans were not aware.
>
> A similar campaign has had greater success in Ambato, a very industrious Andean city and home of three of the ten highest payers of income tax in the country despite its having one-tenth the population of Quito or Guayaquil. The campaign involved several private and public institutions and evoked the civic mystique of Ambato with frequent references to *la hora ambateña* (the hour, by the clock, of the city of Ambato). . . . In Ambato, all public events start on time.[19]

Cultural Change as a By-Product

USAID Democracy Programs

Like other development assistance institutions, the U. S. Agency for International Development (USAID) has supported democratization programs throughout the Third World as well as in the former Communist societies in Eastern Europe and Asia. It often provides such assistance through the international development offices of the Democratic and Republican parties (which became an issue in the disputed Ukraine elections at the end of 2004). Presumably, such programs would promote the values that make democracy work, including trust, association, and respect for the rule of law. But experience suggests that ways must be found to strengthen these values *before*, or at least simultaneously with, the strengthening of democratic institutions.

In 2003, the Government Accountability Office (GAO), formerly the General Accounting Office, completed a study of USAID programs in support of democracy in six Latin American countries. (The GAO is an independent, non-partisan watchdog organization that assesses and reports to the Congress on activities of the federal government.) The six countries are, from north to south, Guatemala, El Salvador, Nicaragua, Colombia, Peru, and Bolivia. Five hundred and eighty million dollars of USAID funds were used to promote "the rule of law, transparent and accountable government institutions, respect for human rights, and free and fair elections"[20] in these countries between 1992 and 2002.

The GAO Report notes some progress in the six countries but concludes that "helping to strengthen democracy can be a difficult and long-term challenge that requires sustained political support from key host country leaders. When this political support wavers, hard-won gains can be quickly lost."[21]

Lurking behind the GAO findings is the message of Alexis de Tocqueville: *It is difficult (and probably impossible from the outside) to build a democracy without a critical mass of democrats.* Disconcerting evidence of the weakness of the democratic vocation in Latin America is, as we mentioned earlier, a recent United Nations survey of 19,000 people in 18 countries that found that "a majority would choose a dictator over an elected leader if that provided economic benefits."[22] Tocqueville's message obviously also applies to other parts of the world, including Afghanistan and Iraq.

As a consultant, I helped the USAID missions in Haiti and Nicaragua design programs in support of democratization in the early 1990s. Both programs included technical assistance, training, and equipment for the legislatures and judiciaries, and for the institutions that managed elections; both also included civic education. In my view, elections are the easiest component of democratization. External organizations with enough money and enough people may be able to assure that the people vote and that the vote is fairly counted. This was true of the elections in Haiti in December of 1990, won by Jean-Bertrand Aristide. But once the elections are over, making a society function democratically is a lot more difficult, above all if there is not a substantial democratic consensus and vocation among the people. Haiti is a case in point. Aristide was removed by the Haitian military in September of 1991 and restored to power through the intervention of U.S. military forces in 1994. Aristide's choice, René Preval, was elected as president in 1995 and was succeeded in 2001 by Aristide. But by then it had become apparent that Aristide was not a democrat. When he was overthrown by force in 2004, Haiti entered yet another chapter in its sad saga.

Of the six countries whose USAID democratization programs were evaluated by the GAO, only El Salvador seems to be making significant progress in the consolidation of democracy. El Salvador's political progress is probably linked to relative economic well-being, in important part the result of more than $2 billion in annual remittances from Salvadorans in the United States—by far the largest source of the country's income and foreign exchange—another case where cultural change and the consolidation of democracy may be driven by prosperity. (The annual remittances work out to about $350 per capita.)

With roughly half its population composed of Indians, many of whom are not fluent in Spanish, Guatemala remains a deeply divided society where crime and violence are rampant. Nicaragua's current president, Enrique Bolaños, prosecuted his predecessor Arnoldo Alemán for corruption—Alemán had apparently misappropriated $100 million of public funds—and Alemán was convicted in March 2004. But some leaders of the opposition Sandinista party as well as Nicaraguan Cardinal Miguel Obando y Bravo have defended Alemán, and Bolaños's crusade has fractured his political base.

Colombia has been wracked for decades by civil war, compounded by its prominent role in the narcotics trade. The current president, Álvaro Uribe, a conservative, is seeking to modify the constitution to permit reelection. The administration of President Alejandro Toledo of Peru has been staggered by corruption scandals, incompetence, and very low popularity ratings, as well as by the resurgence of the Sendero Luminoso Marxist revolutionaries. And in Bolivia, elected President Gonzalo Sánchez de Lozada was forced out of office by street demonstrations in October of 2003. Sánchez de Lozada's successor, Carlos Mesa, resigned in June 2005 under continuing pressure from a strong populist movement. The country continues in turmoil.

The recent U.S. emphasis on democracy is not new. Support for democracy was a central component of John Kennedy's Alliance for Progress, the goal of which was to make Latin America safe for democracy—and safe *from* Cuban-style revolution—within a decade. That was almost a half-century ago. And a half-century before that, the United States tried to impose democratic institutions on the Dominican Republic, Haiti, Nicaragua, and Cuba. The lesson that culture matters is not easily learned.

Bogotá: A Transformed City

In April 2004, Enrique Peñalosa, mayor of Bogotá, Colombia, from 1998 through 2000, spoke at the Fletcher School about a novel approach, at least in Latin America, to urban public investment: giving highest priority to the needs and aspirations of poor people. During his three years in office, Peñalosa built libraries, sidewalks, bike paths, and parks for children in the poor areas of Bogotá. He also installed a modern, efficient system of bus transportation throughout the city. I talked to Peñalosa subsequently and suggested to him that his approach may have had cultural consequences in the sense that people who had never seen significant benefits from government programs were now the principal beneficiaries of such programs. A more optimistic outlook on life, a stronger identification with and trust of government, a sense of empowerment and the ability to influence one's destiny might logically have been a consequence.

A few months later, I asked Miguel Basáñez, who has long been a leader in the measurement of values and value change in Latin America and is the author of the CMRP Mexican case study, to visit Bogotá and assess the impact of the Peñalosa program. Basáñez accepted the assignment, but with skepticism. "When I was thirteen, my father took me to see a Mexican president who was visiting my hometown. There, for the first time, I heard the words: 'Now, things will change in a fundamental way—those who governed before us didn't know how to do it.' I was very impressed. But that impression vanished over the subsequent 34 years as I heard government after government speak of 'profound change' without producing any. I was frankly skeptical about the impact of the Peñalosa program."[23]

Basáñez was startled by the visual impact of Bogotá, which he had not visited for 17 years. "Bogotá was now an impressive, orderly city of modern skyscrapers, wide streets and sidewalks, very clean, no advertisements on walls. People even were respectful of crosswalks."[24] But even more impressive was the broad consensus of some 40 people from many walks of life he interviewed that Bogotá had indeed been transformed and so had the culture of the Bogotanos. "They speak of a new culture of respect for life, the law, and for others."[25] While Peñalosa gets a lot of credit for the transformation, so does Antanas Mockus, the mayor from 1995 through 1997 and from 2001 to 2003. Mockus's slogan was "Law, Morality, Culture." Together, Mockus and Peñalosa, both of whom were independent of the traditional political parties, governed for nine years. "Their admirers attribute to Mockus the disposition to change, to Peñalosa the merit of realizing change."[26]

The number and variety of their reforms are extraordinary, among them:

1. An effective campaign against police corruption.
2. An effective campaign against violent crime: murders declined from 81 to 31 per 100,000 inhabitants from 1993 to 2003.
3. Sweeping fiscal reforms.
4. An effective campaign to increase the yield of property taxes.
5. Creation of a modern, extensive, and efficient system of public transportation.
6. Extensive new paths and facilities for bicycles. (Peñalosa estimates that 300,000 Bogotanos depend on bicycles.)
7. Extensive new public health outreach.
8. Construction of three "mega-libraries" and twelve smaller libraries "of the Anglo-Saxon type with direct access to books."[27] (Latin American libraries typically do not permit direct access, reflecting a culture of mistrust.)
9. Contracting with the most prestigious private secondary schools to administer public secondary schools.
10. Enforcement of parking laws.
11. Obligatory non-use of automobiles (two days per week) at rush hours.
12. Rehabilitation of parks and athletic fields.
13. Prohibition of the use of fireworks. (In Latin America, fireworks are commonly detonated to celebrate birthdays, wed-

dings, and saints' days, among other events, and accidents, sometimes fatal, are frequent.)

14. Restaurants and discotheques must close by 1 A.M.

Deplorable conditions in Bogotá prior to 1988 were in important measure the consequence of the fact that the mayor was theretofore appointed by the president of Colombia. The mayor had to compete with cabinet colleagues for resources.

At the end of his visit, an initially skeptical Basáñez was convinced that profound change *is* possible. Basáñez concludes: "The above list gives us an idea of the surprising cumulative effect the actions of city government can have on citizens unaccustomed to responsive government. . . . The Bogotá experience demonstrates that a city government can not only influence the perceptions and attitudes of city-dwellers but penetrate beyond to the deeper level of values. It's not a question of revealing unknown values. In such circumstances, those values become palpable and functional. The new values were always latent. It would, however, have been absurd to apply them in a cultural environment in which 'the shrewd live off the fools.'"[28]

Promoting Philanthropy

The Random House Dictionary of the English Language defines "philanthropy" as "altruistic concern for human welfare and advancement, usually manifested by donations of money, property, or work to needy persons, by endowment of institutions of learning and hospitals, and by generosity to other socially useful purposes." "Charity," by contrast, is defined as "generous actions or donations to aid the poor, ill, or helpless." Thus, philanthropy usually implies a contribution to social progress while charity responds to an urgent need. The difference is suggested in a metaphor commonly heard in development circles: one can give a hungry person a fish (charity) or teach the person how to fish (philanthropy).

What, in a cultural or psychological sense, motivates philanthropy? Five possible motives occur to me. The philanthropic act may be motivated by a strong identification with and concern for the well-being and advancement of society. The philanthropist may feel guilt for his/ her affluence, hoping to expiate it by philanthropic activity. The philanthropist may wish to make a public demonstration of his/her wealth or goodness as a means of ego gratification. Philanthropic (or charitable) activity may be motivated by the belief that one gains points toward a happy arrival in the afterlife. Or giving may be central to the structure of one's religion, as in the case of tithing for Mormons.

It is clear that some cultures are more prone to philanthropic activity than others. The United States has been notable for its traditions of philanthropy, symbolized by Andrew Carnegie, who, with echoes of Calvinism, believed, "The man who dies rich, dies disgraced."[29] The United Fruit Company's Samuel Zemurray, whose impressive philanthropic record is mentioned in the preceding chapter, apparently felt similarly (though he did not, any more than Carnegie, die poor). According to *The Economist*, "American generosity outstrips that of most other countries, especially in money terms, and particularly if gifts to religious bodies are included."[30]

Philanthropy may be motivated by a general concern for the well-being of one's society, or even of humankind in general. But isn't that the same basic concern that motivates a society to tax itself at high levels for the general welfare? I have in mind particularly the welfare societies of the Nordic countries, where one also finds high levels of volunteer social work and high levels of trust.

In any event, like trust, philanthropy is in short supply in most poor countries, where the upper classes have generally not concerned themselves with the well-being of others in the society they share. The narrow concentration of wealth in all Latin American countries could facilitate the mobilization of very substantial amounts of money from the private sector for education, health, housing, small-business promotion, and other longer-term projects that would promote growth, improve equity, and strengthen democratic institutions.

In February 1999, Harvard University sponsored a workshop on philanthropy in Latin America. As the report of the workshop notes: "Philanthropy, as it is understood in North America, has little solid tradition in Latin America. Typically, philanthropy in Latin America is ... 'passive' ... limited to charitable, clientelistic, or paternalistic practices. Rarely is philanthropy associated with any structured or sustained effort to relieve poverty, or with institutionalized forms of corporate citizenship. ... The Latin American historical tradition has left a weak, fragile, and poorly organized civil society, although with democratization there are now infinitely more opportunities for participation."[31]

Participants included representatives from several Latin American countries who were involved with promotion of philanthropy or the strengthening of the civil sector. Since the blossoming of democratic politics in Latin America, at least in the electoral sense, in the 1980s, the civil-sector vacuum in the region has been the focus of attention from fledgling non-governmental organizations often supported by outside development assistance institutions, both bilateral and multilateral. Philanthropic and philanthropy-promoting organizations have sprung up in many Latin American countries, some dedicated to poverty alleviation, others to the strengthening of the citizen's role in politics, for example, through the development of a broader understanding of participatory politics in the electorate, and through oversight activities focused on transparency, accountability, and corruption.

The findings and recommendations of the workshop include the following:

- Enhance awareness of philanthropic practices through mobilization of the media.
- Work toward better legal frameworks that provide incentives for philanthropy.
- Strengthen alliances among government, business, and nongovernmental organizations. (We are reminded of the problems INDEHU encountered in Peru because of erratic government support and failure to involve other institutions.) "Many countries suffer from an extraordinary lack of trust in public institutions and in their provision of services . . . [and] tax evasion . . ."[32] (A reminder of the importance of an honest and efficient civil service.)
- Encourage civic engagement through "policies that promote a culture of generosity and civic participation. There was unanimous agreement that working to create a more favorable environment for philanthropy requires major cultural and psychological change. . . . It was generally accepted that one should start young."[33]

American and Other Schools Abroad

As I mentioned earlier, my first overseas assignment was in Costa Rica in 1964, where I served as program officer for the USAID mission. I had studied Spanish for four months at the Foreign Service Institute in Washington. While the instruction provided an excellent foundation, it became apparent to me on the first day in Costa Rica that I had a lot more to learn about the language—I had great difficulty in communicating my way through the purchase of diapers in a San José store. So I made a pact with my Costa Rican secretary, Ana Sayaguez, that we would only speak in Spanish and that she would correct me.

Ana spoke English like a native speaker. She had received her primary and secondary education at an American school in Costa Rica named after Abraham Lincoln. While many of the students at the school were Americans, quite a few Costa Rican youngsters also attended. Even though Ana and I mostly communicated in Spanish, I soon found that it was easier for me to communicate with her than with other Costa Ricans, including some with whom I spoke English. The reason was that Ana, because she had been educated in English by mostly American teachers, *thought* like an American—practical, pragmatic, a problem solver.

Language is the conduit of culture. The words, verbal structures, and emphases we use reflect our system of values, attitudes, and beliefs. Recall the observation of the Costa Rican psychiatrist Luis Diego Herrera that the idea of accountability is not highly developed in Hispanic culture, evidenced by the absence of a Spanish word that fully captures the idea.

There was at the time I first lived in Costa Rica a German primary and secondary school named after the German scientist Alexander von Humboldt, which was attended chiefly by the offspring of the numerous German families that had migrated to Costa Rica. (Coffee was first exported from Costa Rica in 1832 by a German, Jorge Stiepel.) Some non-German Costa Ricans also attended the Humboldt School, where they not only acquired the language but also much of the German way of seeing and doing things.

My strong sense is that such primary/secondary schools are powerful instruments of cultural change for students who are nationals of the countries in which the schools are located. My colleague at Fletcher, Georges Prevelakis, who wrote the paper on Greece and Orthodoxy, is a graduate of Athens College in Athens, Greece. Athens College is a high school, founded in 1925, where much of the curriculum is taught in English and where the American influence has been profound. According to Prevelakis, graduates of Athens College are—and are seen by others as—different from other Greeks in their worldview and their pragmatic approach to problem solving.

The American Farm School was established in Thessaloniki, Greece, at the secondary level in 1904. During its hundred years of existence, it has graduated thousands of Greek students who have learned a practical, hands-on approach to agriculture. It now also offers courses at the university level. This brings us back to Samuel Zemurray, the former president of the United Fruit Company, who created the Pan-American Agricultural School in Zamorano, Honduras, in 1941. The "Zamorano School," as it is often referred to, started at the secondary level with heavy emphasis on the practical aspects of agriculture. It subsequently converted itself into an agricultural university, among the best in Latin America. Its students come not only from Honduras and other Central American countries but also South America, Mexico, and the Dominican Republic. Many of its several thousand graduates have served as ministers of agriculture.

The Central American Business Administration Institute (the Spanish acronym is INCAE), with campuses in Nicaragua and Costa Rica, is another example of a high quality institution that promotes progressive cultural change. INCAE was founded in 1963 with substantial assistance from the Harvard Business School, whose influence continues to be felt through several of its professors and graduates who have taught at INCAE. Like the Harvard Business School, INCAE stresses practicality, employing case studies extensively.

Institutions like the Zamorano School and INCAE, and high quality Latin American universities like the Monterrey Technological Institute, with campuses throughout Mexico, and the Catholic University of Caracas, Venezuela, play a crucial role in Latin America's progress. Many Latin American universities, particularly public universities, do not serve their societies well because many of their faculty members, particularly in the social sciences, are committed more to the transmission of left-wing orthodoxies than to the search for truth. I was reminded of this in November 2004 when I led a seminar on culture and development at Harvard. A Mexican and a Brazilian student attended the seminar and both made it clear that dependency theory was still a dominant theme in their universities. Latin America's disenchantment with market economics and even democracy is driven in large measure by intellectuals who continue to pursue utopian socialist visions.[34]

A number of educational institutions in Africa, many of them created by British missionaries, have also provided both quality education and exposure to progressive value systems. Three are located in South Africa: the Tiger Kloof Institute, established by the London Missionary Society in 1904; the Lovedale Institution, established by Scottish Presbyterians in the nineteenth century; and the University of Fort Hare, established by the United Church of Scotland in 1915. Presidents Seretse Khama and Quett Masire of Botswana both attended Tiger Kloof, and Khama went on to Lovedale and Fort Hare. Nelson Mandela is among the illustrious graduates of Fort Hare.

Bogazici University, a premier institution of higher learning in Istanbul, is the outgrowth of Robert College, founded by an American philanthropist in 1863 (it was the first American college overseas), and of the American College for Girls, founded in 1890, and subsequently merged with Robert College. Bogazici was established on the site of the American schools in 1971 and has sustained the philosophy and emphases of Robert College, including exclusive teaching in English, to this day. The principal language of instruction at Bilkent University, established in Ankara in 1984, is English, and Bilkent has ties to a dozen American and Canadian universities as well as to Tel-Aviv University.

The American University of Beirut, established in 1866, and the American University of Cairo, established in 1919, are two more examples of institutions of excellence that have also exposed students to new ways of seeing the world. Other American universities are found in Armenia, Bulgaria, Kyrgyzstan, and the United Arab Emirates.

The foregoing is not intended to suggest expansion of the number of "American" educational institutions around the world. Obvious political and security considerations argue against such an initiative today. But the idea of developing a system of high-quality international universities, under UN or World Bank/IMF auspices, particularly in the Islamic world and Africa, may have merit not only to enhance the professional preparation of the young people who will lead their societies into the future but also to expose them to the values that make democracy, prosperity, and justice a reality.

There may be a downside, as Prevelakis points out: "Graduates of such 'foreign' schools attract hostility and are often perceived as janissaries in their own countries. The opposition to such groups is a function of their number and of their influence. The generalization of the principle in the form of an international network of schools or universities might lead to dangerous reactions. It might be better to leave this phenomenon in its chaotic form rather than try to bring it to a higher level of organization."[35]

Still, it seems to me that the benefits would outweigh the risks, above all in the Islamic world and Africa.

Six Types of Development Assistance That Affect Culture

JAMES W. FOX IS A FORMER USAID ECONOMIST who worked in Costa Rica at the same time as Seligson and who has recently taken on a number of research and evaluation assignments for the World Bank. I originally asked him to look for evaluations of development projects that touched on culture and cultural change. Since development assistance institutions have largely ignored culture, he was unable to find anything useful for our purposes and instead did some generalizing about the cultural impact of six types of development assistance. He then examined the experience of two Costa Rican communities over the second half of the twentieth century based on studies of the two done in 1950 and 1996.

The six types of development assistance:

1. **Agriculture.** There is a presumption that "better technology would demonstrate the value of knowledge in raising incomes, thereby discrediting traditional approaches and fatalism. This would lead to increased investment, greater emphasis on learning and knowledge, and more entrepreneurship. In the wake of these changes, other progress-friendly values would gradually follow."[36] This is likely to have happened to some degree, but it has not been the subject of systematic analysis.
2. **Education.** "The power of literacy as a vehicle for individual empowerment—for connection to world culture and values, and for going beyond village or tribal values—is surely enormous. Literacy may not result in 'development-friendly' cultural values, but it certainly opens the door to such values. Some in every culture will surely walk through."[37]

3. **Family planning.** "Family planning advocates have often claimed some success from direct efforts to change cultural values, but there is only very weak evidence to support this view. The predominant explanation that econometric studies offer for fertility decline largely involves changes in circumstances, rather than culture *per se*."[38] Nevertheless, the very introduction of the idea that family size might be controlled has surely been an important first step in this direction.

4. **Women in development.** Male dominance characterizes many lagging societies, most Islamic countries and India prominently among them. Development assistance institutions have for more than two decades been trying to promote greater gender equality, particularly though female education. But as Fox observes, such programs have run into cultural resistance akin to efforts to promote desegregation in Alabama and Mississippi in the 1950s. Clear progress in the role of women is occurring, faster in some places than others, but usually against heavy resistance.

5. **Microfinance.** The now legendary Grameen Bank in Bangladesh, founded by Mohammed Yunus for poor women, has spawned numerous clones, in Bangladesh and elsewhere. Yunus incorporated a strong component of cultural change in his approach: each borrower had to commit to 16 progress-prone behaviors. Most of the experts who have studied microfinance agree that it is an instrument of cultural change, but "the key tool is cash in the hand, and not commitments to live better, or joint borrowing."[39]

6. **Democracy and governance.** Substantial resources have been devoted by development assistance institutions to promotion of democracy. The results are uncertain. The 2003 report by the U.S. General Accounting Office on democracy programs in Latin America (see above), which is often critical of the programs, laments the "lack of baseline data on attitudes and values at the outset of the intervention."[40]

With respect to the role of development assistance in the two Costa Rican towns, both of which had experienced transforming changes in well-being, including health, education, prosperity, the status of women—and values, including tolerance, Fox notes:

The role of foreign aid cannot be separated from other factors. Nevertheless, some activities left discernable "footprints." In coffee, the quadrupling of yields surely owes a significant amount to donor-promoted initiatives.

Collaborative efforts by USAID, the World Bank, the Inter-American Development Bank, and the Costa Rican Government in rural roads, public health, education, electricity, telephones, and water and sewerage also touched the communities, at least indirectly. In more recent years, the restoration of macroeconomic stability to the country has provided a more favorable environment for people in the villages. . . . The creation of alternative sources of employment, such as at the baseball factory in Turrialba where a dozen women from both villages work, is a legacy of donor-assisted export and investment promotion efforts.[41]

Fox concludes that future development assistance projects should (1) incorporate value/belief baseline data that will facilitate subsequent assessment of cultural change; and (2) adapt the CMRP typology for analysis of impact to assure that project design promotes the progressive rather than the resistant factors.

WHETHER DESIGNED SPECIFICALLY to modify culture or as a by-product of activities with a different primary focus, the foregoing examples, along with the case studies of the two preceding chapters, all provide valuable lessons in formulating guidelines for progressive cultural change—the focus of the concluding chapter.

9

Conclusion: Guidelines for Progressive Cultural Change

THE VAST MAJORITY OF PARTICIPANTS in the CMRP agree that the cultural dimension of human progress has been neglected by the government officials and development institutions who bear the principal responsibility for guiding the policies and programs whose goal is the greater freedom and well-being of humankind. The same is true of other institutions—particularly religious, educational, and the media—that influence popular values, beliefs, and attitudes. None of the CMRP participants believes that the integration of cultural factors into policies and programs will bring about instant development. But most of us do believe that by incorporating culture into the mix of factors that shape development, the *pace* of progress can be accelerated toward the goals of the U.N. Universal Declaration of Human Rights.

I also want to restate a basic CMRP premise: cultural change, like democracy and market economics, cannot be imposed from the outside, except in the most extraordinary circumstances, for example, in Japan after its unconditional surrender in 1945. Progress endures only when it is driven chiefly from within. To be sure, the CMRP success stories underscore the importance of openness to the ideological, political, technological, and institutional lessons learned by more advanced societies. But until a critical mass of awareness emerges in a society, external pressures for change are likely to be resisted. As Daniel

Latouche emphasized in his paper on Quebec, "There can be no cultural transformation without the widely-accepted belief that there is indeed something 'wrong' with the [culture] and without widespread discussion of how to fix it. For culture to matter, there must [first be] a realization that it needs fixing."[1]

Iraq is a case in point. The January 2005 elections and October 2005 constitutional referendum in Iraq have been heralded by the Bush administration as a major turning point toward democracy, or even as the arrival of democracy. I remind the reader of similar "transformations" that have taken place in Latin America in the presence of American troops (for example, in the Dominican Republic, Haiti, Nicaragua in the early decades of the twentieth century, and again in the Dominican Republic in 1966) or with a substantial American civil presence (as in Haiti in 1990). In none of these three countries has democracy been fully consolidated. Haiti is a good deal closer to anarchy than to democracy. And viewed toward the end of 2005, the same might be said for Iraq.

I want to reiterate an observation from chapter 7: cultural change and "development," as it has come to be defined over the past half-century, are closely connected. Initiatives to promote cultural change are likely to promote political, economic, or social development; and initiatives designed to promote development in the traditional sense may also promote progressive cultural change.

I also want to refer to a key finding in the preceding chapter's evaluation of INDEHU: a single instrument like the INDEHU program cannot by itself divert the powerful momentum of culture. What is necessary is a coordinated program that may involve, among other things, child rearing, religion and religious reform, education and education reform, the media, civic groups, and above all, strong political leadership committed to the democratic-capitalist model. Clearly, cost must be taken into consideration, and priorities have to be worked out. It will not, for example, be possible to support education equally at all levels. But our guidelines do offer some building blocks to develop such a program.

I. Child rearing and education

A. End illiteracy

Illiteracy is the single greatest obstacle to progressive cultural change. It enshrouds the human capacity to learn, to change, and it nurtures the perpetuation of traditional culture. Human progress lags the most in societies, above all in Islamic countries and Africa, with high illiteracy levels. In the large majority of these countries, female literacy is sharply lower than male literacy. Yet in terms of cultural change, it can be argued that female literacy is more important than male literacy because of the crucial role women play in child rearing. It is highly relevant that females are more literate than males in Botswana.

The argument that low literacy levels are an inevitable consequence of generalized poverty is not convincing. Its relative poverty notwithstanding, Scotland was the most literate country in the world by the end of the eighteenth century. High levels of literacy were also achieved by the Nordic countries while they were still poor. Japan had substantially eliminated illiteracy by the early years of the twentieth century, long before it could be considered affluent. Chilean men and women were more literate than other Latin Americans in the nineteenth century. Islamic Indonesia's per capita income is one-fifth of Islamic Saudi Arabia's, yet Indonesia is far more literate.

I don't know how much money and time would be necessary to eradicate illiteracy, but I am confident that, given high priority by governments in poor countries and international development institutions, the goal could be substantially reached in a generation, two at the most. Ending illiteracy must embrace plans to assure first a complete primary education for everyone. Because poor parents often keep their children out of school either to earn money or help at home, government grants to parents to keep their children in school may be necessary. Such a program has been instituted by the Da Silva government in Brazil.[2]

Then the goal must be a complete secondary education for everyone; and finally, access for everyone to post-secondary education.

B. Study, then modify child-rearing techniques

Traditional child-rearing patterns are sustained from generation to generation, in large measure because the only preparation most young parents have is the recollection of the way their parents raised them. A friend, Mary Hansen, relates a highly relevant anecdote. She overheard her daughter, then three years old, repeatedly scolding her doll. Mary thought, "She sounds just like my mother." But the daughter had grown up overseas without any significant contact with her grandmother. Yet, as Luis Diego Herrera makes clear, traditional child rearing may inculcate values, beliefs, and attitudes that are obstacles to the progress of the individual and the society, not only through *what* the parent teaches the child but also through *how* the parent relates to the child.

In his CMRP paper "Culture, Values, and the Family," Jerome Kagan suggests what parents can do to strengthen the values that facilitate democracy, social justice, and prosperity.

In order to promote the ethic of democracy, the family must encourage a sense of personal agency in their children by providing experiences that allow sons and daughters to feel they have some power to affect the family. Put simply, consulting the child, asking her opinions, and when appropriate taking the child's preferences into account, should strengthen the child's sense of agency. Psychologists call parents who adopt these practices authoritatively democratic.

The assumption that all members of a community should have equal power to decide on the future of the community is harder to promote than a sense of agency because this premise requires the child to understand the difference between economic gain and symbolic signs of status, on the one hand, and political privilege, on the other. . . . Unlike a sense of agency, which can emerge before age 7, this more abstract idea has to wait until the years before puberty, when the maturing cognitive abilities make it possible for youth to understand that the vitality of the community should sometimes have priority over the desires of the individual. Promotion of this goal requires conversation . . . and is accomplished less easily through parental rewards and punishments.

Nature awarded all children, save a very small proportion with a special biology, the ability to empathize with those in physical or psychic distress. An empathic concern over a whining puppy or a crying infant comes easily to all children. This sentiment, which Hume assumed was the foundation of human morality, represents a significant foundation on which the teaching of social justice rests.

If children are reminded regularly of the deprivation experienced by disenfranchised citizens, they should, by adolescence, create a concern for strangers in need. It helps, of course, if the parents not only promote this ethic in conversation, but also display it in their behavior.

The attainment of economic prosperity requires an ethic that celebrates the intrinsic value of personal accomplishment; that is, a work ethic in which individual accomplishment brings virtue. . . . This standard, common in

North America and parts of Europe, requires suppressing worry over "being better than another."[3]

Parenting education, particularly at the secondary and post-secondary levels, offers a promising instrument for promoting child-rearing techniques that strengthen progressive values. Sharon Lynn Kagan and Amy Lowenstein make clear that although values, beliefs, and attitudes have generally not been addressed by parenting educators, there is no reason why they can't or shouldn't be.

C. Reform education

In their paper "Schooling Open Societies in Latin America," Fernando Reimers and Eleonora Villegas-Reimers suggest six objectives for educational reform in Latin America that will strengthen the values that make democracy work. Their paper has substantial relevance for Africa, the Islamic world, and other lagging areas. The six objectives apply principally to primary and secondary education.

1. A broad commitment to educating all children at high levels.
2. Schools that are themselves open communities with freer communication among administrators, faculty, and students.
3. Stronger relationships between schools and communities.
4. Teachers who are well prepared; who can serve as democratic models; and who value freedom and diversity.
5. Civic education curriculum.
6. Practical experiences to learn well and to learn to make choices.

A seventh objective is the integration of character education into curricula, an initiative discussed by Thomas Lickona in his paper "Character Education: Restoring Virtue to the Mission of Schools."

Finally, I would urge independent assessments of the way that universities are succeeding or failing to meet their responsibilities to produce the leaders, professionals, and technical experts that modern democratic-capitalist societies need. Many of these universities do not serve their societies well, and good universities are crucial to progress.

D. Learn English

The Singaporean and Irish miracles and India's recent economic surge owe a lot to their English-language capabilities. American capital has dominated the heavy flow of foreign investment into Ireland in recent decades, and this was partly owing to Ireland's being a nation of native speakers of English. India's dynamic outsourcing sector has been made possible by the large number of Indians who speak English. In his CMRP paper "India: How a Rich Nation Became Poor and Will Be Rich Again," Gurcharan Das makes the point and underscores the irony: "Ever since the British left, Indians constantly complained against the English language. But in the 1990s this carping seemed to die, and quietly, without ceremony English became one of the Indian languages. . . . Young Indians in the new middle class think of English as a skill, like Windows."[4]

A similar irony is found in Quebec. In their zeal to protect the French language, the Québecois separatist leaders have promoted a campaign to suppress English. Yet the English facility of many Québecois is a valuable resource, for example in the expansion of trade with and tourism from the neighboring United States, not to mention Anglophone Canada. That most people in the Nordic countries are fluent in English has facilitated the access of those countries to the world market in goods and ideas. The left-of-center government of Chile recently announced a program to make Chile bilingual in Spanish and English. The *New York Times* quotes the Chilean Minister of Education Sergio Bitar: "We have some of the most advanced commercial accords in the world, but that is not enough. We know our lives are linked more than ever to an international presence, and if you can't speak English, you can't sell and you can't learn."[5]

English is a resource for both economic development *and* cultural change. If learning from the experience of more advanced societies is crucial to progressive cultural change, command of English today is extremely valuable.

II. Religious reform

A. Islam

Islam is the chief source of values, beliefs, and attitudes for most of its believers. In this respect, Islam is unique: no other religion of worldwide scope today so powerfully influences the culture of its faithful. In the West, with the exception of the United States, the influence of religion has given way to secularism—a secularism, to be sure, that has been influenced profoundly by earlier religiosity, as in the Nordic countries. But the cultural power exerted long ago by religion in Scandinavia is very much a reality in the Islamic world today. And whereas Lutheranism was a force for progress (for example, with respect to universal education and a rigorous ethical code) in the Nordic countries, Islam today, with a few exceptions like Turkey and Indonesia, is not. Unlike medieval Hellenized Islam and even the nineteenth-century Islam of reform and liberal thought, contemporary Safist-Wahhabis and what Bassam Tibi refers to as "Islamist" or radical Islam, reject learning from others.

While there are numerous factors that lie behind the slow progress of the Islamic countries, a major contributor has been clerical interpretations of the Quran that have transmitted fatalistic dogma, permitted adoption of scientific and technological advances from outside but closed the door to the liberalizing cultural forces that made these advances possible, and perpetuated the subordination and illiteracy of women. This condition is not uniform throughout the Islamic world, as Turkey and Indonesia demonstrate. But it is the predominant condition. As Islam has steadily slipped from its early leadership in the arts and sciences, especially so with the collapse of the once-powerful Ottoman Empire, most Muslims today are constantly reminded of how far behind the West and East Asia they have fallen. This insistent insult to self-respect is, in my view, central to the motivation of Osama bin Laden and his followers.

Bassam Tibi's CMRP papers on Islam and Egypt, Robert Hefner's papers on Islam and Indonesia, and the two UNDP Arab Human Development Reports are crystal clear on one point: the reform of Islam is indispensable for accelerated progress toward the goals of democratic governance, social justice, and prosperity. Key elements of reform include: openness to the values, ideas, and institutions of the non-Islamic world; tolerance of other religions; and a broad commitment to excellence, education, and gender equality.

B. Roman Catholicism

As Michael Novak points out in his CMRP paper, the number of people who identify themselves as Catholics is growing with the Church's many new adherents in Africa. But in Europe and Latin America, the number of practicing Catholics is declining, and in Latin America, tens of millions of nominal Catholics have converted to Evangelical and Pentecostal Protestantism. It is highly significant that the transformations of Italy, Spain, Ireland, and Quebec have all involved a substantial loss of influence by the Church.

As I documented in chapter 4, Catholic countries are generally outperformed by Protestant countries in most of the ten indicators that measure democracy, prosperity, social justice, trust, and corruption. That is also true even when assessing only the advanced democracies. But the most compelling evidence of the need for reform in the Catholic Church is the condition of Latin America. Although the Church can take some credit for the advance of electoral democracy in the region in recent decades, it must also assume some responsibility for Latin America's most troubling problems:

- With the exception of Chile, economic growth rates have been insufficient to offer hope of ending poverty.
- Distribution of wealth, income, land, and opportunity is among the most inequitable in the world.
- Levels of trust are among the lowest in the world.
- Levels of corruption are high (Chile being a salient exception).
- Levels of criminal activity, including violent crime, are high, symbolized by the current epidemic of kidnappings, many of short duration and involving petty ransoms.

Michael Novak makes a compelling case for an unqualified commitment by the Church to democratic capitalism. (We are reminded of the title of Miguel Basáñez's CMRP paper on Mexico—"The Camel and the Needle.") Minority elements of the Church support Novak's views, but there are also influential Church leaders driven by utopian socialist ideology who are among those attacking "neoliberal" (read "capitalist") economic policies in Latin America. The irony is that while the Church continues its preference for the poor, Catholic Latin America has produced vastly more poor people than Protestant Canada and the United States, a fact to which the heavy flow of poor Latinos *al norte* is eloquent testimony. And tens of millions of poor Latin Americans have been drawn to Protestant religions that preach a message similar to that of Deng Xiaoping: "To get rich is glorious."

But there is another important aspect of Latin America's problems for which the Church must also assume some responsibility and for which new approaches by the Church could be extremely helpful: the ethical issues underlying Latin America's generally dismal performance with respect to social justice, trust, corruption, and crime. At the root of these phenomena is a too-elastic ethical code that tolerates antisocial behavior—a failure to inculcate the Golden Rule. To be sure, there are other factors in play besides religion, American pop culture—for example, violent movies and rap—among them. But that the Church bears some responsibility is underscored by the Latin Americans, predominantly poor and female, who convert to Protestantism not only because they identify it with prosperity but also because they believe that it will keep their men out of the bars and bordellos and provide a measure of family stability in which their children will have a chance for a better life.

Were the Catholic Church to take a leadership role in a campaign to promote a rigorous ethical standard in Latin America and elsewhere, it could make a huge contribution to progress as well as to its own relevance and credibility.

C. Orthodox Christianity

Orthodox Christianity, an offshoot of Roman Catholicism that became fully independent of Rome in 1054, is the dominant religion in Russia, Greece, Ukraine, Belarus, Romania, and several smaller countries in Eastern Europe and western Asia, including the Republic of Georgia. In his CMRP paper on Georgia, Irakli Chkonia lists a number of progress-resistant characteristics often associated with Orthodox Christianity: "submission to authority, discouragement of dissent and initiative, discouragement of innovation and social change, submissive collectivism rather than individualism, emphasis on ethnic cohesion rather than supranational relationships, isolationism and particularism, spiritual determinism and fatalism. Also embraced in the pattern is the aversion of Orthodoxy to the non-Orthodox Christian West and the Islamic World, political rivals of the past and the present."[6]

But the CMRP papers by Chkonia, Archie Brown on Russia, and Georges Prevelakis on Greece emphasize both significant national variations in Orthodoxy and the considerable diminution of its influence and prevalence over the past century, consistent with secularizing trends in Europe more generally. Brown observes that "the Orthodox religious legacy is almost certainly of less political significance in contemporary Russia than the seven decades of Communist rule, followed by some fifteen years of political pluralism. . . ."[7]

As in other religions, both reformist and conservative currents are found in Orthodoxy, and the two vie for dominance, particularly in Russia. Nikolas Gvosdev concludes that "the foundation for reform [of Orthodoxy] exists, but it is not yet clear that construction will begin."[8] He subsequently elaborated: "Orthodox Christianity today is in a pre–Vatican II state; perhaps on the verge of reforms designed to make relevant its ancient traditions—but not yet clear that it will move in that direction."[9]

The circumstances are similar to those of Roman Catholicism. The influence of the Church is generally in decline. Reform of Orthodox Christianity aimed at support of democracy and market economics could help reverse the erosion of both in Putin's Russia at this crucial moment, as well as having similar positive effects in other Orthodox countries and enhancing the relevance and credibility of the religion.

D. Hinduism

Hinduism has been labelled "anti-progress" by Max Weber and Gunnar Myrdal, among others. Fatalism, the caste system, and the subordination and exploitation of women are the chief characteristics of Hinduism that critics have highlighted. But as Pratap Bhanu Mehta stresses in his CMRP essay on Hinduism, the religion is a good deal more flexible and diverse than many critics appreciate, and it has demonstrated a considerable capacity for change. Moreover, India's democratic politics have had a powerful influence on Hindu practice, for example in breaking down the caste system.

Nonetheless, Hindu leaders might ponder the CMRP typology with a view to doctrinal modifications that support India's quest for modernity.

E. Buddhism

"Buddhist theory for the most part remains resolutely a theory about individual life and practice. In a strictly formal sense, Buddhism and democracy are mutually independent. Buddhism neither precludes nor entails liberal democracy; liberal democracy neither precludes nor entails Buddhism," observes philosophy professor Jay Garfield of Smith

College.[10] Yet there are elements in Buddhist doctrine and practice that are clearly compatible with democracy, above all the egalitarian nature of the *sangha*, the ideal Buddhist community in which seniority matters but not class, caste, wealth, or prestige.

Buddhism expert Christal Whelan, in her CMRP paper on Buddhism, emphasizes the vast variety of Buddhist interpretations and practices, some supporting modernization, others resisting it. That variety is reflected in the performance of Buddhist nations: Freedom House ranks Myanmar (Burma) with the least free countries like North Korea and Cuba. Yet Mongolia and Thailand are listed as "free" countries. Of the seven Buddhist countries included in the chapter 4 analysis, only Thailand has experienced rapid economic development, and that is disproportionately attributable to Thailand's Chinese minority.

There is, of course, a major question as to the extent of contemporary Buddhist influence on politics and economics, considering that so many other forces, globalization among them, are also in play. It seems reasonable to conclude that "reform" of Buddhism is unlikely—and unlikely to have much influence on the paths followed by the countries in which the religion predominates.

F. Confucianism, Judaism, Protestantism

These are the three "religions" (once again, Confucianism is not a religion but an ethical code) whose value systems best correspond with the progress-prone column of the CMRP typology—the "universal progress culture" described in chapter 2. All three promote the ideas/values of individual control of destiny, achievement, education, diligence/work ethic, merit, saving, and social responsibility, although in different degrees. And those values tend to persist even in the face of secularization, as the Nordic countries demonstrate.

All three will confront sooner or later the costs of success in terms of the erosion of the traditional values. This is John Wesley's dilemma. The progress-promoting values produce so much success, so much wealth, that they may undermine themselves, for example diluting the work ethic, frugality, the quest for achievement. As David Martin suggests in his "Note to Mainstream Protestants," success and affluence may also produce disdain for those poorer co-religionists who dedicate themselves to the old values, the old religion.

To be sure, the largest Confucian society, China, remains a one-party dictatorship, lacking in political legitimacy and sustaining itself in power largely through the success of its economic policies: liberalizing markets, encouraging foreign investment, and maintaining stability, policies normally associated with the capitalism that was once its despised enemy. And Singapore has thus far avoided the democratic transition experienced by its fellow "dragons," South Korea and Taiwan. But I believe that Francis Fukuyama is right in his prediction, in *The End of History*, that high rates of economic development will produce a populace accustomed to the freedom of the marketplace, inevitably leading to demands for political freedom.

The general lesson, however, is clear: these cultures share values that work in very different settings. Lagging societies must find ways of strengthening those same values.

G. Animist religions

In his chapter in *Culture Matters*, Daniel Etounga-Manguelle says: "A society in which magic and witchcraft flourish today is a sick society ruled by tension, fear, and moral disorder. Sorcery is a costly mechanism for managing conflict and preserving the status quo, which is, importantly, what African culture is about."[11] Animist religions, in which what happens in life is determined by a pantheon of capricious spirits, present an extreme case of progress-resistant culture, as we have seen in Haitian Voodoo, the roots of which are in Africa. Animist religions are most widely practiced in Africa, although they are also found in the Western hemisphere both in Haitian Voodoo and Brazilian Santería.[12]

The guideline with respect to animism is: encourage conversion of those practicing animist religions to more progress-prone religions.

III. Governments

A. Raise awareness of the key role of culture

Political leaders should be mindful of the implications of their policies, programs, and public appearances for the strengthening of progressive values. (Bogotá's recent progress under the leadership of two enlightened mayors, described in chapter 8, is a case in point.) Leaders should educate the public on the key role progressive values play in the achievement of the goals of a society, and they should sustain a continuing dialogue with the media over the role of the latter in promoting progressive values.

B. Look for historic/mythical precedents for cultural change

As the cases of Botswana, Georgia, Novgorod, and Quebec demonstrate, it will be easier to strengthen progressive values if the initiative involves at least an appearance of continuity—"the creation of new mythologies based on selective memories taken from the past," in Daniel Latouche's words.[13]

C. Be alert to developments in other societies that may be applied beneficially at home

Develop an institutionalized means of monitoring global advances in science, technology, policies, institutions, and cultural change, for example, a coordinating council of government ministries, universities, and think tanks.

D. Give highest priority to education and education reform (See section I-C, page 210)

E. Pursue open economic policies and encourage foreign investment

Several of the transformations, for example, Spain and Ireland, were either driven or facilitated by open economic policies. (In the cases of Japan, Korea, and Taiwan, the opening was more selective.) Such policies should produce more rapid economic development. Higher, steadily growing levels of prosperity are reflected not only in higher standards of living and more effective government action (for example, in education reform); they also help to create a national psychology of optimism and opportunity that sap the strength of fatalism and strengthen the entrepreneurial vocation so central to development. Foreign investment not only produces economic benefits (most of the time) but also often transfers new technologies, new ideas, and new values.

F. Build a competent, honest, respected civil service

Aside from the performance benefits that attend competence and honesty in the public sector, an efficient, professional civil service plays an important role in extending a society's radius of identification and trust—in government and in the broader society. High-quality bureaucracies have contributed much to the success of Sweden, Botswana, Chile, and Singapore, among others.

G. Encourage and facilitate home ownership

Home ownership played a key role in the transformations of Spain and Singapore. In both cases, housing policies were consciously designed to give people a stake in the society, to create a middle class, and to strengthen the family.

H. Regularize property ownership

The advantages that attend Hernando de Soto's emphasis on real property security through legalized registration programs that facilitate market transactions are not only economic. Security and marketability of property are also likely to nurture optimism and the entrepreneurial vocation.

I. Institutionalize periodic surveys of values, beliefs, and attitudes

Miguel Basáñez has created a survey instrument for the CMRP that will enable the development of a national value profile tied to the 25-point typology. Periodic resurveys will permit assessments of cultural change that should be helpful in guiding public policy decisions.

IV. Development Assistance Institutions

A. Confront culture

Development assistance institutions, both multilateral and bilateral, have thus far failed to address cultural change, chiefly because anthropologists and other social scientists committed to cultural relativism have dominated policy. That some cultures are more prone to progress than others is a message that goes down very hard in development circles, all evidence to the contrary notwithstanding. This obstacle is magnified by the politics of the international institutions, where both donors and recipients have a voice and where it is much more interpersonally comfortable, and less threatening to self-esteem, to view the countries lagging behind as either the victims of the more successful countries or as merely having failed so far to find the proper content and mix of policies, incentives, and institutions. Evidence of this intellectual/emotional obstacle is the response to the two UNDP Arab Human Development Reports, both of which focus on the need for cultural change and have provoked outspoken criticism from many Arabs.

I can only hope that the persistent, widespread dissatisfaction and frustration with the sluggish pace of progress in most poor countries will cause development professionals to ponder the messages of *Culture Matters* and *The Central Liberal Truth*. The considerable intelligence, creativity, and dedication of development professionals over the past half-century have not succeeded in transforming the large majority of poor, authoritarian societies. Where transformations have occurred, they either have been nurtured by cultures that contain progress-prone elements (for example, the Confucian societies of East Asia) or have been cases where cultural change was central to the transformation (for example, Spain, Ireland, and Quebec).

B. Integrate cultural change analysis into research programs, strategies, and project design

Development-assistance institutions should acquire the doctrine and staff that will enable them to help countries integrate cultural change into their policies and programs. They should be prepared to provide technical assistance for baseline value/belief/attitude surveys that can subsequently be reiterated to assess change, and they should integrate cultural change into their research agendas, including economic analysis, along the lines of Yoshihara Kunio's discussion of Japan. The development-assistance institutions should also examine the impact that the projects they support will have on values/beliefs/attitudes and be mindful of such impact in project design. Project evaluations should address the impact on culture along with the other objectives of a project.

C. Consider establishing a network of quality universities under international institutional auspices

The discussion in chapter 8 of the positive impact of American and other universities overseas, in terms both of quality education and cultural change, suggests the desirability of establishing a network of universities, dedicated to excellence, in lagging areas. Such a network might be particularly helpful in the Islamic world and Africa. The United Nations would be one possible home for the network, the World Bank/IMF another.

V. Universities

A. Confront culture

Like the development institutions, universities around the world have avoided addressing culture, because of the dominance of cultural relativism in the social sciences. The *Culture Matters* view is politically incorrect and often associated—incorrectly—with a right-wing agenda. I am aware of only three courses that address the relationship between culture and development: one offered by Samuel Huntington at Harvard; another by Harvey Nelson at the University of South Florida; the third by me at the Fletcher School at Tufts. On the other hand, *Culture Matters* is in use in universities throughout the United States, and there may be other such courses, or parts of courses, that address the issue.

It should be crystal clear from *The Central Liberal Truth* that the CMRP agenda is not conservative. I know of no one associated with the CMRP who believes in cultural determinism—that is, that culture is immutable, perhaps even genetically rooted. All of us believe that culture is acquired, that it changes, and that cultural change may offer a vehicle for accelerated progress toward the elimination of tyranny, injustice, and poverty. If we are right, it behooves the universities, like the development institutions, to take culture and cultural change seriously. That means developing courses and research programs on the role of culture and cultural change in human progress. Child rearing is one of several aspects of the CMRP in which universities should take the lead.

VI. The media

THE POWER OF THE MEDIA, above all television, to influence not only the views and opinions of people but also their values is enormous. Mariano Grondona and Carlos Alberto Montaner argue, from their own considerable experience as columnists, that the influence of opinion writers is limited by the tendency of most people to read, listen to, or watch only those with whom they agree. But there are two other dimensions of the media whose impact can be far greater: news and entertainment.

The degree of objectivity with which news is presented is a central issue. Because reporters and editors are human beings, complete objectivity is unattainable, and the substance of news stories and the prominence given to them will inevitably reflect bias. The problem becomes acute when bias becomes policy, and the newspaper or television channel pursues an ideological "line" that confounds objectivity and may reinforce both prejudice and error. This is the case in the Arab world today with respect to al Jazeera, which former CNN President Reese Schonfeld describes (in his CMRP essay on entertainment media) as "respectable but slanted."[14] Al Jazeera's reporting—not to mention the violently anti-American, anti-Semitic, anti-Israel programming of al Manar, a Hezbollah network recently banned in France and the United States—reinforces the prevalent Arab "victim" self-image that presents such a huge obstacle to progress in the Arab world, and in doing so, runs contrary to the internal reform thrust of the two UNDP Arab Human Development reports. In sharp contrast, Schonfeld points to highly popular talent shows broadcast by Lebanon's Future TV and the Lebanon Broadcast Company in which viewers participate through voting to decide the winners. The message of these shows is one of modernity, upward mobility, and participation.

A similar competition in values is found today in China. The domination of the media by the government is threatened by all the foreign channels beamed through satellites, not to mention the Falun Gong's New Tang Dynasty Televison (NTDT) network, which, Schonfeld notes, "features Hollywood movies from the thirties through the fifties, partly because they are affordable but, more importantly, because they conform to NTDT's avowed intention to promote democratic cultural change [so that] 'more people can enjoy peace and freedom and live harmoniously among different races and beliefs.'"[15]

Schonfeld suggests that ideally a government in a developing nation committed to the goals of the UN Universal Declaration of Human Rights would ban commercial TV channels for at least twenty years and would rely on a public broadcasting network whose programs would be designed to communicate the values that nurture progress toward the goals of the UN Declaration. Some will judge Schonfeld's approach as unacceptable in a free society and fraught with the danger of abuse of the TV monopoly for political ends, citing, perhaps, Myanmar and Russia, where chiefs of state have renationalized private networks and maintain strangleholds on television content. But in a setting of truly inspired leadership—say the Botswana of Seretse Khama and Quett Masire—a dominant role for government television might well make sense. (Interestingly, the Botswana leaders emphasized radio because it was so much more widely accessible.)

What about the advanced democracies? In Britain, Germany, Sweden, and Japan, public networks still dominate TV viewing. In other Western countries, they have been increasingly marginalized. The tendency is toward privatization and competition, which is surely consistent with the sacrosanct principle of freedom of the press. There are, however, risks that either public or private television may be sending messages that undermine the values that nurture democracy, prosperity, and justice. One possible innovation would be an institutionalized continuing dialogue on the role and impact of the media on values involving people concerned about national well-being and progress from government, the private media, and universities/research institutions.

VII. The Private Sector

WE HAVE TOUCHED ON TWO OPPORTUNITIES for the private sector to play a part in the promotion of progressive values: philanthropy and participatory management.

A. Philanthropy

Philanthropy has made a huge contribution to progress in the United States, through, for example, financial support of universities, libraries, hospitals, and museums. But philanthropy also has an important cultural effect by reinforcing the national social fabric. Philanthropic traditions encourage the affluent to reflect and act on their sense of obligation to the broader society and its values, for example by making a university education, and the upward mobility it implies, possible for people who would otherwise not be able to afford it. On the

other hand, the beneficiaries of philanthropy see new horizons opening up to them that reinforce their sense of identification with the society and its values.

The Harvard workshop mentioned in chapter 8 developed some
helpful recommendations for the promotion of philanthropy:

- Enhance awareness of philanthropic practices through mobilization of the media.
- Work toward better legal frameworks that provide incentives
  for philanthropy.
- Strengthen alliances among government, business, and non-
  governmental organizations.
- Encourage civic engagement through "public and other policies that promote a culture of generosity and civic participation. . . . [W]orking to create a more favorable environment for
  philanthropy requires a major cultural and psychological
  change."[16]

B. Participatory management

In most poor countries, the authoritarianism found in government is
repeated in all human relationships. That is particularly true of relationships in the workplace. The boss's word is law, and anything other
than blind obedience can result in severe consequences.

Modern participatory management, of the kind we now associate
with Japanese industry, Toyota, for example, can precipitate cultural
change. The manager who explains rather than commands, who encourages communication in his organization, who encourages and rewards initiative, can create an environment in which, as Argentine
writer Tomás Roberto Fillol notes, "workers feel they are recognized
by their superiors; responsibilities and a certain degree of autonomy
are . . . delegated by all levels of management; all levels of personnel
identify with their jobs, the enterprise, and its goals; workers willingly
cooperate with each other and with all levels of management in the
pursuit of personal, but common, advantages; individuals are free to
discuss problems arising from their jobs with superiors and workmates
and willingly take advantage of such opportunities."[17]

Such has been the experience in Peru's Furukawa Corporation (see
chapter 8), where there is strong evidence that enlightened manage-

ment has led to a new and more progressive set of values on the part of the Furukawa employees.

Conclusion

WHAT WE HAVE LEARNED FROM THE CULTURE MATTERS RESEARCH PROJECT is that culture does matter, particularly in the long run. Daniel Patrick Moynihan was right: Politics *can* change culture, enabling more rapid progress. Societies *can* be substantially transformed within a generation. We have also been reminded that numerous other factors are in play, geography and natural environment prominent among them, and that culture can be trumped, for example, by adverse ideologies, as in the case of North Korea. But we have also seen how powerful culture can be, both as a facilitator of or an obstacle to progress.

The anguish of the American adventure in Iraq, the chaos of Haiti, genocide and famine in Africa, and the huge flow of poor people seeking a better life in rich countries are among the constant reminders of the enormity of the task of creating a more democratic, just, and prosperous world. Fifty years ago, the experts, mostly economists, were confident that poverty, authoritarianism, and injustice would have been substantially eradicated by the end of the twentieth century. That optimism was unfounded, and their prescriptions, while helpful, have fallen far short. So have the prescriptions of other social scientists, who have since influenced development theory and practice. Those who have advocated attention to the role of culture and cultural change in human progress have found increasing receptivity to their arguments but have inevitably come up against the question, "OK, we believe you, but what can be done about it?"

While there is still a lot to learn, *The Central Liberal Truth* offers some strategies and tools that can help convert cultural theory into beneficial practice.

Notes

Preface

1. I was the deputy director and then acting director of the USAID mission during the period 1965–68. In the other four countries, I was the director.
2. Teodoro Moscoso, "The Will to Economic Development," in *The Alliance for Progress—A Retrospective,* ed. L. Ronald Scheman (New York: Praeger 1988), 86.
3. The book was published in English as Carlos Rangel, *The Latin Americans: Their Love-Hate Relationship with the United States* (New York: Harcourt Brace Jovanovich, 1977).
4. In June of 2005, Nicholas Wade of the *New York Times* reported on a study by three researchers at the University of Utah that presents evidence that higher-than-average IQs of Ashkenazic Jews are the result of a centuries-long process of genetic selection ("Researchers Say Intelligence and Disease May Be Linked in Ashkenazic Genes," *New York Times,* June 3, 2005, A21). But one wonders how the comparably high IQs of East Asians would then be explained.
5. Brief biographic sketches of participants appear in the Appendix.

Introduction

1. Alexis de Tocqueville, *Democracy in America* (London: David Campbell Publishers/ Everyman's Library, 1994), 322–23.
2. From the Bush 2002 National Security Strategy, quoted by David M. Kennedy in "What 'W' Owes to 'WW,'" *The Atlantic* (March 2005): 36.

3. Jared Diamond, *Guns, Germs, and Steel* (New York: W. W. Norton, 1997), 417–18.

4. Lawrence Harrison and Samuel Huntington, eds., *Culture Matters: How Values Shape Human Progress* (New York: Basic Books, 2000), xv.

5. Lawrence Harrison, *Underdevelopment Is a State of Mind—The Latin American Case* (Cambridge, Mass.: Harvard Center for International Affairs, 1985), xvii.

6. "Norway Looks for Ways to Keep Its Workers on the Job," *New York Times*, July 25, 2004, 4.

7. See Ronald Inglehart, *Modernization and Postmodernization* (Princeton: Princeton University Press, 1997), 325.

8. Arthur W. Lewis, *The Theory of Economic Growth* (Homewood, Ill.: Richard D. Irwin, Inc., 1955), 14.

9. Piero Gleijeses, *Shattered Hope: The Guatemalan Revolution and the United States 1944–54* (Princeton: Princeton University Press, 1991), 89: "Managed with ruthlessness, skill, and ambition, [United Fruit] earned its sobriquet: the Octopus."

10. Lucian Pye, with Mary Pye, *Asian Power and Politics—The Cultural Dimensions of Authority* (Cambridge, Mass.: Belknap Press of Harvard University Press, 1985), 4.

11. Bernard Lewis, "The West and the Middle East," *Foreign Affairs* (January–February 1997): 121.

12. David Landes, "Culture Makes Almost All the Difference," *Culture Matters*, 7.

13. Vijayendra Rao and Michael Walton, *Culture and Public Action* (Stanford, Calif.: Stanford University Press, 2004), 4.

14. Samuel P. Huntington, *The Clash of Civilizations and the Remaking of World Order* (New York: Simon and Schuster, 1997).

15. Geert Hofstede has articulated a view of the sources of human behavior that is instructive here. In his milestone work *Culture's Consequences* (London: SAGE Publications, 2001), Hofstede presents a triangle with three horizontal sectors that describe the sources of human behavior: the foundation level is labeled "universal"—human nature; the middle level is labeled "collective"—culture; and the apex level is labeled "individual"—personality.

16. United Nations Development Program and Arab Fund for Economic and Social Development, *Arab Human Development Report 2002* (New York: UNDP, 2002), 8.

17. Hefner e-mail to Harrison, April 28, 2004.

18. See, for example, Geert Hofstede, *Culture's Consequences: Comparing Values, Behaviors, Institutions and Organizations Across Nations* (London: SAGE Publications, 2003).

19. Richard Shweder, "Moral Maps, 'First World' Conceits, and the New Evangelists," in *Culture Matters*, 163.

20. The Declaration did not address the environment, which has since become a major development issue, witness the frequently used term "*sustainable development*."

21. Shweder, "Moral Maps," 164.

22. Ibid., 167.
23. Ibid., 164.
24. Rhoda E. Howard. "Cultural Absolutism and the Nostalgia for Community," *Human Rights Quarterly* 15:2 (May 1993): 315.
25. I did not attend the Shweder lecture. The comment was conveyed to me orally by a friend, Robert Iadicicco, who did.
26. Shweder, "Moral Maps," 172.
27. Daniel Etounga Manguelle, "Does Africa Need a Cultural Adjustment Program?" in *Culture Matters*, 56–77.
28. Ibid., 173.
29. William Easterly, *The Elusive Quest for Growth: Economists' Adventures and Misadventures in the Tropics* (Cambridge, Mass.: MIT Press, 2002); The World Bank and the IMF, *Finance and Development*, March 1994, 51.
30. Chile's exceptionalism is addressed in the CMRP paper on Chile by economist David Hojman. It is summarized in chapter 6.
31. Samuel Huntington, *Who Are We?: The Challenges to America's National Identity* (New York: Simon and Schuster, 2004), 254.
32. Jeffrey D. Sachs, *The End of Poverty: Economic Possibilities for Our Time* (New York: Penguin, 2005).
33. Ibid., 60, 72.
34. Daniel Drezner, "Brother, Can You Spare $195 billion?" *New York Times*, Sunday Book Section, April 24, 2005.
35. Robert Putnam, *Making Democracy Work* (Princeton: Princeton University Press, 1993).
36. José Enrique Rodó, *Ariel* (Madrid: Espasa-Calpe S. A., 1971).
37. Yoshihara Kunio, *Asia Per Capita* (Singapore: Curzon Press, 2000).
38. Ibid., 211–16, passim.
39. Sachs, *The End of Poverty*, 218.
40. See, for example, Jeffrey Sachs, "Don't Know, Should Care" *New York Times*, op-ed page, June 5, 2004, A25.
41. Sachs, *The End of Poverty*, 317.
42. I again take note of the June 3, 2005, *New York Times* report on a study by three researchers at the University of Utah, Gregory Cochran, Jason Hardy, and Henry Harpendina, that presents evidence that higher-than-average IQs of Ashkenazic Jews are the result of a centuries-long process of genetic selection ("Researchers Say Intelligence and Disease May Be Linked in Ashkenazic Genes," A21). But, again, one wonders how the comparably high IQs of East Asians would then be explained.
43. Samuel Huntington, *The Clash of Civilizations and the Remaking of World Order*, 43.

Chapter 1

1. Frank Moya Pons, *Historia Colonial de Santo Domingo* (Santiago de los Caballeros: Universidad Católica Madre y Maestra, 1974).

2. Adam Smith, *Wealth of Nations* (New York: Random House, 1937), 538.
3. The population estimates derive from Frank Moya Pons, *Historia Colonial*, 303–14 passim, and Samuel Hazard, *Santo Domingo Past and Present with a Glance at Hayti* (1873; reprint Santo Domingo: Editoria de Santo Domingo, 1974), 105.
4. I was assigned to the Dominican Republic three weeks after the outbreak of the revolution and remained there until the end of 1968 as the deputy and acting director of the USAID mission.
5. U.S. Census Bureau 2002 data show about 650,000 Dominican-born and 570,000 Haitian-born in the United States.
6. I was the U.S. member of an Organization of American States team that tried to negotiate the return of Jean-Bertrand Aristide to power in 1991–92. I directed the USAID mission to Haiti from 1977 to 1979.
7. United Nations, *Human Development Report 2003* (New York: Oxford University Press, 2003), 238–39.
8. Jeffrey Sachs, "Notes on a New Sociology of Economic Development," in eds. Lawrence Harrison and Samuel Huntington, *Culture Matters* (New York: Basic Books, 2000), 31.
9. Angus Maddison, *The World Economy in the Twentieth Century* (Paris: OECD, 1989), 19.
10. James Leyburn, *The Haitian People* (New Haven: Yale University Press, 1966), 144.
11. Daniel Etounga-Manguelle, "Does Africa Need a Cultural Adjustment Program?" *Culture Matters*, 65–77.
12. Ibid., 71.
13. "Poverty Linked to Voodoo Spirits," *The Baltimore Sun*, November 15, 1981.
14. Quoted in Lawrence Harrison, *Underdevelopment Is a State of Mind* (Cambridge: The Center for International Affairs, Harvard University, 1985), 22.
15. Hazard, *Santo Domingo*, 103.
16. Carlos Rangel, *The Latin Americans: Their Love-Hate Relationship With the United States* (New York: Harcourt Brace Jovanovich, 1977), 193.
17. Sachs mentioned these factors in a debate with me at Harvard in 2001.
18. The principal U.S. motive in both cases, and in the simultaneous intervention in Nicaragua, was the security of the Panama Canal, fearing that the chaotic financial management of all three countries would be seized upon by European creditors, above all Germany, to install military bases that would threaten the Panama Canal, which was inaugurated in 1914.
19. Daniel Etounga-Manguelle, "Does Africa Need a Cultural Adjustment Program?" 75.
20. A member of the Colgate University faculty argued this point when I spoke there in the fall of 2001.
21. This is central to the argument of David Nicholls in *From Dessalines to Duvalier* (New Brunswick, N.J.: Rutgers University Press, 1996).
22. Jared Diamond, *Collapse: How Societies Choose to Fail or Succeed* (New York: Viking, 2005).
23. Ibid., 333.

Chapter 2

1. Mariano Grondona, "A Cultural Typology of Economic Development," in Lawrence Harrison and Samuel Huntington, eds., *Culture Matters* (New York: Basic Books, 2000), 46–7.
2. Memo to author from Robert Hefner, April 28, 2004.
3. Ronald Inglehart, "Testing the Progress Typology," presented at the final Culture Matters Research Project conference at the Fletcher School, Tufts University, March 27–28, 2004, 10.
4. Ibid., 6.
5. Alexis de Tocqueville, *Democracy in America* (London: David Campbell Publishers, 1994), 300. De Tocqueville goes on to assert that Catholicism is also nurturing of democracy so long as it is separated from the state.
6. Bassam Tibi, "Political Innovation in the Gulf: Society and State in a Changing World," presented at the ninth annual conference of the Emirate Center for Strategic Studies, Abu Dhabi, January 10–13, 2004.
7. Inglehart, "Testing the Progress Typology," Table 5.
8. Quoted in Max Weber, *The Protestant Ethic and the Spirit of Capitalism* (New York: HarperCollins Academic, 1992), 175.
9. Tibi, "Political Innovation in the Gulf," 13.
10. Ibid.
11. The words are those of a former Chief Rabbi of Great Britain in J. H. Hertz, ed., *The Pentateuch and Haftorahs* (London: Soncino Press, 1960), 196.
12. George M. Foster, "Peasant Society and the Image of the Limited Good," in Jack M. Potter, May N. Diaz, and George M. Foster, eds., *Peasant Society: A Reader* (Boston: Little Brown, 1967), 304.
13. Weber, *The Protestant Ethic*, 48–50.
14. Ibid., 117.
15. "The price of lateness," *The Economist*, November 22, 2003, 38.
16. James Surowiecki, "The Financial Page—Punctuality Pays," *The New Yorker*, April 5, 2004.
17. See Arthur Herman, *How the Scots Invented the Modern World* (New York: Three Rivers Press, 2001)
18. Hara Hiroko and Managawa Mieko, "Japanese Childhood Since 1600," English manuscript version of a chapter in Jochen Martin and August Nitschke, eds., *Zur Sozialgeschicte der Kindhet* (Freiburg/Munchen: Verlag Karl Alber, 1985), 176.
19. Edward Banfield, *The Moral Basis of a Backward Society* (New York: The Free Press, 1958), and Mariano Grondona, *Las Condiciones Culturales del Desarrollo Económico* (Buenos Aires: Ariel/Planeta, 1999).
20. Inglehart, "Testing the Progress Typology," Table 5.
21. The World Bank, *World Development Indicators 2003* (Washington, D.C.: The World Bank), Table 3.15.
22. Joseph A. Schumpeter, *Capitalism, Socialism, and Democracy* (New York: Harper Bros., 1950), 132.
23. Ibid.

24. See Magnus Blomsröm and Patricio Meller, eds., *Diverging Paths: Comparing a Century of Scandinavian and Latin American Development* (Washington, D.C.: Inter-American Development Bank, 1991).

25. Hernando De Soto, *The Mystery of Capital: Why Capitalism Triumphs in the West and Fails Everywhere Else* (New York: Basic Books, 2000).

26. John L. Stephens, *Incidents of Travel in Central America, Chiapas and Yucatan*, vol. II (New York: Dover Publications, 1969), 13.

27. Mariano Grondona, "A Cultural Typology of Economic Development," *Culture Matters*, 49.

28. United Nations Development Program, *Arab Human Development Report 2003* (New York: United Nations, 2003), 8.

29. Today the Catholic populations of the Netherlands and Switzerland may outnumber the Protestant, but the value systems of both societies have been largely shaped by Protestantism. What matters, as Ronald Inglehart points out in his chapter in *Culture Matters* is "the historical impact . . . on the societies as a whole."

30. Inglehart, "Testing the Progress Typology," 4.

31. Ibid., 2.

32. From "Putting the Good in Good Government," *Washington Post*, November 1, 1998, C5. The writers of the report included Rafael LaPorta, Florencio López de Silanes, and Andrei Schleifer of Harvard and Robert Vishny of the University of Chicago.

33. David Hackett Fischer, *Albion's Seed: Four British Folkways in America* (New York: Oxford University Press, 1989), 24.

34. Edward Banfield, *The Moral Basis of a Backward Society* (New York: The Free Press, 1958).

35. Roberto DaMatta, *A Casa e a Rua* (São Paulo: Editora Brasiliense, 1985), 40.

36. Cited by Francis Fukuyama in *Trust: The Social Virtues and the Creation of Prosperity* (New York: The Free Press, 1995), 10.

37. Robert Putnam, *Making Democracy Work* (Princeton: Princeton University Press, 1993), 170.

38. José Ortega y Gasset, *Invertebrate Spain* (New York: Norton, 1937), 152–53.

39. Daniel Etounga-Manguelle, "Does Africa Need a Cultural Adjustment Program?" in *Culture Matters*, 71.

40. Tu Weiming, "Multiple Modernities: A Preliminary Inquiry into the Implications of East Asian Modernity," in *Culture Matters*, 264.

41. Magnus Blomström and Patricio Meller, *Diverging Paths* (Washington, D.C.: The Inter-American Development Bank, 1991).

42. E-mail to author from Robert Hefner, April 28, 2004.

43. Alfred Stepan, *Arguing Comparative Politics* (New York: Oxford University Press, 2001), 217.

44. Yilmaz Esmer, "Turkey Torn Between Two Civilizations," 13. (Paper prepared for CMRP conference, March 2004.)

45. World Bank, *World Development Indicators 2003*, Table 2.14.

46. Steven A. Camarota, "Birth Rates Among Immigrants in America"— www.cis.org/articles/back1105.html.

Chapter 3

1. The term "cultural black hole" is discussed in Richard Lewis, *The Cultural Imperative* (Yarmouth, Maine: Intercultural Press Inc., 2003), 115–28
2. Harvey Nelsen, "A Cultural Change Model," essay written for Culture Matters Research Project, 5.
3. Ibid.
4. Lawrence Harrison and Samuel Huntington, eds., *Culture Matters: How Values Shape Human Progress* (New York: Basic Books, 2000), 211.
5. Ibid., 212.
6. Ibid., 214.
7. Ibid., 217.
8. Luis Diego Herrera Amighetti, "Parenting Practices in Latin America and Governance: The Case of Costa Rica," essay written for the Culture Matters Research Project, 4.
9. Ibid., 5.
10. Ibid., 6.
11. Ibid., 7.
12. Ibid., 8.
13. Ibid., 8–9
14. D. Baumrind, "Current Patterns of Parental Authority," *Developmental Psychology Monograph*, 4,1, part 2 (1971).
15. Herrera Amighetti, "Parenting Practices in Latin America and Governance: The Case of Costa Rica," 9.
16. Ibid., 9–10.
17. Ibid. 11.
18. Ibid., 11–12
19. UNDP, *Arab Human Development Report 2003* (New York: United Nations, 2003): 3.
20. Ibid., 20.
21. Carlos Alberto Montaner, *Libertad—La Clave de la Prosperidad* (Madrid: Fundación Liberal José Martí, 1994), 140.
22. "Character Education—Restoring Virtue to the Mission of the Schools," essay written for the Culture Matters Research Project, 1, 2.
23. Ibid., 7.
24. Thomas Lickona, *Educating for Character: How Our Schools Can Teach Respect and Responsibility* (New York: Bantam Books, 1991): 395; cited in Herrera, ibid., 12.
25. Richard Niemi and Steven Finkel, "Civic Education and the Development of Civic Knowledge and Attitudes," essay written for the Culture Matters Research Project, 23–25.
26. Fernando Reimers and Eleonora Villegas-Reimers "Schooling Open Societies in Latin America," essay written for the Culture Matters Research Project, 1, 2.
27. F. Reimers, "The Social Context of Educational Evaluation in Latin America," in T. Kellaghan and D. Stufflebeam, eds., *International Handbook of Educational Evaluation* (Boston: Kluwer Academic Press, 2003): 450–51.
28. "Schooling Open Societies in Latin America," 16.

29. Grondona and Montaner, "Journalism and Values," essay written for the Culture Matters Research Project, 2.
30. Ibid., 3.
31. Ibid., 6.
32. Ibid., 4–5.
33. Ibid., 13.
34. Ibid., 14.
35. John Berger in *The Guardian,* August 24, 2005.
36. Schonfeld, "The Entertainment Invasion," essay written for the Culture Matters Research Project, 1.
37. Ibid., 2–3.
38. Thomas Friedman, "52–48," column in the *New York Times,* September 3, 2003, A19.
39. Schonfeld, "The Entertainment Invasion," 7.
40. Ibid., 6.
41. Ibid., 7.
42. Ibid., 9.
43. Ibid., 10–11.
44. Ibid., 22.
45. Ibid., 23.
46. Richard Lamm, "Public Policy and Culture," essay written for the Culture Matters Research Project, 7.
47. Ibid., 10.
48. Ibid.
49. Teodoro Moscoso, "The Will to Economic Development" in ed. L. Ronald Scheman, *The Alliance for Progress: A Retrospective* (New York: Praeger, 1988), 83; Lamm, "Public Policy and Culture," 12–13.
50. Lamm, "Public Policy and Culture," 13.

Chapter 4

1. The per-capita income purchasing power parity and income distribution data for Taiwan are extrapolated estimates from other sources, since the World Bank no longer publishes data for Taiwan. The per capita income figure, also purchasing power parity, for Hong Kong is drawn from the *UN Human Development Report 2001.*
2. Ronald Inglehart, "Culture and Democracy," in *Culture Matters,* Lawrence Harrison and Samuel Huntington, eds. (New York: Basic Books, 2000), 91.
3. The Protestant First World countries, in the order of their appearance in the 2001 UN Human Development Index, include Norway, Australia, Canada, Sweden, United States, Netherlands, Finland, Switzerland, United Kingdom, Denmark, Germany, and New Zealand. The Catholic First World countries are Belgium, France, Austria, Ireland, Italy, Spain, and Portugal.

4. "France's Protestants—Prim but Punchy," *The Economist*, April 18, 1998, 48.
5. Richard Morin, "Putting the Good in Good Government," *The Washington Post*, November 1, 1998, C5.
6. Published by the World Economic Forum on October 13, 2004, on its website.
7. Tom Phelan and Stephen Cole, "Why Are There Top Dogs in Global Science," *Times Higher Education Supplement*, June 18, 1999.
8. Centre for Global Development and *Foreign Policy Magazine*, website of latter, October 2004.
9. Rodger Doyle, "Civic Culture," *Scientific American* (June 2004): 34.
10. The fertility data in Table 4.1 were drawn from the UN's *Human Development Report 2002*; the *Human Development Report 2003* contains the 2000–2005 estimates.
11. See, for example, Yoshihara Kunio, *Asia Per Capita* (Singapore: Curzon Press, 2000), 127 ff.
12. David Martin, "Evangelical Expansion and 'Progressive Values' in the Developing World," essay written for Culture Matters Research Project, 2–3.
13. Ibid., 11.
14. Ibid., 25–27.
15. Samuel Huntington, *Who Are We? The Challenges to America's National Identity* (New York: Simon and Schuster, 2004), 59.
16. Ibid., 75.
17. Gunnar Myrdal, *An American Dilemma*, vol. 1 (New York: Harper, 1944), 495.
18. Huntington, *Who Are We?*, 71.
19. Ibid., 68–9.
20. Ibid, 79.
21. Edward Rothstein, "Jews in the New Wilderness," *New York Times*, September 24, 2004, 29.
22. Max Weber, *The Protestant Ethic and the Spirit of Capitalism* (New York: HarperCollins Academic, 1992), 188–89.
23. One is reminded of the Calvinist doctrine of "calling"—that humans are put on earth to do something to enhance the glory of God.
24. Jim Lederman, "The Development of the Jews," essay written for the Culture Matters Research Project, passim.
25. Alexis de Tocqueville, *Democracy in America* (London: David Campbell Publishers/Everyman's Library, 1994), 300–301.
26. "Contradictions," *The Economist*, April 12, 2003, 48.
27. Marlise Simmons, "Spain Is Seeking to Integrate Growing Muslim Population," *New York Times*, October 24, 2004.
28. *UN Human Development Report 2003*, Table 13.
29. Irakli Chkonia, "Timeless Identity Versus Final Modernity: Identity Master Myth and Social Change in Georgia," essay written for the Culture Matters Research Project, 5.
30. Nikolas Gvosdev, "Re-Imagining the Orthodox Tradition: Nurturing Democratic Values in Orthodox Christian Civilization," essay written for the Culture Matters Research Project, 10–11.

31. Georges Prevelakis, "Greece, Orthodoxy, Culture, and the Economy," essay written for the Culture Matters Research Project, 2.

32. Robert Weller, "Market Development, Political Change, and Chinese Cultures," essay written for the Culture Matters Research Project, 20, 22–23.

33. Christal Whelan, "Buddhism and Development in Asia," essay written for the Culture Matters Research Project, 1.

34. Ibid., 2.

35. Ibid., 9.

36. Ibid.

37. Hedley Bull, "The Revolt Against the West," in H. Bull and A. Watson, eds., *The Expansion of International Society* (Oxford: Clarendon Press, 1984), 223.

38. Bassam Tibi, "Cultural Change in Islamic Civilization Requires Value Changes, Not Semi-Modernity," essay written for the Culture Matters Research Project, 19–20.

39. Hefner e-mail to Harrison, April 28, 2004.

40. Robert Hefner, "Culture and Progress in the Muslim World," essay written for the Culture Matters Research Project, 24–25.

41. Personal e-mail communication with Adil Najam, The Fletcher School, November 11, 2004.

42. Cited by David Landes in *Culture Matters*, 7. The quote is elaborated upon by Lewis in Bernard Lewis, *What Went Wrong?* (New York: HarperCollins Perennial, 2002), concluding chapter.

43. E-mail from Pratap Bhanu Mehta to author, November 19, 2004.

44. Pratap Bhanu Mehta, "Hinduism and Modernity," essay written for the Culture Matters Research Project, 1.

45. Ibid., 5–6.

46. Ibid., 16.

47. World Bank, *World Development Indicators 2003* (Washington, D.C.: World Bank, 2003), 89, table 2.14.

48. Mehta, "Hinduism and Modernity," 17–18.

49. Ibid., 18.

50. Alfred Stepan, *Arguing Comparative Politics* (New York: Oxford University Press, 2001), chapter 11; a version of the chapter was published in *Journal of Democracy*, vol. 11, no. 4 (2000): 37–57.

51. Ibid., 213.

52. Ibid., 226–7.

53. Bernard Lewis, "Freedom and Justice in the Modern Middle East," *Foreign Affairs* (May/June 2005): 37. Lewis's observation evokes Tocqueville's similar comment about Catholicism.

Chapter 5

1. Martin Meredith, *The Fate of Africa* (New York: Public Affairs, 2005), cited by Janet Maslin in *New York Times* review (see note 2).

2. Janet Maslin, "Africa and Its Rapacious Leaders," *New York Times*, August 8, 2005, B6.

3. Stephen Lewis, "Explaining Botswana's Success," essay written for Culture Matters Research Project, 6.

4. Ibid., 9.

5. Ann Bernstein, "Culture and Development: Questions from South Africa," essay written for Culture Matters Research Project, 1.

6. Ibid., 3.

7. Ibid., 8.

8. Ibid., 21. The source is a South African participant in a workshop sponsored by Bernstein's organization, the Centre for Development and Enterprise in Johannesburg.

9. Elisha Renne, "The Culture of Development in a Southwestern Nigerian Town," essay written for Culture Matters Research Project, 1.

10. Lawrence Harrison, *Who Prospers?* (New York: Basic Books, 1992), 79–80.

11. Renne, "The Culture of Development," 29.

12. Tu Weiming, "A Preliminary Inquiry into China's Cultural Renaissance," essay written for Culture Matters Research Project, 15.

13. Ibid., 13.

14. Ibid., 17.

15. Ibid., 34.

16. Yoshihara Kunio, "Japanese Culture and Postwar Economic Growth," essay written for Culture Matters Research Project, 2.

17. Ibid., 16–18.

18. Chua Beng-Huat, "Culture Matters: Values and Development in Singapore," essay written for Culture Matters Research Project, 9.

19. Ibid., 22.

20. Ibid., 27.

21. Robert Weller, "Market Development, Political Change, and Taiwanese Culture," essay written for Culture Matters Research Project, 1.

22. Ibid., 2.

23. Ibid., 3.

24. Ibid., 26.

25. Angus Maddison, *Monitoring the World Economy, 1820–1992* (Paris: OECD, 1995), 30.

26. Gurcharan Das, "India: How a Rich Nation Became Poor and Will Be Rich Again," essay written for Culture Matters Research Project, 3.

27. Ibid., 6.

28. Ibid., 9.

29. Ibid., 14.

30. Deepak Lal, *Unintended Consequences: The Impact of Factor Endowments, Culture and Politics on Long-Run Economic Performance* (New Delhi: Oxford University Press, 1999), 8.

31. Das, "India," 12.

32. Bassam Tibi, "Egypt as a Model of Development for the World of Islam?" essay written for Culture Matters Research Project, 3.

33. Ibid., 4.

34. Ibid., 14.

35. Ibid., 44.
36. Robert Hefner, "Cultural Matters and Developmental Dilemmas in Indonesia," essay written for Culture Matters Research Project, 21–2.
37. UNDP, *Human Development Report 2004* (New York: Oxford University Press), Tables 11 and 26.
38. F. S. Aijazuddin, "Two Halves Did Not Make a Whole—Pakistan Before and After Bangladesh," essay written for Culture Matters Research Project, 1.
39. The data on literacy and fertility are drawn from the tabular section of UNDP, *Human Development Report 2003* (New York: Oxford University Press), 2003.
40. UNDP, *Human Development in South Asia 2003: The Employment Challenge* (Karachi: Oxford University Press, 2004). Published for the Mahbub ul Haq Human Development Centre, Islamabad.
41. Microcredit programs, despite their apparent success, have their critics for failing to create asset generation or provide sustained employment opportunities.
42. Aijazuddin, "Two Halves Did Not Make a Whole," 20.
43. Yilmaz Esmer, "Turkey: Torn Between Two Civilizations," essay written for Culture Matters Research Project, 1–14, passim.

Chapter 6

1. Maria Lucia Victor Barbosa, "The Importance of Culture—The Brazilian Case," essay written for Culture Matters Research Project, 14–15.
2. Ibid., 17–18.
3. David Hojman, "Economic Development and the Evolution of National Culture: the Case of Chile," essay written for Culture Matters Research Project, 2.
4. Arnold J. Bauer, *Chilean Rural Society* (Cambridge: Cambridge University Press, 1975), 16, 24.
5. See Lawrence Harrison, *Underdevelopment Is a State of Mind* (Cambridge: Harvard Center for International Affairs, 1985): 48–49. In her book *Political Culture and Institutional Development* (New York: Cambridge University Press, 2005), Consuelo Cruz attributes Costa Rica's exceptionalism to the success of Costa Rica's Spanish conquerors in forging "a virtuous collective identity" (40), which Nicaragua's conquerors failed to do. "Costa Ricans set out to protect their 'virtuous' people from external contamination by other Central Americans—a goal they maintained was realistic only if Costa Rica, traditionally poor and militarily weak, grew socio-economically strong" (41). Interestingly, in a telephone conversation with me in the summer of 2005, Cruz stressed Costa Rica's success, unique in Central America, in integrating the Anglo-Saxon concept of "compromise" into political and popular behavior in a manner similar to Chile's experience.
6. Simon Collier, Thomas Skidmore, and Harold Blakemore, eds., "Chile," in *Cambridge Encyclopedia of Latin America* (Cambridge, UK: Cambridge University Press, 1992), 263.

7. Francisco Encina, *Nuestra Inferioridad Económica* (Santiago: Editorial Universitaria, 1978): 107–9. Encina cites an estimate that there were 32,000 Chileans and children of Chilean parents in the south of Argentina in 1905.

8. François Depons, *Viaje a la Parte Oriental de la Tierra Firme en la América Meridional* (Caracas: Banco Central de Venezuela, 1960), 85.

9. Ibid., 105. Note the use of the word "customs," the same word Tocqueville used for "culture."

10. Hojman, "Economic Development and the Evolution of National Culture," 16–17.

11. Miguel Basáñez, "The Camel and the Needle," essay written for the Culture Matters Research Project, 1–2.

12. See Ronald Inglehart, Miguel Basáñez, and Neil Nevitte, *Convergencia en Norteamérica* (Mexico City: Siglo Veintiuno, 1994).

13. Basáñez, "The Camel and the Needle," 16.

14. Barry Edmonston and Jeffrey S. Passel, "Ethnic Demography: U.S. Immigration and Ethnic Variations," in Edmonston and Passell, eds., *Immigration and Ethnicity: The Integration of America's Newest Arrivals* (Washington, D.C.: Urban Institute Press, 1994), 8.

15. Janos Matyas Kovacs, "Which Past Matters? Culture and Economic Development in Eastern Europe after 1989," essay written for the Culture Matters Research Project, 21–22.

16. Ibid.

17. Irakli Chkonia, "Timeless Identity Versus Another Final Modernity: Identity Master Myth and Social Change in Georgia," essay written for the Culture Matters Research Project, 17–18.

18. Nicolai Petro, "A Tale of Two Regions: Novgorod and Pskov as Models of Symbolic Development," essay written for the Culture Matters Research Project, 10.

19. "Getting back together is so hard," *The Economist*, September 18, 2004, 58.

20. See Thane Gustafson, *Capitalism Russian-Style* (Cambridge: Cambridge University Press, 1999).

21. Archie Brown, "Cultural Change and Continuity in the Transition from Communism: The Russian Case," essay written for the Culture Matters Research Project, 17–21, passim.

22. John McWhorter, "Scene From a Fast-Food Restaurant: Signs of the Times in Black America and the Path Beyond," essay written for the Culture Matters Research Project, 2.

23. Ibid., 4–6, passim.

24. Ibid., 21.

25. Matteo Marini, "The Long and Winding Road: The Italian Path to Modernization," essay written for the Culture Matters Research Project, 3.

26. Ibid. 7.

27. Ibid., 21–23, passim.

28. Data are from Daniel Latouche's CMRP paper, "Culture and the Pursuit of Success: The Case of Quebec in the Twentieth Century."

29. See Alexis de Tocqueville, *Democracy in America* (New York: Harper & Row, 1969), 284, 306, 409.
30. Latouche, "Culture and the Pursuit of Success," 12–13.
31. Carlos Alberto Montaner, "The Spanish Transition (1975–82): Did Prevailing Values Bring Forth Change or Did Change Bring Forth New Values in Spanish Society?"essay written for the Culture Matters Research Project, 9.
32. Ibid., 12.
33. Ibid., 21–22.
34. In the article "Civic Culture" in *Scientific American* (June 2004): 34, Rodger Doyle writes, "Political scientists Tom W. Rice of the University of Iowa and Jan L. Feldman of the University of Vermont have measured civic culture among ancestry groups in the U.S. They find that Americans of Scandinavian and British descent have the highest levels of civic culture. . . ."
35. Dag Blanck and Thorleif Pettersson, "Strong Governance and Civic Participation," essay written for the Culture Matters Research Project.
36. Quoted by Blanck and Pettersson, in "Strong Governance," 9.

Chapter 7

1. Amartya Sen, *Development As Freedom* (New York: Anchor Books, 2000), 31–32.
2. Bernard Lewis, *What Went Wrong?* (New York: HarperCollins Perennial, 2002), 6.
3. Stephen Lewis, "Explaining Botswana's Successes," paper written for Culture Matters Research Project, 14–15.
4. Nicolai Petro, "A Tale of Two Regions: Novgorod and Pskov as Models of Symbolic Development," paper written for Culture Matters Research Project, 10.
5. Daniel Latouche, "Culture and the Pursuit of Success: The Case of Québec in the Twentieth Century," paper written for Culture Matters Research Project, 8.
6. Irakli Chkonia, "Timeless Identity versus Another Final Modernity: Identity Master Myth and Social Change in Georgia," paper written for Culture Matters Research Project, 17.
7. Cited by Thomas McGann in *Argentina: The Divided Land* (Princeton: Van Norstrand Company, 1966), 30.
8. Robert Edgerton, *Sick Societies* (New York: Free Press, 1992).
9. Sen, *Development as Freedom*, 143.
10. Hara Hiroko and Managawa Mieko, "Japanese Childhood Since 1600," English manuscript version of a chapter in *Zur Sozialgeschicte der Kindheit*, ed. Jochen Martin and August Nitschke (Freiburg: Verlag Karl Alber. 1985), 176.
11. Larry Rohter, "Learn English, Says Chile, Thinking Upwardly Global," *New York Times*, December 29, 2004, A4.

12. Ibid.
13. David Hojman, "Economic Development and the Evolution of National Culture," paper written for Culture Matters Research Project, 6.
14. World Bank, *World Development Report 1980* (Washington, D.C.: The World Bank, 1980), Table 23.
15. Dick Spring, "The Celtic Tiger: How Did It Happen?" paper written for Culture Matters Research Project, 5.
16. Dag Blanck and Thorleif Pettersson, "Strong Governance and Civic Participation: Some Notes on the Cultural Dimension of the Swedish Model," paper written for Culture Matters Research Project, 8.
17. Arthur Herman, *How the Scots Invented the Modern World* (New York: Three Rivers Press, 2001), 23, 25.
18. Fox e-mail attachment, March 31, 2005.
19. Spring, "The Celtic Tiger," 2.
20. Stacy May and Galo Plaza, *The United Fruit Company in Latin America* (Washington D.C.: National Planning Association, 1958).
21. Ibid., 229
22. Ibid., 232.
23. Carlos Alberto Montaner, "The Spanish Transition," paper written for Culture Matters Research Project, 19.
24. Chua Beng-Huat, "Culture Matters: Values and Development in Singapore," paper written for Culture Matters Research Project, 21–22.
25. "Housing in Mexico: An Overlooked Revolution," *The Economist*, August 26, 2004, 32.
26. See Robert Samuelson's joint review of *The Mystery of Capital* and *Culture Matters*, "The Spirit of Capitalism," *Foreign Affairs* (January–February 2001): 211.
27. Ibid., 205–211; Michael Novak, "The Poverty of Nations," *The Weekly Standard*, January 15, 2001, 36–37.
28. Lawrence Harrison, "Some Hidden Costs of the Public Investment Fixation," *International Development Review* (1970/2): 20–23.
29. Dag Blanck and Thorleif Pettersson, "Strong Governance and Civic Participation: Some Notes on the Cultural Dimension of the Swedish Model," paper written for Culture Matters Research Project, 5.
30. Ibid., 16.
31. E-mail from Stephen Lewis, January 5, 2005.
32. See "Putting Presidents on Trial Can Hurt Your Reputation," *New York Times*, November 3, 2004, A4.
33. E-mail from David Hojman, January 11, 2005.

Chapter 8

1. Quoted in Maria Rocio Romero, "Discurso y práctica de una experiencia de cambio cultural, desde el mundo empresarial peruano: El Decálogo del Desarrollo y el Instituto de Desarrollo Humano INDEHU" (evaluation commissioned by CMRP), November 2004, 5.

2. Ibid.

3. Ibid., 15.

4. Roy Godson, "Guide to Developing a Culture of Lawfulness," December 14, 2000 (Washington, D.C.: National Strategy Information Center, 2000), 1.

5. Ibid., 4.

6. Ibid.

7. Ibid., 8.

8. Ibid., 10.

9. NSIC, "Culture of Lawfulness Update," June 2002 (Washington, D.C.: National Strategy Information Center, 2000), 2.

10. Mitchell Seligson, "Can Social Capital Be Constructed? Decentralization and Social Capital Formation in Latin America," paper written for Culture Matters Research Project, 10.

11. Ibid., 32.

12. Fernando Díaz-Plaja, *El Español y los Siete Pecados Capitales* (1966; reprint, Madrid: Alianza Editorial, 1985).

13. Ibid., 76; José Ortega y Gasset, *Invertebrate Spain* (New York: Norton, 1937), 47–50.

14. Benwick McLean, "Spaniards Dare to Question the Way the Day is Ordered," *New York Times*, January 12, 2005, A4.

15. "Ecuadorean Time—The Price of Lateness," *The Economist*, November 22, 2003, 38.

16. James Surowiecki, "The Financial Page—Punctuality Pays," *The New Yorker*, April 5, 2004, 31.

17. Ibid.

18. Ibid.

19. E-mail to author from Osvaldo Hurtado, October 26, 2004.

20. GAO, "U. S. Democracy Programs in Six Latin American Countries Have Yielded Modest Results" (forwarded to the Congress on March 18, 2003), 3.

21. Ibid.

22. Juan Forero, "Latin America Graft and Poverty Trying Patience with Democracy," *New York Times*, June 24, 2004, 1.

23. Basáñez report for CMRP of November 30, 2004, 1.

24. Ibid.

25. Ibid., 2.

26. Ibid.

27. Ibid., 4.

28. Ibid., 5.

29. "Doing Well and Doing Good," *The Economist*, July 31, 2004, 57.

30. Ibid.

31. David Rockefeller Center for Latin American Studies and Hauser Center for Nonprofit Organizations, Cambridge, Harvard University, "Strengthening Philanthropy in Latin America—Executive Summary" (1999), 4.

32. Ibid., 11, 12.

33. Ibid.

34. Stephen Lewis believes that the costly pursuit of Fabian socialism in South Asia and Africa, similar to that ideological current in Latin America, is the result of many leaders "trained by the soft Marxists at the London School of Economics." (E-mail to author, April 11, 2005.)

35. E-mail from Prevelakis to author, February 2, 2005.

36. James Fox, "Donor Projects and Culture Change: The Case of Costa Rica," paper written for Culture Matters Research Project, 2.

37. Ibid., 2.

38. Ibid., 3.

39. Ibid., 5.

40. Ibid.

41. Ibid., 13–14.

Chapter 9

1. Daniel Latouche, "Culture and the Pursuit of Success," paper written for Culture Matters Research Project, 12–13.

2. See Celia Dugger, "To Help Poor Be Pupils, Not Earners, Brazil Pays Parents," *New York Times*, January 3, 2004, 1.

3. Jerome Kagan, "Culture, Values, and the Family," paper written for Culture Matters Research Project, 9–15 passim.

4. Gurcharan Das, "India: How a Rich Nation Became Poor and Will Be Rich Again," paper written for Culture Matters Research Project, 9.

5. Larry Rohter, "Learn English, Says Chile, Thinking Upwardly Global," *New York Times*, December 29, 2004, A4. A front-page article of February 15, 2005, reported on a Mongolian government program to promote mastery of English.

6. Irakli Chkonia, "Timeless Identity Versus Another Final Modernity: Identity, Master Myth, and Social Change in Georgia," paper written for Culture Matters Research Project, 7–8.

7. Archie Brown, "Cultural Change and Continuity in the Transition from Communism: The Russian Case," paper written for Culture Matters Research Project, 9.

8. Nikolas Gvosdev, "Re-imagining the Orthodox Tradition: Nurturing Democratic Values in Orthodox Christian Civilization," paper written for Culture Matters Research Project, 12.

9. E-mail from Gvosdev to author, February 8, 2005.

10. Jay L. Garfield, "Buddhism and Democracy," http://www.buddhist information.com/buddhism_and_democracy.htm, part 1.

11. Daniel Etounga-Manguelle, "Does Africa Need a Cultural Adjustment Program?" in *Culture Matters*, ed. Lawrence Harrison and Samuel Huntington (New York: Basic Books, 2000): 73.

12. Animism also finds some adherents in Asia—see, for example, Robert Weller's CMRP paper on Taiwan.

13. Daniel Latouche, "Culture and the Pursuit of Success: The Case of Québec in the Twentieth Century," paper written for Culture Matters Research Project, 8.

14. Reese Schonfeld, " Entertainment Supremacy (Or The Entertainment Invasion): The Global Battle for Cultural Domination," paper written for Culture Matters Research Project, 2.

15. Ibid., 9.

16. David Rockefeller Center for Latin American Studies and Hauser Center for Nonprofit Organizations, Cambridge, Harvard University, "Strengthening Philanthropy in Latin America" (1999), 11.

17. Tomás Roberto Fillol, *Social Factors in Economic Development* (Cambridge, Mass.: MIT Press, 1961), 97.

APPENDIX:
BIOGRAPHICAL SKETCHES OF CULTURE MATTERS RESEARCH PROJECT PARTICIPANTS

Developing Cultures: Essays on Cultural Change

Contributors

Jerome Kagan (co-editor) is the Daniel and Amy Starch Research Professor of Psychology at Harvard University, where his work has focused on child development. He has long been interested in the contribution of cultural variation to the character and personality of children. His most recent book, with Nancy Snidman, is *The Long Shadow of Temperament.*

Steven Finkel is Professor and Daniel Wallace Chair in Political Science, University of Pittsburgh, and, jointly from 2005 through 2008, Professor of Quantitative and Qualitative Methods at the Hertie School of Governance, Berlin, Germany. His research interests are in the areas of political participation, voting behavior, the development of democratic attitudes and values, and research methodology.

James W. Fox is a former chief economist for the Latin American region for USAID and former head of USAID's evaluation unit for economic growth activities. He has also worked as an economist for the State and Treasury Departments and the Senate Foreign Relations Committee.

Mariano Grondona is the host of the weekly public affairs television program *Hora Clave* in Argentina. He is Professor of Government at the National University of Buenos Aires and a columnist for the newspaper *La Nación*. A contributor to *Culture Matters*, his most recent book is *The Cultural Conditions of Economic Development.*

Nikolas Gvosdev, Senior Fellow in Strategic Studies at the Nixon Center and editor of *The National Interest*, is a specialist in Eurasian and Balkan affairs with emphasis on how the historical, cultural, and religious inheritance of the region affects current developments. His most recent book is *Receding Shadow of the Prophet: The Rise and Fall of Radical Political Islam*.

Robert Hefner is Professor of Anthropology and Associate Director of the Institute on Culture, Religion and World Affairs at Boston University. The author of many books on Islam, he recently completed a multi-country, collaborative project on civil democratic Islam and is completing a book, *Muslim Politics and the Quandary of Modernity*.

Luis Diego Herrera is a Costa Rican psychiatrist specializing in children and adolescents. He has served as Chief of the Department of Psychology and Psychiatry at the National Children's Hospital in San José, Costa Rica, also as the Chief of the Department of Adolescents at the Gaebler Center for Children in Waltham, Massachusetts. He is President of the Paniamor Foundation for the Promotion of Children's Rights.

Samuel Huntington is Albert J. Weatherhead III University Professor at Harvard University, where he was also director of the Center for International Affairs for eleven years and Chairman of the Academy for International and Area Studies for eight years. He is the author, most recently, of *Who Are We? The Challenges to America's National Identity* and is the co-editor, with Lawrence Harrison, of *Culture Matters*.

Sharon Lynn Kagan is the Virginia and Leonard Marx Professor of Early Childhood and Family Policy at Teachers College, Columbia University, where she is Associate Dean for Policy. She is also Professor Adjunct at Yale University's Child Study Center. She is past president of the National Association for the Education of Young Children. Her most recent book is *Children, Families, and Government: Preparing for the Twenty-first Century*.

Richard Lamm is Co-Director of the Institute for Public Policy Studies of the University of Denver. He was Governor of Colorado from 1975 to 1987 and also served in the Colorado legislature. His most recent book is *The Brave New World of Health Care*.

James Lederman is a Canadian journalist who resides in Israel. He is the author of *Battle Lines: The American Media and the Intifada*.

Thomas Lickona is a developmental psychologist and professor of education at the State University of New York at Cortland, where he directs the Center for the 4th and 5th Rs. A member of the board of directors of the Character Education Partnership, he is the author, most recently, of the book *Character Matters* and, with Matthew Davidson, the report *Smart & Good High Schools*.

Amy E. Lowenstein is pursuing a joint Ph.D. in developmental psychology and master's in public policy at Georgetown University. Her main research interests are early childhood development and programs and policies to support low-income children and families.

David Martin is an English sociologist and theologian. He is the author of *Tongues of Fire: The Explosion of Protestantism in Latin America* and *Pentecostalism: The World Their Parish*, and most recently, *On Secularization*.

Pratap Bhanu Mehta is President, Center for Policy Research, Delhi. He has also been a visiting professor at Harvard. His most recent book is *The Burden of Democracy*.

Carlos Alberto Montaner is the most widely read columnist in the Spanish language. A contributor to *Culture Matters*, he is the co-author, with Plinio Apuleyo Mendoza and Álvaro Vargas Llosa, of *Guide to the Perfect Latin American Idiot*. His most recent books are *Latin America and the West* and *La Libertad y Sus Enemigos*.

Richard Niemi is Don Alonzo Watson Professor of Political Science at the University of Rochester, where he has also served as Department Chair, Associate Dean, and Interim Dean. Among his fields of concentration are political socialization and civic education. He is recently the co-author, with Jane Junn, of *Civic Education—What Makes Students Learn*.

Michael Novak holds the George Frederick Jewett Chair in Religion and Public Policy at the American Enterprise Institute. He has written 29 books on the philosophy and theology of culture, among them *The Catholic Ethic and the Spirit of Capitalism* and *The Spirit of Democratic Capitalism*.

Georges Prevelakis is Professor of Human and Regional Geography at the Sorbonne. He is the author, among others, of *Athènes: Urbanisme, Culture et Politique*; *Géopolitique de la Grèce*; and *Les Balkans, cultures et géopolitique*. He has edited *The Networks of Diasporas*.

Fernando Reimers is the Ford Foundation Professor of International Education at the Harvard Graduate School of Education, where he directs the Global Education Office and the International Education Policy Program. He specializes in the study of the contributions of education to social and political development and is currently studying the contributions of civic education to democratic citizenship. He is the author of several books and articles and is an advisor to governments, universities, and development agencies.

Reese Schonfeld was the founding president and chief executive officer of the Cable News Network. He also founded the Television Food Network. He is the author of *Me and Ted Against the World: The Unauthorized Story of the Founding of CNN*.

Mitchell Seligson is Centennial Professor of Political Science and Fellow, Center for the Americas, at Vanderbilt University. He is the Director of the Latin American Public Opinion Project (LAPOP) and is co-editor, with John Booth, of *Elections and Democracy in Central America, Revisited*.

Bassam Tibi is Professor of International Relations at the University of Göttingen, Germany. He is also the A. D. White Professor-at-Large at Cornell University. He has been Visiting Professor at Bilkent University in Ankara, Turkey, the University of California (Berkeley), Harvard University, and the National University of Singapore. Among his recent publications are *The Challenge of Fundamentalism: Political Islam and the New World Disorder* and *Islam between Culture and Politics*, both recently republished in updated editions.

Eleonora Villegas-Reimers is Associate Professor of Human Development and Acting Dean of the Division of Child and Family Studies at Wheelock College. She specializes in moral and civic education. She has published a book and several articles on civic education and teacher professional development and consults for a number of development organizations on issues of teacher professional development, curriculum development, and civic education.

Robert Weller is Professor of Anthropology and Research Associate at the Institute on Culture, Religion, and World Affairs at Boston University. He works on the relations among culture, society, and political change in China and Taiwan. His most recent books include *Civil Life, Globalization, and Political Change in Asia: Organizing Between Family and State* (editor) and *Discovering Nature: Globalization and Environmental Culture in China and Taiwan*.

Christal Whelan is an Earhart Fellow at the Institute on Culture, Religion, and World Affairs at Boston University. She specializes in Japanese religion, cultural change, and visual anthropology. Her book *The Beginning of Heaven and Earth* and companion film *Otaiya* deal with the cultural history of Christianity in Japan. Her current research is on Buddhist-oriented new religious movements.

Developing Cultures: Case Studies

Contributors

Peter Berger (co-editor) is University Professor and Professor of Sociology and Theology at Boston University, where he also directs the Institute for the Study of Economic Culture and the Institute on Religion and World Affairs. He is the author most recently of *The Capitalist Revolution* and co-editor, with Samuel Huntington, of *Many Globalizations*.

F. S. Aijazuddin OBE, FCA is a Pakistani author and journalist. Recent books include *From a Head, Through a Head, to a Head: The Secret Channel between* *the U.S. and China Through Pakistan,* and *The White House & Pakistan: Secret Declassified Documents 1969–74.*

Maria Lucia Victor Barbosa is a sociologist, columnist, and author. Her most recent books are *O Voto da Pobreza e a Pobreza do Voto: A Éiica da Malandragem* and *América Latina em Busca de Paraíso Perdido.*

Miguel Basáñez is president of the Global Quality Research Corporation and was executive vice president of MORI International from 1993 to 2000. He is the co-author, with Ronald Inglehart, of *Human Values and Beliefs* most recently, and he is the founding publisher of the Mexican monthly magazine *Este País,* specializing in public opinion polls.

Ann Bernstein is founding executive director of the Centre for Development and Enterprise in Johannesburg, South Africa. CDE is an independent and influential think tank working on critical national challenges for a newly democratic country.

Dag Blanck is a university lecturer in history at the Center for Multiethnic Research at Uppsala University and Director of the Swenson Swedish Immigration Research Center at Augustana College in Rock Island, Illinois. His research interests are in international migration and transcultural processes, with a special focus on Sweden and the United States.

Archie Brown is Professor of Politics at Oxford University and has been a Fellow of St Antony's College, Oxford, since 1971. His recent books include *The Gorbachev Factor* and, as editor, *Contemporary Russian Politics.*

Irakli Chkonia was an advisor to the Speaker of the Georgian Parliament from 1995 to 2000. He is a graduate of the Fletcher School.

Chua Beng Huat is Professor of Sociology and leads the Cultural Studies research group in the Asia Research Institute at the National University of Singapore. His most recent book, as editor, is *Communitarian Politics in Asia,* and he is the founding co-executive editor of the journal *Inter-Asia Cultural Studies.*

Gurcharan Das is a columnist for the *Times* of India and former CEO of Proctor and Gamble India. He is the author of *India Unbound.*

Yilmaz Esmer is a professor in the Department of Political Science and International Relations, Bogazici University, Istanbul. He is a member of the Executive Committee of the World Values Survey Association and, since 1990, Principal Investigator for the Turkish Values Survey.

Mariano Grondona (see page 245).

Robert Hefner (see page 246).

David Hojman grew up in Valparaiso and Santiago de Chile and completed his education at the University of Edinburgh. He is Professor of Economics and International Business at the University of Liverpool Management School. He has done research and published in areas including political economy, public choice, labor markets, poverty and inequality, trade, international development, and international business.

Janos Matyas Kovacs is Professor of Economics and Permanent Fellow at the Vienna Institute for Human Sciences and member of the Institute of Economics, Budapest. His recent publications on cultural issues include "Rival Temptations—Passive Resistance: Cultural Globalization in Hungary" in Peter Berger and Samuel Huntington (eds.), *Many Globalizations* and "Approaching the EU and Reaching the US? Transforming Welfare Regimes in East-Central Europe": Rival Narratives, *West European Politics* (April 2002).

Daniel Latouche is Research Professor of Political Science at the Urban and Culture Studies Center of the National Institute of Scientific Research, affiliated with the University of Québec. He taught at McGill from 1970 to 1987. His interests include Québec, Canadian politics, urban issues, and economic development and governance in Africa.

Stephen Lewis is President Emeritus and Professor of Economics at Carleton College in Minnesota. He has worked as an economist/consultant in a number of countries in Asia and Africa since 1963 and has served as economic consultant to the Government of Botswana since 1975.

Matteo Marini is Professor of Economic Development Theories at the University of Calabria, Cosenza, Italy. He is the principal investigator of a research project on local cultures and economic growth in three Italian regions and is the author of "Cultural Evolution and Economic Growth," published in *The Journal of Socio-Economics*.

John McWhorter is Senior Fellow at the Manhattan Institute and was Associate Professor of Linguistics at the University of California at Berkeley. He is the author of *Losing the Race: Self-Sabotage in Black America, Authentically Black, The Power of Babe,* and *Doing Our Own Thing*; has written for various national publications; and appears regularly on National Public Radio.

Carlos Alberto Montaner (see page 247).

Adil Najam, a Pakistani, is Associate Professor of International Negotiation and Diplomacy at the Fletcher School of Law and Diplomacy, Tufts University. His recent books include, *Civic Entrepreneurship* and *Environment, Development and Human Security: Perspectives from South Asia.*

Nicolai Petro is Professor of Political Science at the University of Rhode Island. In 1989–90 he served as Special Assistant for Policy in the State Department's Office of Soviet Affairs, also as Political Attaché at the U.S. Embassy in Moscow. He is the author of *Rebirth of Russian Democracy—An Interpretation of Political Culture* and *Crafting Democracy: How Novgorod Has Coped with Rapid Social Change.*

Thorleif Pettersson is a professor in the sociology of religion at Uppsala University. Previously he has worked as a researcher at the Stockholm Institute for Future Studies, the Swedish Council for Research in Humanities and Social Sciences, and the Stockholm Institute for the Sociology of Religion. He has also been a research fellow at the Swedish Collegium for Advanced Studies in the Social Sciences and has been involved in the World Values Survey for many years.

Elisha Renne is an associate professor in the Department of Anthropology and the Center for Afroamerican and African Studies at the University of Michigan. Her research focuses on fertility and reproductive health, gender relations, the anthropology of development, and religion and social change, specifically in Nigeria. Her most recent book, *Population and Progress in a Yoruba Town*, was published in 2003.

Dick Spring was a member of the Irish Parliament for 21 years and is a former leader of the Labour Party. He served as Deputy Prime Minister and as cabinet minister for ten years. He is chairman and director of numerous companies and leads Realta, an Irish Global HIV/AIDS Foundation.

Bassam Tibi (see page 248).

Tu Weiming is Professor of Chinese History and Philosophy and of Confucian Studies at Harvard, where he is also Director of the Yenching Institute. He is currently working on the modern transformation of the Confucian tradition. He is the author of several books in English. A five-volume collection of his works was published in China in 2002.

Luis Ugalde, S. J., is rector of the Catholic University Andrés Bello of Caracas, Venezuela, and president of the Association of Jesuit Universities of Latin America.

Robert Weller (see page 248).

Yoshihara Kunio is Professor of Asian Economic Development at the Faculty of Environmental Engineering in the University of Kitakyushu, Japan, and Professor Emeritus of Kyoto University. He has specialized in the economies of Southeast Asia and the influence of culture on their performance. His most recent book is *Asia Per Capita: Why National Incomes Differ in East Asia*.

Advisory Board and Other Participants

Morris Altman is Professor of Economics and the Head of the Department of Economics at the University of Saskatchewan. He is also the editor of the *Journal of Socio-Economics* and the author, most recently, of *Worker Satisfaction and Economic Performance*.

Stephen Bosworth is Dean of the Fletcher School at Tufts University. A former career foreign service officer, he has served as the U.S. ambassador to

Korea, the Philippines, and Tunisia as well as Director of Policy Planning in the State Department. He was President/CEO of the United States–Japan Foundation from 1988 to 1996 and Executive Director of the Korean Peninsula Energy Development Organization from 1995 to 1997.

Harold Caballeros, attorney and theologian, is the founder of the El Shaddai Church in Guatemala, an Evangelical Church with some 30,000 members and branches in several Spanish-speaking countries. He sponsored a conference on the role of culture and cultural change in Guatemala in 2001 and was a fellow at the Weatherhead Center for International Affairs at Harvard University in 2004–5.

Houchang Chehabi is Professor of International Relations and History at Boston University. He is the author of *Iranian Politics and Religious Modernism* and coeditor of *Politics, Society, and Democracy* and *Sultanistic Regimes.*

Kent R. Hill is the Assistant Administrator for Global Health of the U.S. Agency for International Development. He served as president of Eastern Nazarene College in Quincy, Massachusetts, from 1992 to 2001 and was president of the Institute on Religion and Democracy in Washington, DC, from 1986 to 1992.

Robert Hodam is the CEO of the International Center for Economic Growth, a network of 419 economic policy institutes in 104 countries. He is the founder of six private sector companies in three countries and has had 25 years of experience as a consultant to multilateral and bilateral development assistance organizations.

Ronald Inglehart is Professor of Political Science and Program Director at the Institute of Social Research at the University of Michigan. He helped found the Euro-Barometer Surveys and is chair of the steering committee of the World Values Survey. He is most recently the author, with Pippa Norris, of *Rising Tide: Gender Equality and Cultural Change Around the World* and *Sacred and Secular: Religion and Politics Worldwide*; and with Christian Welzel, of *Modernization, Cultural Change and Democracy.* He is a contributor to *Culture Matters.*

Tamar Jacoby is Senior Fellow at the Manhattan Institute. She has also written for *Newsweek* and was for six years the Deputy Editor of the op-ed page of the *New York Times.* Her most recent books are *Someone Else's House: America's Unfinished Struggle for Integration* and *Reinventing the Melting Pot: The New Immigrants and What It Means to be American.*

Timur Kuran is Professor of Economics and Law and King Faisal Professor of Islamic Thought and Culture at the University of Southern California. He has written on the evolution of preferences, the functions of institutions, the economic effects of Islam, and economic development of the Middle East. He is the author most recently of *Private Truths, Public Lies:*

The Social Consequences of Preference Falsification and *Islam and Mammon: The Economic Predicaments of Islamism.*

Roderick MacFarquhar is Leroy B. Williams Professor of History and Political Science at Harvard, where he has been chair of the Department of Government and, earlier, director of the Fairbank Center for East Asian Research. His book on the Cultural Revolution, co-authored with Michael Schoenhals, will be published by Harvard University Press in 2006.

Harvey Nelsen teaches a course on political cultures at the University of South Florida, where he is a professor in the International Studies Program, Department of Government and International Affairs. He has just completed a textbook on political culture.

Lucian Pye is Ford Professor of Political Science Emeritus at MIT. He is a past president of the American Political Science Association; chairman of the National Committee on US–China Relations; and an advisor to the National Security Council and the State Department. He is the author / co-author or editor / co-editor of more than 25 books, prominently among them *Asian Power and Politics.*

Robert Rotberg is director of the Program on Intrastate Conflict and Conflict Resolution of Harvard's JFK School. He is also President of the World Peace Foundation. He is the editor, most recently, of *When States Fail: Causes and Consequences.*

John Sanbrailo is executive director of the Pan American Development Foundation (PADF), a nonprofit organization affiliated with the Organization of American States. He served with the U.S. Agency for International Development for three decades during which he directed missions in Ecuador, Peru, Honduras, and El Salvador.

Index

Note: Page numbers in *italics* refer to graphs, charts or maps.

absolutism, cultural, 10
A Casa e a Rua (*At Home and on the Street*)
    (DaMatta), 50
accountability, 66
achievement, 36, 43–44, 176
The Achieving Society (McClelland), 66
activism, 103, 104
advancement, 37, 47
Afghanistan, 15
Africa. *See also specific countries*
    African Renaissance, 124
    authoritarianism, 27
    case studies, 120, 121–26
    civic education, 74
    colonialism, 5, 6
    cultural relativism, 10–11
    democracy, 64
    education, 125, 202, 221
    fertility, 54
    literacy, 208
    religion, 30, 98, 99, 104, 212, 217
    Sahel countries, 27
    slavery, 24
African Americans, *59*, 59–61, 121, 154–
    55
agriculture, 203
AIDS/HIV, 123, 125

Aijazuddin, F. S., 138–39, 248–49
Alemán, Arnoldo, 180, 194
Algeria, *96*
al Jazeera, 222
Alliance for Progress, xi–xii, 15, 168, 195
Al Manar, 83
Al-Shattat, 83
Altman, Morris, 14, 251
altruism, 129, 197–99
American Anthropological Association,
    8
American College for Girls, Turkey, 202
American Creed, 101
The American Dilemma (Myrdal), 101
American Farm School, Greece, 201
American University of Beirut, Lebanon,
    202
American University of Cairo, Egypt,
    202
ancestor worship, 29n, 90–91
Anglicanism, 98
Anglo-Protestant culture, 101–2
Anthony, Susan B., 58
Arab countries, 2, 7–8, 82, *88–89*, *96–97*.
    See also specific countries
Arab Human Development Reports, 7–8,
    47, 69, 112, 115, 220, 222

Argentina, 28, 45, 48, 120, 142–43
Arguing Comparative Politics (Stepan), 118
Ariel (Rodó), 13
Aristide, Jean-Bertrand, 26, 193–94
Armenia, 202
Asia, 5, 56, 74, 99, 214. *See also specific countries*
Asia Per Capita (Yoshihara), 14
assertiveness, 67
assimilation, 151
assistance institutions, 219–21
association, 37, 41
attitudes, 7, 163
Australia, 28, 48, 98
Austria, 105
authoritarianism
    in Africa, 122
    in Brazil, 143, 144
    in Confucian societies, 52, 56
    and education, 76
    in families, 67–68
    and geography, 27–28
    in Haiti, 33
    and Islam, 52
    in Latin America, 169
    in Quebec, 158
    and religion, 39, 104, 114
    and social revolutions, 59
    in Taiwan, 131
    in Venezuela, 149
authority, 37, 52, 107
autonomy, 66–67, 157
Aylwin, Patricio, 165

Bai Xiang (*Ordinary People*), 84
Balaguer, Joaquín, 25
Bandaranaike, Sirimavo, 111–12
Banfield, Edward, 43, 49, 50, 125, 157
Bangladesh, 96, 138–39, 173
Barbados, 16–17
Barbosa, Maria Lucia Victor, 143–45, 249
Basáñez, Miguel
    biographical sketch, 249
    on Bogotá, Colombia, 195–97
    CMRP typology questionnaire, 38, 219
    on Mexico, 148–49, 213
Basques, 91, 119, 145, 146, 152
Bauer, Arnold J., 146
Baumrind, Diana, 67, 70
BBC (British Broadcasting Corporation), 84

Belarus, 214
Belgium, 5
beliefs, 7, 163
Belli, Humberto, 186
Benin, 29, *29*
Berger, John, 81–85, 248
Berger, Peter, 19
Bernstein, Ann, 124, 249
Bhutan, 97
bicycles, 196
Bilkent University, Turkey, 202
Bin Laden, Osama, 114, 115, 212
Bitar, Sergio, 171, 211
blacks. *See* African Americans
Blanck, Dag, 52, 161–62, 172, 180–81, 249
Bloodbowl Sutra, 112
Bogazici University, Turkey, 202
Bogotá, Colombia, 195–97, 217
Bolaños, Enrique, 194
Bolivia, 92, 189–90, 193
Bosworth, Stephen, 251
Botswana
    case studies, 120, 122–23
    civil service, 181–82
    democracy, 168
    foreign investment, 176
    leadership, 164
    media, 223
    and precedents for change, 218
    prosperity, 64
bourgeois societies, 101
Bowling Alone (Putnam), 50
Boyer, Jean Pierre, 24–25, 32
Boy Scout Law, 70
Brazil
    case studies, 120, 143–45
    education, 208
    income distribution, 105
    literacy, 92
    religion, 99, 217
Britain
    colonialism, 133
    democracy, 42, 91
    economy, 58
    media, 223
    religion, 98
Brown, Archie, 153–54, 214–15, 249
Buddenbrooks (Mann), 4
Buddhism, 6, 110–12
    and democracy, 215
    influence of, 29n
    and modernization, 94, 97–98

reforms, 215–16
summary, *88–89*, 90
Bulgaria, 202
Bull, Hedley, 112–13
Burma (Myanmar), 27, 97, 111, 216, 223
Bush, George W., 2, 53, 207

Caballeros, Harold, 252
Calvinism, 40, 42, 98, 106
Cambodia, 97, 111
Campos, Roberto, 144–45
Canada, 48, 98, 172, 211
capitalism
    and Catholicism, 43, 105, 109, 144, 213
    and competition, 46
    in Confucian societies, 127
    in Eastern Europe, 150
    in India, 12
    and media, 80–81
    in Nordic countries, 106
    in Russia, 152
Caribbean, 22
Carlos, Juan, 58, 160, 165, 168
Carnegie, Andrew, 198
Carrillo, Santiago, 160
caste systems, 115, 116–17, 133, 134, 215
cataclysmic events, 58
Catalans, 152
The Catholic Ethic and the Spirit of
    Capitalism (Novak), 105, 118
Catholicism, 6, 104–7
    and authority, 52
    in Brazil, 143–44
    and capitalism, 43, 105, 109, 144, 213
    and corruption, 47–48, 106
    and democracy, 105
    and education, 43, 156
    ethical code, 106
    and income distribution, 105–6
    and INDEHU project, 187
    influence, 54
    in Ireland, 156
    in Mexico, 148
    and modernization, 92–94
    and prosperity, 105
    in Quebec, 158, 159
    reforms, 212–14
    summary, *88–89*, 90
    and trust, 106
Catholic University of Caracas,
    Venezuela, 201
Central America, 15, 16, 45. *See also*
    specific countries

Central American Business
    Administration Institute
    (INCAE), 201
Character Counts! Coalition, 72
character education, 71
Chávez, Hugo, 149
Chehabi, Houchang, 252
Chiang Ching-Kuo, 131
Chiang Kai-Shek, 131
child rearing, 61–69, 174, 187, 207–11
Chile
    case studies, 120, 145–47
    civil service, 182
    corruption, 48, 145
    economy, 12, 213
    English language, 171, 211
    gender relationships, 54
    leadership, 58, 165
    literacy, 54, 145, 171, 208
    religion, 119
    social justice, 64
    success, 168
China
    authoritarianism, 27, 96
    case studies, 120
    communitarianism, 51
    Confucianism, 29n, 109–10, 217
    culture of progress, 56
    economic growth, 44, 122, 176
    education, 43
    filial piety, 7
    immigrants, 12, 97
    influence of intellectuals, 127–28
    leadership, 58, 164
    media, 83–84, 222
    modernization, 95
    social justice, 64
    Western intrusiveness, 167
Chkonia, Irakli
    biographical sketch, 249
    on Georgia, 151–52, 169
    on Grondona's typology, 38
    on Orthodox Christianity, 107, 214–15
Chua, Beng-Huat, 130–31, 249
church-state relations, 37, 53–54, 93
civic education, 72–74, 77, 210
civility, 132
civilizations, 7
civil liberties, 94
civil service, 123, 130, 179–83, 218–19
The Clash of Civilizations and the Remaking
    of World Order (Huntington), 7,
    118

climate, 2–3, 27
Coleman, James, 50
*Collapse: How Societies Choose to Fail or
    Succeed* (Diamond), 33–34
Colombia, 178, 186, 187, 193–97, 217
colonialism, 5–6
Columbus, Christopher, 23
communications, 27, 67. *See also*
    language
Communism, 4, 95, 150, 156, 177
communitarianism. *See also*
    individualism
    in Africa, 122
    of early humans, 61
    in Grondona's typology, 37, 51–52
    in Japan, 129
    in Judaism, 104
    and religion, 107
community service, 73–74
competition, 36, 46, 94
conflict resolution, 123
conformism, 156
confrontation, 122
Confucian societies, 6, 29n, 90, 109–10
    authoritarianism, 3
    authority, 52, 56
    case studies, 120, 126–32
    civil service, 182–83
    communitarianism, 51
    economic growth, 2, 43
    education, 43
    filial piety, 7, 52
    and Golden Rule, 55
    merit emphasis, 47
    modernization, 94
    social progress, 216–17
    summary, *88–89*
    time orientation, 40
Congo, 5
consumerism, 122, 128. *See also*
    capitalism
continuities, 168–70
contraception, 93
corruption. *See also* Transparency
    International's Corruption
    Perceptions Index
    anti-corruption campaigns, 187–89
    in Bogotá, Colombia, 196
    in Brazil, 144
    in Chile, 48, 145
    in China, 128
    in Costa Rica, 182
    and cultural costs, 180

and economy, 48
    in Grondona's typology, 37, 41, 47–
        48, 93
    in Italy, 48
    in Latin America, 169, 213, 214
    in Nordic countries, 48
    in politics, 166
    and religions or ethical codes, 47–48,
        89, 94, 95, 96, 97, 106, 114
    in Singapore, 48, 93, 130, 183
    in Sweden, 48
    in Third World countries, 166
    in United States, 48
    in Venezuela, 149
Costa Rica
    child rearing, 65–69
    Chile compared to, 145–46
    corruption, 182
    development assistance, 203–5
    language, 199–200
    prosperity, 64
    success, 28, 238n5
    and United Fruit Company, 177–78
crime, 187–88, 196, 213, 214
crises and traumas, 4
Cronkite, Walter, 79
Cruz, Consuelo, 238n5
Cuba, 28, 195
cultural restriction, 143
Cultural Revolution, 58
Culture Matters Research Project
    (CMRP), xiv
curfews, 197

Dada, Samuel Ayoola, 125
Dahomey region of Africa, 29
DaMatta, Roberto, 50
Das, Gurcharan, 132–34, 211, 249
DeBeers company, 123
Del Buen Salvaje al Buen Revolucionario
    (Rangel), xii
democracy. *See also under specific
    countries*
    and Bush administration, 2
    and child rearing, 61–62, 209
    and competition, 46
    and Confucianism, 128
    and education, 73, 77, 173, 202, 210
    and ideology, 3
    and literacy, 170
    and religions or ethical codes, 53, *89*,
        90, 92, 104, 105, 107, 111, 114, 116,
        118–19, 215
    and trust, 42

Democracy in America (Tocqueville), 39
Deng Xiaoping, 44, 58, 127, 164, 213
Denmark, 42, 94
Dependency Theory, xi, 5–6, 80, 106, 201
Depons, François, 147
Dessalines, Jean-Jacques, 24
destiny, 36, 40
DeValera, Eamon, 175
developing countries. *See* Third World countries
Developing Cultures: Case Studies (Berger and Harrison), 19
Developing Cultures: Essays on Cultural Change (Kagan and Harrison), 18, 120
development, social, 7
Development As Freedom (Sen), 166
development assistance, 14–16, 203–5
Diamond, Jared, 3, 27, 33–34
Díaz-Plaja, Fernando, 191
dissent, 46, 158
Dominican Republic, 22, 29
    democratization in, 195
    Diamond on, 33–34
    geography, 23, 27–29
    Haitian invasion, 24–25
    literacy, 92
    population, 31
    status, 2
    trade, 32
Doyle, Rodger, 94
Drake, Francis, 24
Duvalier, François, 26, 33

East Asia. *See also specific countries*
    economic growth, 2, 29, 176
    education, 170
    intelligence in, 227n4, 229n42
    transformations in, 122
Easterly, William, 11–12
Eastern Europe. *See also specific countries*
    case studies, 120, 150–51
    civic education, 74
    foreign investment, 177
    religion, 214
East Germany, 5, 150–51
Economist, 105, 179, 191
economists, 11–14
economy. *See also* gross domestic product; *specific countries*
    of Confucian societies, 126–27
    and corruption, 48
    economic growth, 4

economic policies, 174–76, 218
    and education, 172
    and English language, 171
    foreign investment, 108, 130, 155, 156, 175–78, 218
    Great Depression, 4, 58
    in Grondona's typology, 36–37, 43–47
    income distribution data, 90, 93, 95, 97, 144
    market economics, 201
    and microfinancing, 204
    prosperity, 63, 65, 105, 173, 197 (*see also* poverty)
    and religions or ethical codes, 93
    and trust, 49
Ecuador, 42, 50, 178, 190–92
Edgerton, Robert, 169
education. *See also* literacy
    in Africa, 125, 202, 221
    in Bogotá, Colombia, 196
    in Brazil, 208
    in China, 43
    civic education, 72–74, 77, 210
    in Confucian societies, 43
    and cultural change, 200–203
    and democracy, 73, 77, 173, 202, 210
    and economy, 172
    in Egypt, 202
    and elites, 174
    and families, 76
    in Grondona's typology, 36, 43
    in Haiti, 174
    importance of, 64, 203, 207–11, 218, 220–21
    as instrument of change, 69–78
    in Ireland, 156, 171, 210–11
    and Islam, 202, 221
    in Japan, 43, 54, 128, 168, 170, 176
    in Latin America, 74–78, 171, 201, 210
    and lawfulness culture, 189
    in Mexico, 201
    parenting education, 70, 174, 210
    and poverty, 170
    and prosperity, 173
    in Quebec, 158, 159, 171
    and religions or ethical codes, 43, 93, 97, 103–4, 125, 156, 162, 172
    role, 170–74, 187
    in Russia, 173
    in Singapore, 130, 170, 210
    and social mobilization, 188
    in Sweden, 172
    in Taiwan, 132

education (*continued*)
  in Turkey, 202
  and values, 69
  of women, 54, 96, 97, 125, 172–73, 208
egalitarianism, 103
Egypt
  case studies, 121, 134–36
  education, 202
  gender issues, 54
  literacy, 54, 96, 173
Ekedahl, Niles, 161
elections, 193
El Español y los Siete Pecados Capitales
  (Díaz-Plaja), 191
elites
  and education, 174
  in Grondona's typology, 37, 52–53
  in Italy, 156
  and religions or ethical codes, 100–
    101
  in Russia, 152
  in Spain, 159–60
El Salvador, 187, 193, 194
emigration. *See* immigration and
    emigration
The End of History (Fukuyama), 217
The End of Poverty (Sachs), 12–13
English language, 171
  in Greece, 200–201
  in India, 133, 210–11
  in Ireland, 155
  in Quebec, 159
  in Singapore, 131
entertainment media, 81–85, 222
entrepreneurship. *See also* capitalism
  in Chile, 146–47
  in Eastern Europe, 177
  in Grondona's typology, 36, 44–45
  home ownership, 179
  in Mexico, 148
  in Quebec, 158
environmentalism, 59
Episcopalianism, 98
equality, 76, 102, 119, 159
Erdogan, Tayyip Recip, 54, 141
Esmer, Yilmaz, 140–41, 249
ethics, 103. *See also* religions and ethical
    codes
ethnocentrism, 8
Etounga-Manguelle, Daniel
  on African poverty, 12
  on individual responsibility, 51
  on institutions, 32

on magic and witchcraft, 30, 87, 217
  on obstacles to progress in Africa,
    121–22
  on South Africa, 125
Europe. *See also specific countries*
  church-state relations, 53
  population, 55
  religion, 104, 106, 212–13
  resources, 15–16
European Economic Community, 155
Eutelsat, 83–84
Evangelical Protestantism, 98–102, 107,
    144, 145, 213

Falun Gong cult, 83, 222
families
  in Africa, 126
  and child rearing, 61–69, 174, 187,
    207–11
  and education, 76
  family planning, 93, 204
  in Grondona's typology, 37, 49–50
  and INDEHU project, 187
  literacy, 173
  parenting education, 70, 174, 210
  paternity, 59–61
  and political development, 74
  in Singapore, 130, 178
  and social development, 74
Fascism, 156
The Fate of Africa (Meredith), 122
Fawcus, Peter, 123
female genital cutting, 10
feminism, 59
fertility, *96*
  in Algeria, *96*
  in Bangladesh, 138
  in Grondona's typology, 37, 54–55
  in Indonesia, *96*
  in Iran, *96*
  in Morocco, *96*
  in Pakistan, *96*, 138
  in Quebec, 158
  and religion, *89*, 90, 96, 114
  in Yemen, *96*
filial piety, 7, 52
Fillol, Tomás Roberto, 224
Finkel, Steven, 72–74, 245
Finland, 42, 48, 94
fireworks, 196–97
First World countries, 92–93, 95, 98, 166,
    234n3
Fischer, David Hackett, 49, 161

Fletcher School conferences, 17
foreign aid, 14–16
foreign investment, 176–78, 218
  in Ireland, 155, 156
  in Russia, 108
  in Singapore, 130
foreign policy, 2, 102, 152
Foster, George, 41
Fox, James W., 14, 173, 203, 204–5, 245
Fox, Vicente, 149
fragmentation, cultural, 113
France
  economic growth, 4, 94
  and Haiti, 24, 33
  religion, 93, 98
Franco, Francisco, 105, 160, 178
Franklin, Benjamin, 42, 70, 99
Freedom House
  on Bangladesh, 138
  on Barbados, 17
  on Botswana, 122–23
  on Dominican Republic, 25
  on Haiti, 17, 26
  on Myanmar, 216
  on Pakistan, 138
  and religions or ethical codes, 90, 92,
    95, 96, 97, 111, 118
  on Singapore, 130
  summary, *89*
Friedman, Thomas, 35, 82
From the Noble Savage to the Noble
  Revolutionary (Rangel), xii
From Third World to First (Lee), 130
frugality, 36, 44, 130
Fujimori, Alberto, 186
Fukuyama, Francis, 1, 50, 51, 132, 217
Furukawa Corporation, 187, 224–25

Garfield, Jay, 215–16
gender relationships. *See also* women
  in Africa, 122, 126
  in Bangladesh, 138
  changes, 166
  in Grondona's typology, 37, 54
  in Mexico, 148
  in Pakistan, 138
  in Quebec, 159
  and religions or ethical codes, 111–12,
    114, 117
  in Turkey, 140, 141
geography, 2–3, 27–29
Georgia, 120, 151–52, 188, 214, 218

Germany
  association, 50
  and Berlin Wall, 82
  democracy, 16
  East and West Germany, 5, 150–51
  ideology, 5
  individualism, 51
  media, 223
  military defeats, 58
  religion, 91, 102
globalization, 113
Godson, Roy, 188–89
Golden Rule, 55
Gorbachev, Mikhail, 4, 153, 165
government
  in Argentina, 143
  in Bogotá, Colombia, 196
  in Brazil, 144
  corruption, 48
  and cultural costs, 180
  in Haiti, 32
  influence on culture, 8
  in Japan, 168
  in Latin America, 193
  in Mexico, 148
  policies, 3
  and punctuality, 191
  role, 217–19
  in Venezuela, 149
Grameen Bank, 138, 204
gratification, delayed, 68
Great Britain. *See* Britain
Great Depression, 4, 58
Greece, 46, 95, 108–9, 214
Greenspan, Alan, 13n
Grondona, Mariano
  on Argentina, 142–43
  biographical sketch, 245
  on cultural costs, 180
  on Latin American issues, xii
  on news and opinion media, 78–81,
    221–22
  on prestige, 43
  typology of cultural values, 18, 35–
    38, *36–37*
gross domestic product (GDP)
  of India, 133
  of Mexico, 148
  of Nordic countries, 94
  and religions or ethical codes, *89*, 92–
    93, 95, 96, 97
Guatemala
  democracy, 193, 194

Guatemala (*continued*)
  literacy, 92
  prosperity, 64
  religion, 99
  and United Fruit Company, 178
Guicciardini, Francesco, 157
guilt, 197
Guns, Germs, and Steel (Diamond), 3
Gupta, Maithli Sharan, 117
Gutiérrez, Lucio, 191
Gvosdev, Nikolas, 107, 108, 215, 246

Haiti, 22, 29
  compared to Barbados, 16–17
  democracy, 193–94, 195
  Diamond on, 33–34
  education, 174
  emigration from, 179
  Freedom House on, 17, 26
  geography, 27–29
  history, 23–25
  home ownership, 179
  investment climate of, 45
  issues, xii, 2, 21–34
  literacy, 92
  religion, 29–31, 32, 39, 42, 87
  Sachs on, 13
  slavery, 24, 31, 32, 33
Hansen, Mary, 208
Hansson, Albin, 162
Hawaii, 28
health, 65–66, 196
Hefner, Robert
  biographical sketch, 246
  on church-state relations, 53
  on Indonesia, 136–38
  on Islam, 112, 113, 115, 212
  on pluralism, 8
  on variety within cultures, 38
helplessness ideology, 64
Herman, Arthur, 172
Herrera, Luis Diego, 65–69, 72, 200, 208–9, 246
hierarchy, 101, 122, 148, 158
Hill, Kent R., 252
Hinduism, 6, 115–17
  in India, 97
  and modernization, 94
  reforms, 215
  summary, *88–89*, 90
Hispanic culture, 66, 169
Hispaniola, 21–34, 22. *See also* Dominican Republic; Haiti

Hitler, Adolf, 102
HIV/AIDS, 123, 125
Hodam, Robert, 14, 252
Hodges, Wallace, 30
Hofstede, Geert, 8
Hojman, David
  biographical sketch, 249
  on Chile, 145, 147
  on civil service, 182
  economics background, 14
  on literacy, 171
  home ownership, 130–31, 178–79, 219
Honduras, 92, 178
Hong Kong
  economic growth, 28, 29, 44, 126, 176
  and filial piety, 7
  modernization, 95
Howard, Rhoda, 10
How the Scots Invented the Modern World (Herman), 172
Human Development Index
  on Bangladesh, 138
  on Barbados, 17
  on Haiti, 17
  on Ireland, 155
  on Nordic countries, 94
  on Pakistan, 138
  on religions or ethical codes, 92, 95, 96, 111
  on Singapore, 130
  on South Africa, 124
  summary, *89*
  on Uzbekistan, 173
Human Development Report 2003, 26
human rights, 8, 76, 193
Humboldt, Alexander von, 200
Hume, David, 63, 209
Huntington, Samuel
  biographical sketch, 246
  on civilizations, 7
  courses on culture and development, 221
  and Latin American issues, xiii
  on religion, 101, 118, 119
  research, 1
  on societal crises, 4
Hurtado, Osvaldo, 192

Iceland, 42, 48, 94, 95
identity and identification
  in Africa, 122
  of African Americans, 154–55
  and civil service, 180

and cultural change, 163
cultural identity, 151–52
ethnocentrism, 8
in Grondona's typology, 37, 41, 49, 52
and philanthropy, 197
immigration and emigration
from China, 12, 97
from East Asia, 2
from Haiti, 26
immigrant remittances, 15n
to Ireland, 156
to Nordic countries, 161
and U.S., 55, 161
imperialism, 5–6
income distribution data
in Brazil, 144
in Confucian societies, 95, 97
in Latin America, 93
and religion, 105–6
in Spain, 159
summary, 90
in United States, 97
independent thinking skills, 77–78
India
capitalism, 12
case studies, 121, 132–34
colonialism, 6
democracy, 27, 133
economy, 122, 171
English language, 171, 211
gender issues, 204
leadership, 165
literacy, 172–73
minorities in, 56
poverty, 27, 133
religion, 90, 97, 215
indigenous people, 11–12
individualism. *See also*
communitarianism
in Africa, 122
in Grondona's typology, 37, 51–52
in Japan, 129
and religions or ethical codes, 103,
104, 107, 110
in Taiwan, 132
in United States, 51, 58
Indonesia
case studies, 121, 136–38
Chinese minorities in, 12, 97
fertility, *96*
literacy, 138, 208
religion, 91, 113, 114, 212
Industrial Development Authority, 155

industrial revolution, 98
Inglehart, Ronald
biographical sketch, 252
on corruption measures, 48
and Grondona's typology, 38
on motivations for work, 44
on quality of life, 4
on religion, 39, 91
innovation, 37, 46–47, 107, 112, 168
Institute of Human Development in
Peru (INDEHU), 185–87, 199, 207
institution building, 153
intelligence, 227n4, 229n42
Inter-American Development Bank, 52
Iran, *96*
Iraq, 15, 80, 83, 207
Ireland
case studies, 121, 155–56
church-state relations, 54
economy, 44, 166, 171, 175, 218
education, 156, 171, 210–11
English language, 171
foreign investment, 176
leadership, 165, 175
religion, 105, 213
Islam, 6, 112–15
and al Jazeera, 222
authoritarianism, 52
case studies, 121, 134–41
and democracy, 118
early progress, 167
and education, 202, 221
and entertainment media, 83
equality, 119
fatalism, 40
gender issues, 54, 163, 173, 204
and literacy, 173, 208
and modernization, 94
obstacles to progress, 46–47
precepts, 39
Quran, 115, 163, 212
reforms, 211–12
sects, 91
social progress, 96–97
summary, *88–89*, 90
trust, 49
Israel, 83, 90, 94, 102, 114
Italy
case studies, 121, 156–57
church-state relations, 54
civic engagement, 50
corruption, 48
economy, 44, 166, 175

Italy (*continued*)
   leadership, 165
   Norman influence, 32
   poverty, 3
   religion, 98, 105, 213
   social progress, 13
   trust, 49

Jacoby, Tamar, 252
Jains, 56
Japan
   association, 50
   case studies, 120, 128–29
   competitiveness, 94
   and Confucianism, 29n
   cultural change, 206
   culture of progress, 56
   democracy, 15, 16, 56, 170
   economic growth, 4, 43–44, 126, 176,
     218
   education, 43, 54, 128, 168, 170, 176
   entrepreneurship, 45
   gender relationships, 112
   individualism and
     communitarianism, 52
   leadership, 3–4, 46, 133, 164, 167, 168,
     170
   literacy, 172, 208
   media, 223
   military defeats, 58
   modernization, 95
   national crisis, 4, 6
   population, 55
   punctuality, 42–43
   resources, 185
   social capital, 51
   success, 15–16, 185
   and Western intrusiveness, 167
Jews and Judaism, 6, 102–4
   culture of progress, 56
   education, 43, 103–4
   intelligence, 227n4, 229n42
   merit emphasis, 47
   and social progress, 216–17
   success, 2, 102
   summary, *88–89*
   time orientation in, 40
John XXIII, 160
journalism. *See* media
Judeo-Christian traditions, 30

Kagan, Jerome, 18, 61–69, 209, 245
Kagan, Sharon Lynn, 69–70, 210, 246

Kemal, Mustafa, 3–4, 165, 167
Kennedy, John F., xi, 15, 168, 195
kgotla, 123
Khama, Seretse
   and civil service, 181–82
   education, 202
   leadership, 123, 164, 167
   use of *kgotla*, 168
Khouri, Rami, 82
King, Larry, 79
King, Martin Luther, Jr., 13, 58, 166
knowledge, 36, 41
Knox, John, 172
Korea, 29n, 56, 218. *See also* North Korea;
   South Korea
Kovacs, Janos Matyas, 150–51, 250
Kuran, Timur, 14, 252
Kurdish Muslims, 91
Kyrgyzstan, 202

LaFraniere, Sharon, 126
Lal, Deepak, 134
Lamm, Richard, 85–86, 246
Landes, David, 1, 6, 169
language
   as conduit of culture, 200
   and economic growth, 171
   English language, 131, 133, 155, 159,
     171, 200–201, 210–11
   in Quebec, 159
Laos, 27, 97, 111
Latin America. *See also specific countries*
   and Alliance for Progress, xi–xii, 15,
     168, 195
   association, 50
   case studies, 120, 142–49
   and child rearing, 65–69
   civic education, 74
   corruption, 169, 213, 214
   democracy, 64, 105, 118, 199, 201
   economy, 93
   education, 74–78, 171, 201, 210
   elites, 52
   fertility, 54
   fireworks, 196–97
   income distribution, 105–6
   individualism, 51
   libraries, 196
   literacy, 171, 208
   and media, 80, 81
   and philanthropy, 198–99
   poverty, 213

prosperity, 105
punctuality, 190–92
religion, 98, 99, 104, 105–7, 119, 212–14
Rodó's allegory, 13
social progress, 122
trust, 49, 196, 213
use of continuities, 169
and Washington Consensus, 12
Yankee imperialism, 5
Latouche, Daniel, 158–59, 169, 206–7, 218, 250
law, rule of
  in Argentina, 143
  in Bogotá, Colombia, 196
  in Brazil, 144
  in Grondona's typology, 37, 41, 47–48
  importance, 153
  in Latin America, 193
  and NSIC, 188
leadership
  in Africa, 125
  in Argentina, 142
  in Botswana, 123
  in Brazil, 143
  in Egypt, 135
  in Indonesia, 137
  as instrument of change, 58, 84–85
  in Japan, 129
  in Judaism, 103
  race leadership, 155
  role, 164–66, 187
Lebanon, 83, 187, 202, 222
Lederman, Jim, 102–3, 246
Lee, Kuan Yew, 3, 91, 130, 164, 168
Lemass, Sean, 165, 175
The Leopard (Lampedusa), 156–57
Lesage, Jean, 158, 165
Lewis, Bernard, 6, 114–15, 119, 167
Lewis, Sir Arthur, 5, 31
Lewis, Stephen, 14, 123, 181–82, 243n35, 250
Liberation Theology, 106
libraries, 196
Lickona, Thomas, 71–72, 210, 246
literacy
  in Africa, 208
  in Bangladesh, 138
  in Brazil, 92
  in Chile, 54, 145, 171, 208
  and democracy, 170
  in Dominican Republic, 92
  in Egypt, 54, 96, 173

in Guatemala, 92
in Haiti, 92
importance of, 203, 207–8
in India, 172–73
in Indonesia, 138, 208
in Ireland, 171
in Japan, 172, 208
in Latin America, 171, 208
in Nicaragua, 92
in Nordic countries, 208
in Pakistan, 54, 96, 138, 173
in Peru, 92
and poverty, 172–73, 208
in Quebec, 171
and religions or ethical codes, 88, 90, 92, 95, 96, 97, 114, 117
in Scotland, 172
in Sweden, 161–62, 172
of women, 54, 96, 97, 172, 208
Llosa, Mario Vargas, xii
Losing the Race (McWhorter), 154–55
L'Ouverture, Toussaint, 24, 32
Lovedale Institution, 202
Lowenstein, Amy, 69–70, 210, 246–47
Luther, Martin, 63
Lutheranism, 53, 98, 161, 172, 212
Luxembourg, 93

MacFarquhar, Roderick, 253
Maddison, Angus, 28, 93
magic and witchcraft, 30, 87, 122, 217
Making Democracy Work (Putnam), 13, 32, 50, 157
Malaysia, 12, 97
Mali, 96, 118
Mandela, Nelson, 166, 202
Manguelle, Daniel Etounga, 11
Mann, Horace, 71
Mann, Thomas, 4
Mao Zedong, 3, 58, 64, 128
Marín, Luis Muñoz, 85–86
Marini, Matteo, 38, 156–57, 250
Marshall Plan, 14–16, 175
Martin, David, 99–102, 144, 216, 247
Marxist-Leninist model, 127
Masire, Quett, 123, 167, 181, 202
Maslin, Janet, 122
matutinal cultures, 143
Mavila, Octavio, 185, 186
May, Stacy, 178
Mbeki, Thabo, 124
McClelland, David, 66
McWhorter, John, 154–55, 250

media, 18
    influence on culture, 69, 221–23
    news and opinion media, 78–85
    and philanthropy, 199
    and popular culture, 189
    role, 187
Mehta, Pratap Bhanu, 115, 116–17, 215, 247
Menem, Carlos Saúl, 143
Meredith, Martin, 122
merit, 47, 103, 130, 176, 181
Mesa, Carlos, 194
Mexico
    case studies, 120, 148–49
    cultural history of, 169
    democracy, 148–49, 179
    education, 201
    home ownership, 179
    and NSIC, 187
    pluralism, 27–28
    and rule of law, 189
    and Spain, 24
    and time orientation, 40
microfinancing, 204
Middle East, 82–83, 119. See also specific countries
Mockus, Antanas, 196
modernization, 92–94
Mogae, Festus, 123
Mongolia, 97, 111, 216
Montaner, Carlos Alberto
    biographical sketch, 247
    on education, 71
    on home ownership, 178
    on Latin American issues, xii
    on news and opinion media, 78–81, 221–22
    on Spain, 159–60
Monterrey Institute of Technology and Higher Studies (ITESM), 186, 201
moral authority, 188–89
The Moral Basis of a Backward Society (Banfield), 49, 50, 125, 157
mores, importance of, 1
Morocco, 54, 96, 96, 173
Moscoso, Teodoro, xi–xii, 86
mountain ranges, 27
Moynihan, Daniel Patrick, xvi, 13, 18, 153, 225
Mubarak, Hosni, 135, 137
multivocality, 118
Muslim Brotherhood, 135, 136

Myanmar (Burma), 27, 97, 111, 216, 223
Myrdal, Gunnar, 101, 116, 134, 215
The Mystery of Capital (Soto), 45, 179
myths and traditions, 168–70

Najam, Adil, 114, 138, 250
Nasser, Gamal Abdel, 135
National Bureau of Economic Research, 94
nationalism, 148, 159
natural resources, 2–3, 25, 27, 185
Nelsen, Harvey, 57–59, 221, 253
nepotism, 144
Neruda, Pablo, 177
Netherlands, 48, 91, 94, 232n29
news media, 222
New Tang Dynasty Television, 83
New Zealand, 48, 94, 98
Nicaragua
    conquerors, 238n5
    democracy, 193, 194, 195
    development assistance, 16
    and government, 180
    intervention, 230n18
    issues, 28
    literacy, 92
    resources, 45
    and USAID, 193
Niemi, Richard, 72–74, 247
Nigeria, 55, 64, 120, 125–26
nongovernmental organizations (NGOs), 199
Nordic countries. See also specific countries
    capitalism, 106
    corruption, 48
    democracy, 56
    and economic indices, 42
    elites, 52
    English language, 171, 211
    immigrants, 161
    individualism and communitarianism, 52
    literacy, 208
    media coverage, 80
    religion, 94–95, 98, 212
    social progress, 2, 94–95
    welfare systems, 198
North America, 99. See also specific countries
Northern Europe, 98
North Korea, 3, 5, 29n, 127
Norway, 4, 42, 48, 94, 111

Novak, Michael
    biographical sketch, 247
    book reviews, 179
    on Catholicism, 104–7, 118, 212–13
    on church-state relations, 53
    on fertility, 55
    and Grondona's typology, 38
Novgorod, Russia, 152–53
    case studies, 120
    democracy, 108
    foreign investment, 176
    identity, 168–69
    leadership, 165
    Orthodox Christianity, 107–8
    precedents for change, 218

Obando y Bravo, Miguel, 194
Ojeda, Luis Thayer, 146
opportunism, 156
Organization of European Economic
        Cooperation, 15, 52
Orlando, Leoluca, 189
Ortega y Gasset, José, 51, 112n, 160, 191
Orthodox Christianity, 6, 107–9
    and economic performance, 95
    reforms, 214–15
    summary, 88–89, 90
Orthodox/Eastern Europe, 120, 150–54
Ottoman Empire, 4

Pakistan
    case studies, 121, 138–39
    colonialism, 6
    fertility, 96
    gender issues, 54
    literacy, 54, 96, 138, 173
    religion, 114
Panama, 178
Panama Canal, 230n18
Pan-American Agricultural School,
        Honduras, 178, 201
Pappalardo, Salvatore, 188–89
participatory management, 224–25
paternalism, 53, 143
paternity, 59–61. See also families
Patterson, Orlando, 59, 59–61
Paul VI, 160
Paz, Octavio, xii
Peña, Ramón de la, 186
Peñalosa, Enrique, 195
Pentecostal Protestantism, 98–102, 107,
        144, 145, 213

Peru
    cultural history of, 169
    and INDEHU project, 185–87, 199
    literacy, 92
    and NSIC, 187
    and Spain, 24
    and USAID, 193
Pétion, Alexandre, 32
Petro, Nicolai, 151, 152–53, 168, 250
Pettersson, Thorleif, 52, 161–62, 172,
        180–81, 251
philanthropy, 197–99, 223–24
Philippines, 12, 97
Pinochet Ugarte, Augusto, 145, 165
Plaza, Galo, 178
pluralism in cultures, 8
    in China, 128
    in Indonesia, 136
    Shweder on, 9–10
    in Taiwan, 131
    and tolerance, 142
Poland, 59, 177
political leadership, 3–4, 18
political participation, 190
popular culture, 189, 214
population, 54–55, 88
Population Communications
        International (PCI), 84
population growth, 25
populism, 81
Portugal, 98
poverty. See also prosperity
    and climate, 3
    and development assistance, 15
    and education, 170
    and fertility, 55
    and geography, 27–28
    in Haiti, 26
    in India, 27, 133
    in Latin America, 213
    and literacy, 172–73, 208
    in Mexico, 149
    and religion, 99, 114
    and societal values, 12–13
Presbyterianism, 98, 172
Preval, René, 194
Prevelakis, Georges, 108, 200, 202–3,
        214–15, 247
private sector, 223–25
procrastination, 68
progress, societal, 2, 8–9
progressive traditions, 101–2, 168–70

prosperity. *See also* poverty
 and child rearing, 63
 and education, 173
 in Grondona's typology, 36
 and philanthropy, 197
 and religion, 63, 105
*The Protestant Ethic and the Spirit of
 Capitalism* (Weber), 102
Protestantism, 6, *88–89*, 98–102
 and authority, 52
 and corruption, 47–48, 106
 and democracy, 105
 and education, 43, 125, 162
 ethical code, 44, 106
 Evangelical Protestantism, 98–102,
 107, 144, 145, 213
 and income distribution, 105–6
 and INDEHU project, 187
 and individualism, 51
 in Latin America, 145, 214
 merit emphasis, 47
 missionaries in Africa, 123
 and modernization, 92–94
 and Nordic countries, 94–95
 Pentecostal Protestantism, 98–102,
 107, 144, 145, 213
 and prosperity, 63, 105
 and social progress, 216–17
 summary, *88–89*, 90
 time orientation in, 40
 and trust, 106
 values, 176
Prusak, Mikhail, 165
Pskov, Russia, 152
public broadcasting, 84, 222–23
public health, 196
public sector, 179–80
Puerto Rico, 85–86
punctuality, 42–43, 50, 190–92
Puritanism, 49, 161
Putnam, Robert, 1, 13, 32, 50, 157
Pye, Lucian, 1, 6, 253–54

quality of life, 4
Quebec
 case studies, 121, 157–59
 church-state relations, 54
 cultural reconstruction, 158–59, 169,
 218
 economy, 44
 education, 171
 English language, 211

 leadership, 165
 religion, 105, 213
Quiet Revolution of Quebec, 158
Quran, 115, 163, 212

racism, 16–17, 155
Rangel, Carlos, 31
reality television, 82
Reimers, Fernando, 74–78, 180, 210, 247
reinterpretations of culture, 159
relativism, cultural, 8–11, 219
The Religion of China (Weber), 109
religions and ethical codes, 18. *See also
 specific religions and sects*
 ancestor worship, 29n, 90–91
 animist religions, 29–30, 87, 118, 124,
 173, 217
 and authority, 52
 and corruption, 47–48, 106
 and education, 43, 93, 97, 103–4, 125,
 156, 162, 172
 and entertainment media, 83
 and fertility, 54
 in Grondona's typology, 36, 39–40,
 41–42, 43, 47, 49
 and identification and trust, 49
 and INDEHU project, 187
 influence on culture, 6–7
 and literacy, *88*, 90, 92, 95, 96, 97, 114,
 117
 and moral authority, 188–89
 and philanthropy, 198
 reforms, 211–17
 relativism in, 118
 role, 187
 summary, *88–89*
 and women, 99, 100, 215
Renne, Elisha, 55, 125–26, 251
republican spirit, 142
responsibility, 101, 103, 144, 157, 161
revolutionary ideologies, 148
risk propensity, 36, 46
Robert College, Turkey, 202
Rodó, José Enrique, 13
Romania, 214
Romero, María Rocio, 186–87
Roosevelt, Franklin, 3–4, 58, 59, 85
Rotberg, Robert, 253
Russia. *See also* Novgorod, Russia;
 Soviet Union
 and Canada, 28
 case studies, 121, 153–54
 democracy, 118, 152, 173

economy, 13
education, 173
and Georgia, 151
media, 223
prosperity, 64
religion, 108, 214, 215
Rwanda, 64, 124

Sachs, Jeffrey
on development assistance, 14–15, 16
on geography, 27
on Haiti, 31–32
Harvard discussion series, 29
on obstacles to development, 12–13
on racism, 16
Sadat, Anwar, 135
Safran, Nadav, 135
Sahel countries, 27
Samuelson, Robert, 179
Sanbrailo, John, 253
Sánchez de Lozada, Gonzalo, 194
Santería, 217
Sarmiento, Domingo Faustino, 169
Saudi Arabia, 27, 91, 173, 208
Sayaguez, Ana, 200
schadenfreude, 41
Schiphorsst, Bernd, 81–82
Schonfeld, Reese, 81–85, 222–23, 247
Schumacher, E. F., 111
Schumpeter, Joseph, 44–45
Scotland, 172, 208
secularism, 212
Seligson, Mitchell, 189–90, 247
Sen, Amartya, 166, 170
sexuality, 59–61
Shia Muslims, 91
Shweder, Richard, 9–11
Sierra Leone, 111
Sikhs, 56
Simons, Marlise, 105
Singapore
case studies, 120, 129–30
civil service, 182–83
Confucianism, 29n, 217
corruption, 48, 93, 130, 183
economic growth, 29, 44, 126, 176
education, 170, 210
filial piety, 7
foreign investment, 176
home ownership, 178, 219
leadership, 91, 164
modernization, 95
religion, 95

slavery
in Brazil, 144
Haiti's slave rebellion, 33
importation of African slaves, 24
in Latin America, 53
Patterson Model, 59, 59–61
relevancy, 32
and religion, 93, 101
and value systems, 31
Smith, Adam, 24
social behavior, 37, 47–55
social capital, 51, 76, 94, 132, 190
socialism, 106
social justice
and Buddhism, 111
and child rearing, 62–63, 209
in Chile, 64
in China, 64
in Latin America, 149, 214
in Russia, 173
"Third Way" social justice, 106
social movements, 58, 59, 188–89
"Some Hidden Costs of the Public
Investment Fixation" (Harrison),
179–80
Sosa, Lionel, 12
Soto, Hernando de, 45, 179, 219
South Africa, 120, 124–25, 166, 202
South Korea
Confucianism, 29n, 217
democracy, 56
economic growth, 44, 126, 176
filial piety, 7
governmental policies, 3
leadership, 165
modernization, 95
Soviet Union, 153–54, 165, 173. See also
Russia
Spain
case studies, 121, 159–60
church-state relations, 54
corruption, 48
democracy, 2, 160
economy, 44, 166, 175, 218
foreign investment, 176
and Haiti, 23–24
home ownership, 178, 219
individualism, 51
leadership, 165
modernization, 152–53
poverty, 3
and punctuality, 191
religion, 98, 105, 213

The Spaniard and the Seven Deadly Sins (Díaz-Plaja), 191
Spring, Dick, 155–56, 171, 175, 251
Sri Lanka, 97, 111
Stanton, Elizabeth Cady, 58
state, role of, 143
Stepan, Alfred, 53–54, 118–19
Stephens, John L., 45
Stiepel, Jorge, 200
Stuyvesant, Peter, 102
suffrage, 116, 140, 161
Sunni Muslims, 91
Super-Star, 82
Surowiecki, James, 42–43, 191
Sweden
    case studies, 121, 161–62
    civil service, 180–81
    corruption, 48
    economy, 42
    education, 172
    elites' role, 52–53
    entrepreneurship, 45
    leadership, 165
    media, 223
    social progress, 94
Switzerland, 48, 91, 232n29

Taino civilization, 23
Taiwan
    case studies, 120, 131–32
    communitarianism, 51
    Confucianism, 29n, 217
    democracy, 56, 131
    economic growth, 44, 126, 176, 218
    income distribution, 234n1
    leadership, 165
    modernization, 95
Taoism, 29n, 90
Tarancón, Vincente Enrique y, 105, 160
Ten Commandments of Development, 185–87
Thailand, 12, 27, 97, 111, 216
Thatcher, Margaret, 58
"Third Way" social justice, 106
Third World countries. *See also specific countries*
    corruption, 166
    issues, 5–6
    politics, 166
    religion and ethical codes, 92–93, 100, 145

Tibi, Bassam
    biographical sketch, 248
    on Egypt, 134–36
    and Grondona's typology, 38
    on Islam, 39, 40, 47, 112–13, 115, 212
    on time orientation, 43
Tiger Kloof Institute, 202
Tikkun Olam, 103
time orientation, 36, 40, 122
Tocqueville, Alexis de
    on democratization, 118, 193
    on mores, 1, 2
    on national identification, 64–65
    on Protestantism, 52
    on religion, 39, 42, 92, 104, 231n5
Toledo, Alejandro, 194
tolerance, 142, 159
toxic cultures, 169
Toyota, 224
traditions and myths, 168–70
Transparency International's Corruption Perceptions Index, 47–48. *See also* corruption
    on Chile, 168, 182
    on India, 97
    on religions or ethical codes, 93, 95
    on Singapore, 130, 183
    summary, 90
    on Venezuela, 149
traumas. *See* crises and traumas
trust
    in Africa, 122
    in Brazil, 144
    and civil service, 180
    in Grondona's typology, 37, 41–42, 49
    in Italy, 157
    in Latin America, 49, 196, 213, 214
    and religions or ethical codes, *89*, 90, 93, 95, 96, 106, 110, 114
    in Taiwan, 132
Trust (Fukuyama), 50, 51, 132
Tu, Weiming, 51–52, 56, 127–28, 251
Turkey
    case studies, 121, 140–41
    church-state relations, 54
    education, 202
    leadership, 165, 167
    religion, 114, 212

ubuntu, 124
Ugalde, Luis, 149, 251
Ukraine, 214
Unamuno, Miguel de, 146

underdeveloped countries. *See* Third World countries
Underdevelopment Is a State of Mind (Harrison), 4
United Arab Emirates, 202
"The United Fruit Co." (Neruda), 177
United Fruit Company, 5–6, 177
United Kingdom, 48
United Nations, 202
United States
    association, 50
    competitiveness, 94–95
    corruption, 48
    democracy emphasis, 195
    development assistance, 14–16
    and Dominican Republic, 25
    entrepreneurship, 45
    Great Depression, 4, 58
    and Haiti, 26
    immigrants, 55, 161
    income distribution, 93, 105
    individualism, 51, 58
    and outsourcing to India, 133
    philanthropy, 198, 223
    population, 55
    poverty, 3
    race relations, 166
    religion, 39–40, 92, 98, 101–2, 104
    Rodó's allegory, 13
    social capital, 94
    and terrorism, 114
United States Agency for International Development (USAID), xi, 192–95
United States General Accounting Office, 204
United States Government Accountability Office, 193, 194
United States National Strategy Information Center (NSIC), 187–88
Universal Declaration of Human Rights, 8–9, 39, 93, 111, 204, 222
Universal Progress Culture, 55–56
university courses on culture and development, 221
University of Fort Hare, 202
Uribe, Álvaro, 194
Uzbekistan, 173

values. *See also specific values*
    and cultural change, 7, 163
    in Grondona's typology, 36–37, 41–43
    in Japan, 128, 129

    in Mexico, 148
    and social development, 7
Venezuela, 12, 149, 201
vespertine cultures, 143
victim self-image, 6
Vietnam, 127
Villegas-Reimers, Eleonora, 74–78, 180, 210, 248
virtues, 36, 41–43, 50
Voodoo, 29–31
    and democracy, 118
    effects, 39, 42, 87
    and progress-resistant cultures, 217

Washington Consensus, 12
wealth, 36, 65, 111, 197–98
Weber, Max
    on capitalism, 39
    on Franklin's ethical exhortation, 41–42
    on orientation to the future, 40
    on prestige, 43
    on religion, 42, 47, 99, 102, 106, 109, 116, 215
welfare systems, 161
Weller, Robert, 109–10, 131–32, 248
Wesley, John, 40, 162, 216
West, 10, 121, 154–62
Western Europe, 53, 55, 152, 175. *See also specific countries*
West Germany, 150–51
West Indies, 22
Whelan, Christal, 110–11, 216, 248
Who Are We? The Challenges to America's National Identity (Huntington), 101
witchcraft, 30, 87, 122, 217
women. *See also* gender relationships
    education of, 54, 96, 97, 125, 172–73, 208
    female genital cutting, 10
    and feminism/women's movement, 59, 166
    literacy, 54, 96, 97, 172, 208
    and religions or ethical codes, 99, 100, 215
    roles, 204
work
    in Africa, 122
    in Grondona's typology, 36, 43–44
    in Japan, 128
    in Singapore, 130
    in Taiwan, 132
    work ethic, 63, 101, 110
World Bank, 6, 14, 90, 202

World Economic Forum, 42, 94
World Values Survey, 8
    and Grondona's typology, 38
    on standard of living, 129
    summary, 90
    on trust, 42, 96
    on work ethic, 44
worldviews, 36, 39–41
World War I, 4
World War II, 4

Yankee imperialism, 5
Yemen, *96*
Yoruba community in Nigeria, 120, 125–26
Yoshihara Kunio, 14, 128–29, 130, 220, 251
Yunus, Mohammed, 204

Zemurray, Samuel, 177–78, 198, 201
zero-sum worldview, 40–41